Asian Americans
in the
Twenty-first Century

ALSO BY JOANN FAUNG JEAN LEE

Asian American Actors:
Oral Histories from Stage, Screen, and Television

Asian Americans: Oral Histories of First- to Fourth-
Generation Americans from China, the Philippines, Japan,
India, the Pacific Islands, Vietnam, and Cambodia

Asian Americans in the Twenty-first Century

Oral Histories of First- to
Fourth-Generation Americans
from China, Japan, India, Korea,
the Philippines, Vietnam, and Laos

Joann Faung Jean Lee

THE NEW PRESS

NEW YORK
LONDON

Requests for permission to reproduce selections from this book should be
mailed to: Permissions Department, The New Press, 120 Wall Street, 31st
floor, New York, NY 10005.

First published in the United States by The New Press, New York, 2008
This paperback edition published by The New Press, 2009
Distributed by Two Rivers Distribution

LIBRARY OF CONGRESS CATALOGING-IN-PUBLICATION DATA

Asian Americans in the twenty-first century : oral histories of first- to fourth-
generation Americans from China, Japan, India, Korea, the Philippines,
Vietnam,
and Laos / [compiled] by Joann Faung Jean Lee.
    p. cm.
  Includes index.
  ISBN 978-1-59558-152-5 (hc)
  ISBN 978-1-59558-478-6 (pb)
1. Asian Americans—Biography. 2. Asian Americans—Social conditions.
3. Asian Americans—Ethnic identity. 4. Asian Americans—
Cultural assimilation. 5. Oral history—United States. I. Lee, Joann
Faung Jean, 1950–
  E184.A75A8434   2008
  920'.0095073—dc22

                                            2008020422

The New Press publishes books that promote and enrich public discussion
and understanding of the issues vital to our democracy and to a more
equitable world. These books are made possible by the enthusiasm of our
readers; the support of a committed group of donors, large and small; the
collaboration of our many partners in the independent media and the
not-for-profit sector; booksellers, who often hand-sell New Press books;
librarians; and above all by our authors.

www.thenewpress.com

Compostion by NK Graphics

Printed in the United States of America

To the Lee family,
past, present, future . . .

Contents

III. JOURNEYS AND PASSAGES

Introduction

Gold Mountain, or *Gum San*—that's what the Cantonese who first arrived called America. They came with the dream of striking it rich in the California Gold Rush. Documented records have three Chinese landing in San Francisco Harbor in 1848. Today, there are over 12 million Asian Pacific Americans. Many more are waiting to enter the United States, but the gate has tightened even further in the wake of the attacks of September 11, 2001.

This book is a twenty-first-century snapshot of Asian Pacific Americans inside the gates of Gold Mountain. It is a tapestry of tales reflecting their lives, experiences, hopes, and dreams. Ultimately the spectrum of values—in education, family, work—form a remarkable mosaic of the Asian American experience, distinct in many ways from that of Asians living either in Asia or as immigrants encountering diaspora elsewhere in the world.

A powerful stereotype of the Asian Pacific American (APA) over the past few decades has been the model minority myth of the hardworking superstudent or well-educated professional from a strong family unit, limited in cultural exposure, and all but invisible in the mass media. Yet today's APAs see their futures through a more diverse prism, one that reflects a global matrix. Places such as Chinatowns or Koreatowns are for food, or friends, or family gatherings perhaps, but cultural space and identity have moved beyond ethnic enclaves; the cultural box has been redefined.

Much has happened to Asian American identity as a cultural touchstone since my last book was written twenty years ago. As Dale Minami, one of the interviewees for this updated volume, said, "For people today it's much more about empowerment and financial success."

While the line for entry into the United States continues to get longer, APAs—those born and raised in the United States, as well as those recently arrived—have a stronger sense of the possible: that first-generation Asians need not cling as tightly to the old country's ways, and that the world has become more global. Hence, the notion of being a racial minority in the United States is but one aspect of being in a larger universe.

This is witnessed in the lives and outlooks of first-generation APAs such as Albert Lee, a Korean American journalist. His parents came from Seoul to settle in Harlan, Kentucky, one of the poorest parts of the nation, so his father could serve as a doctor there. Albert left Kentucky as a teenager, and the road he traveled led him to Princeton University and to the bright lights of New York City, where he is a senior editor for *Us Weekly*, an entertainment magazine. In his eyes, Asian American identity is far less a determining factor in his life than that of being a gay man.

There is Hank Sasaki, who grew up in Japan during a time of heavy American military presence. As a teenager he listened to the music of Hank Williams and Johnny Cash, songs that he heard on Armed Forces Radio. He was drawn to country-and-western music in clubs that brought a taste of home to American GIs. At age fifty he finally embarked on an all-consuming passion: moving to Nashville, Tennessee, and becoming a "cowboy from Japan."

Laura Jung attends Harvard's Graduate School of Education in the risk and prevention program, hopes eventually to go into counseling psychology, "to work with Asian American and immigrant adolescents, because I think there's such a stigma against mental health assistance and I think Asian adolescents do need it."

Recent immigrants to the United States face a mixed arena of transitional challenges. In the past, Chinese women (those who spoke little or no English) settled in New York's Chinatown and pretty much ended up working in sewing factories. Today, there are far fewer jobs in New York's garment industry; over forty factories have shut down since September 11. Yet Chinatowns outside Manhattan are expanding, providing employment opportunities in businesses such as restaurants, pastry shops, and grocery stores (it seems that wherever large populations of Chinese settle, Chinese supermarket chains appear—in Boston, New York, the San Francisco Bay Area, and Los Angeles). For many new immigrants, such as Qing Shan Liang, opportunities to work, albeit it at minimum wage, have fostered such practices as sending newborn children back to China to be reared by grandparents so that both parents can work full time. The migration is temporary, however, because children return to this country in time to begin kindergarten in the United States.

Both Karl Ludwig and Kristen Houghton were adopted from Korea as children. The quest to search for one's birth parents remains a difficult path, as both describe. Karl's and Kristen's perspectives add a greater understanding to aspects of adoption at a time when more and more children are being adopted from China and elsewhere in Asia.

Naomi McWatt's experience growing up as a child of an interracial marriage—her father was African American, her mother, Japanese—is in stark contrast to that of Susha Pratt—her dad was Caucasian, her mom, Chinese. McWatt is in her fifties; she was raised in Florida by a loving woman, her father's ex-girlfriend. Pratt, in her twenties, grew up on the Olympic Peninsula in Washington; even though her parents divorced when she was five, she remained linked to both her Chinese and American worlds.

The evolution of Asian American experiences also includes such issues of mainstream discourse as gay marriage. Gita Deane grew up in India and came to the United States as a student. Here, she met her life mate, Lisa, and together they are raising a family and asserting their rights by bringing suit to legalize gay marriage in Maryland.

A section of the book includes three interviews with Asian Americans who ran successfully for public office: Gary Locke, the first Asian American governor in the continental United States; Ruby Chow, the first Chinese American woman to serve as a council member for King County (Seattle, Washington); and Cheryl Chow (Ruby's daughter), a former Seattle city council member. What rings clear throughout these interviews is a strong sense of civic responsibility, of giving back to the community. Ruby Chow, who is in her eighties, started out as a restaurateur. Her path to public service was triggered by a sense of injustice that emerged soon after World War II. "My sister was pushed out of her seat on a bus," she said. "A white male ordered her out so he could sit, thinking she was Japanese. Those incidences happened and some of the Chinese were worried, so they would say, 'but I'm Chinese.' I thought at that time that's why we need public relations."

When I began recounting the oral histories of Asian Americans two decades ago, the Internet explosion was yet in its infancy. Today, the global possibilities of communication within the World Wide Web have redefined the meaning of community. Dale Minami touches on the potential power of community activism and organization through the Internet.

In a global context, the Internet has enabled the reframing of the concept of "foreign" into a more user-friendly sense of internationalism. The infusion of Asian films into American cinemas is but one instance of such trends, with names like Jackie Chan and Michelle Yeoh becoming synonymous with celebrity.

The book's interviewees hail from a broad cross section of occupations: I spoke with students, politicians, a lawyer, an educator, a photographer, musicians, a corporate professional, an engineer, a restaurant owner, a deliveryman, and a law enforcement officer, to name a few. Some, like Frank Bai, are immigrants who arrived in the United States as adults and who continue to grapple with transition and adjustment. Others, such as Vietnamese-born Hoan Dang, came as children, were raised in the United States, and are now fully acculturated with successful careers. Still others were born and raised in the United States, like Susha Pratt. She is third generation, and her experiences are in stark contrast to those of her grandfather, Ark Chin, and her mother, Candace Chin.

The subthemes that emerge throughout the interviews illuminate the values of education, family, work, and identity. Ultimately, they are all elements of the American Dream; the most prevalent is a faith in education as the great enabler.

Those I interviewed were proud to be Americans. For those who were born and raised in the United States, knowledge of their Asian culture wasn't all that important. Some saw their Asian heritage as an enriching aspect to their identities. Few could speak a second language fluently or felt that it was an absolute need.

Interviewees were chosen randomly across the country, but primarily on the East and West Coasts. The overwhelming majority were people I did not know—names I gathered from friends and colleagues. Of the two exceptions, one is a relative and the other, a very old friend; I felt both their stories contributed to a deeper view of the Asian American portrait. I am not related to any of the Lees interviewed; Lee is a common surname among Chinese and Koreans. Because of the uniqueness of my experience as a teenager, however, I included my own story of singing in a girls' rock-and-roll group.

This book is divided into three parts: Living in America, which addresses arrival, resettlement, and growing up; Aspects of Americanization, focusing on specific events and topics such as personal career choices, passions, and values; and Journeys and Passages, which addresses the challenges and joys of family relationships across cultures.

I'd like to thank all who shared so willingly their lives and feelings with me. From the outset, I wanted to write a book with broad-based appeal. As with my first book, I sought with this project to capture the individual voices of Asian Americans through their stories.

Being part of a culture is different than owning the culture. In that sense, growing up in New York City's Chinatown as first generation, I felt *a part of* American culture—an example is my story about the Fortune Cookies, a girl singing group my friends and I formed—but as an Asian American, I realize that I grew up with two cultures, the culture of my parents and heritage (which I *owned*), as well as the culture of the mainstream.

In school I spoke English. At home, with my mom, I'd speak Chinese. At lunchtime, my mother would rush home from the sewing factory and serve my sisters and me rice dishes. We would eat in ten minutes and rush back to school. I'd like to think that my mom wanted to make sure we had a decent hot meal every noontime, but I can't rule out the reality that this also saved lunch money for four girls every week. By high school, I was working on weekends as a cashier in a Chinese restaurant to earn spending money. My experience is probably very commonplace for first-generation Chinese Americans growing up in Chinatown.

Back then, Chinatown was a tiny enclave that stretched for three blocks down Mott Street. Today, there are essentially three Chinatowns in New York City: Manhattan, Flushing (Queens), and Brooklyn all have pockets where Chinese can buy groceries and eat Chinatown-style food. The landscape of what it means to be Chinese in America today has clearly changed. Much of that is because the world around us is so very different.

Owning the culture means not just assimilating, but also contributing to, defining, and shaping it. If mainstream culture is about what we wear, how we look, the books we read, the movies we see, and what we talk about, then Asians have made major strides in recent years. There are new sets of cultural images—ones that project far greater range and outreach in terms of expectations, hopes, and accomplishments. Over the past two decades, APAs have come to occupy the cultural forefront with increased visibility. Young brides covet Vera Wang gowns; basketball fans cheer for the Houston Rockets' seven-foot six-inch center, Yao Ming; and the Yankees' starting lineup features names like Chien-Ming Wang and Hideki Matsui. In the corporate world, India-born Indra Nooyi made headlines as the new CEO of Pepsico, as did Jerry Yang, CEO and co-founder of Yahoo. Examples abound. Clearly, Asians are no longer just sojourners to the Gold Mountain. APAs are claiming space in American mainstream culture, and this ownership has rendered new definitions and outlooks of the Asian American experience as reflected in this book.

And yet, lest I leave the reader with the impression that APA stereotypes no longer cast shadows over our cultural landscape, my closing reference here is to just such a stereotypical Asian American experience that occurred on the East Coast. A Chinese man walks out of an Italian restaurant after lunch and is approached by a mop-headed boy of about eleven years of age. The man is a few steps from his news van, which is clearly marked. (He is a cameraman for one of the New York news programs and is walking with an African American reporter.) The boy approaches, somewhat hesitant. The man, accustomed to small talk about the news business, expects a friendly encounter and smiles. The boy says to the man, "Can I kick you?"

The man, thinking he didn't hear correctly, says, "Pardon me?"

"Can I kick you? My dad said that if I kicked you, I wouldn't have to get a haircut," replied the boy, pointing to a middle-aged man standing and staring by a car across the street.

The man, stunned, said, "Absolutely not."

The boy, not to be deterred, says, "Can I at least kick at you, and you pretend that I hurt you so my dad can see. . . ."

The man leans over and stares into the boy's face, saying, "Son, tell your dad if you kick me, or touch me, I will have to hit you back, hard. . . ."

The boy, looking disappointed, crosses the street and walks back to his father.

This actually happened, in the winter of 2007, in Newton, New Jersey.

—Joann Faung Jean Lee

I. Living in America

The first Chinese to come to this country came, lured by rumors of gold in California. Documented accounts list three Chinese arriving in San Francisco Harbor in 1848. By 1852, twenty thousand more had arrived.

—*Guide to the Chinese American Experience*

Total Asian American population in 2000, including hapas [Asian Pacific Americans of mixed heritage]: 12,504,636.

—*The New Face of Asian Pacific America*

CIRCLE OF LIFE

Asian Americans as a Movement
Dale Minami

Dale Minami is an attorney in San Francisco and has practiced law for thirty-five years. He received the American Bar Association's Thurgood Marshall Award in 2003.

Any Asian in this country with the intent to live here permanently is an Asian American. I don't think of it just as a political term anymore. It's a social term that disregards the [specific] demographics of people who come from certain parts of the world.

Things change and things evolve. When you talk about Asian Americans in the sixties and seventies I think that was a narrow demographic compared to the numbers we have now. More than 60 percent of Asian Americans now are immigrants. They don't have the experience of the sixties. They don't have the chance to see what African Americans or Latino Americans did. They don't understand the struggle just to get equal dignity. They have their own struggles. So a lot of immigrants are not taught or not given the advantage of that historical perspective. It's become much more diffuse.

But what you do have is a lot of groups that want to help the notion of community improve in power, immigrant or nonimmigrant. We have bigger numbers now; we have more people who are politically active. So it has gotten better to the extent that we have more people and those people are more willing to do community work or get involved in some way.

I think there's less anger today. I mean, we were angry back then—when you learn about the history of what you've gone through and what your parents have gone through. In our day it was about overturning the whole system to make it more equitable economically and socially. For people today it's much more about empowerment and financial success.

As long as you realize where you came from, and that somewhere, sometime, someone has helped you to create that circle of history then it is really incumbent on you to sometime, somewhere, help somebody else. If you're a famous Asian American who isolates yourself from the community, you're probably having some good effect on the perception of Americans—that this is a successful Asian American who is probably a role model for somebody. But I have much more respect for those who try to come back and help.

Now I see people engaging in social services, fighting racism at the legislative level. So it's the same kind of notion—that we need to help people who are less fortunate, or who need help.

Race: I still think race is a major question that needs to be resolved in this country. It's been submerged but it's always going to come back in some form until you see a more proportional [representation] of people in society. If you're talking about the immigration debate—that's about race, it's not just about immigration. It's not about Canadian or French people coming; it's about Mexicans coming over here, people from South America. That's a question of race because it's a question of what our culture is going to be in the future.

As Pat Buchanan said, we have a cultural war going on here. What he's really saying is that white people are feeling threatened by the number of minorities who are now in this country, that are growing at a huge rate, and that soon we may not see the Anglo-Saxon culture survive. So I think that the issue of race is being submerged or it's not being talked about as directly; it's camouflaged into other issues. Take the whole immigration debate that's still going on. I think we've made great progress, don't get me wrong on that. I think as a country we've really made wonderful improve-

Dale Minami

ments, if you think about it from the lynchings to the internment camps to some of the really overt racism. But what you find is that it's a little bit more submerged, a little more subtle; it's going to be camouflaged as an immigration issue, not a race issue.

I've seen some improvement in America's understanding of the racial paradigm, which was always black and white. Now we occasionally get a notion that there's more than black and white, that it's technicolor, with Latinos and Asian Americans represented at the table when you see diversity. But it's not improved nearly to the degree that I would've liked.

We still see hate crimes and see anecdotal evidence, including personal episodes, where white America sees us as perpetual foreigners. To that extent there's still a lot that needs to be done and progress to be made.

Born in the U.S.A: I think in some ways I feel really lucky to have Japanese ancestry; it traces back thousands of years, just like if you were Chinese. It's something to be proud of; civilizations and cultures can bring pride out of you in terms of what your people have done.

As an American I would never have wanted to have been born in any other country. I'm really lucky to be here. I think about people who were born in Somalia just by accident of birth, or they're in Pakistan or Bangladesh—I just think about that, and the greatness of our country. We're criticized over and over because we always want it to be better, and we said it was perfect, even though it wasn't. We thought we could try to make it perfect, so I think this country has tried to adapt and incorporate people from diverse cultures to the extent that I have both a Japanese background and an American background. I really feel fortunate.

I feel fortunate too because I was able to grow up with a diverse group of people—African Americans, Latino Americans—that helped me to understand why diversity is so important to this country. It's the only way this country will survive without more racial havoc or tension. W.E.B. DuBois always wrote about the color line and the great issue of the nineteenth century. It became a great issue in the twentieth century with the riots in the sixties and the issue of affirmative action thereafter. I think race is always going to be an issue.

But I think the greater issues that are coming up are economic issues. I always feel that when you have economic issues or crises then you have tensions. It brings out the worst in a country, the worst in its people. That's what happened to my parents in Japan after Pearl Harbor. People couldn't distinguish Japanese Americans from the Japanese. I worry that the same thing might happen with China. With the strength of China, the power it has economically, politically (not militarily), I think that's going to impact us all as Asian Americans here.

As far as the future of Asian Americans, I do see younger people with a little different perspective. But I think the bottom line is they want to see a more equitable society, a society with a lot less racism—a society with people who are not spending their money on wars or military contractors, but on social services that are helping the people. They do have that sense of social justice that is perhaps even broader than the sense that we grew up with because they have a broader experience. I think the issue for all of us is the Internet.

Community Building, Political Activism, and the Internet: What I saw in the Abercrombie & Fitch boycott was a terrific model for Asian Americans to follow, one that fits more of their personalities, their skills, their propensities. [The retailer launched a line of T-shirts depicting what some Asians feel to be stereotypical images.] That boycott was started, spread, and won through the Internet and use of e-mail in almost an organic way. I've always talked about trying to create an organization that enforced a boycott against an offending politician, company, or DJ because I think Asian Americans have buying power. If they could apply that toward social justice by use of the Internet, that kind of power would be really formidable. I don't think we've even begun to tap that power. Through Web sites like MySpace or Facebook or Friendster, they have built these virtual communities of Asian Americans that aren't just Japanese, Chinese, or Korean communities. The aim is to reach out. You find them creating this idea of Asian American online. College campuses are probably where most of the organizing takes place. I think that's why the Abercrombie & Fitch boycott was so successful. Organizers were able to reach thousands of people in a matter of days, maybe even hours. I think if you set up those kinds of networks it's going to help people understand the commonalities of being Asian Americans rather than the differences. To that extent the computer and the Internet are going to be the X factor in what happens to our Asian American community.

From Toi Shan to the Olympic Peninsula Gateway

Ark Chin

*Ark Chin is a Chinese American living in Seattle, Washington. He has had an excep-
tionally successful career as a structural engineer spanning over four decades. His life
as a Chinese American started in the 1930s.*

I came to the United States in 1934. I was ten years old. It was a
frightening experience because my father was released as soon as
he passed through customs in Seattle, whereas I was held in a jail-
like setting with a whole bunch of adults. There were very few
young people. They kept me there for two weeks. There was no ex-
planation of what was going on. You're just totally at a loss. There
were bars on the window, just like a jail.

Every so often they would pick you out for interrogation. There
would be a Chinese interpreter, and in my case they would ask
questions about my village, the number of houses, my neighbors,
who did the plowing, what kind of animals were used.

They asked questions that required detailed answers because,
as I understood later on, they brought my father in for interrogation to see if they matched up. If there were any discrepancies,
they would hone in on that and ask more questions.

Finally they figured I was a true son of my father. And whether
it was maybe through some greasing of the palm or whatever, my
father never told me.

My grandfather was the first one to come to this country—
from Toi Shan, China, in the late 1800s or early 1900s—he and his

big brother. The oldest brother came first and started a laundry, so grandfather worked in this laundry and then later established his own laundry on Broadway near Republican Street. The storefront is still there. It's gone through a number of transitions. I think it is a TV store now.

My grandfather luckily became a citizen as a result of the San Francisco earthquake disaster. What apparently happened was that all the immigration records that were held in San Francisco got burned up. A lot of the people found out about it and had neighbors go with them into court and swear on an affidavit that they were born on that street in such and such house number. The judge had no way of refuting it, so he issued a court order that this person is a U.S. citizen. So henceforth my dad was an American citizen. And the same applied to me.

My father came in 1917 when he was fourteen years old. He worked until 1922 and returned to China to marry. I was the first male of my generation so I was really a highly prized person, so to speak. After my birth, my father came back to the U.S. in 1926. By then he already had a restaurant in Aberdeen (Washington).

When my dad brought me here, he waited and waited until I was released from the immigration station and then we stayed with my grandfather for about a week. After that, we went to Aberdeen, where I grew up.

I was the only Chinese in the school system for a good number of years. From time to time there may have been one to two others, but most of the time there was just me. Aberdeen was a redneck city, and so the Chinese were looked upon as subhuman. I was stigmatized being a Chinese and they would yell "Ching Chong Chinaman" at me, but what could you do? Nothing. So I was fortunate there were a few friends and several teachers that took real interest in me and gave me a great deal of encouragement.

There wasn't that much racism, but when there was, it was severe. In junior high school I called this girl to ask her to go to the dance with me. She was talking to me, and unbeknownst to me her mother was listening on the extension. All of a sudden the mother yelled out "no" and slammed the phone down. It was just like being looked upon as a social outcast.

So you have to have a certain mental toughness to survive that kind of environment. Physically I was a very slight individual when I graduated from high school: five-foot ten-inches and a hundred and nineteen pounds. So you can't really fight with kids that are approaching six feet, a hundred and eighty pounds. This was from 1934 to 1943. That's when I graduated.

Since then there's been a huge change. I think the primary factor was World War II, when many Chinese went into service and many were wounded and killed.

There was this anti–Chinese immigration law that was enacted back in the 1800s, and the womenfolk could not even come to this country unless you were a wife of a merchant or diplomat. It didn't matter that your husband was a citizen. So, in effect, the people's conscience said that was wrong. Here you ask the Chinese to sacrifice and perhaps give their lives for this country, but then they're not good enough citizens to have their family with them. So they repealed that act.

No doubt the civil rights movement had an impact. Meanwhile the Chinese became more educated, they went into more professions, and they demonstrated that they are equal to any racial group in terms of intelligence and ability. The willingness to work, a constant sacrifice by the family to push their kids to get an education—all these factors gradually brought about a change. There also was more interaction, so that people realized you didn't change color by touching a Chinese, you're not in any way threatened or degraded by being next to a Chinese. In the old days it was almost like, being Chinese, you were stigmatized as kind of a subhuman.

The Army: I think the changes really started to take place after the war was over. In the beginning of the war I felt racism against me, but because of my actions in battle and so forth I kind of "earned my place." I was given a battlefield promotion to squad leader.

I was a grunt, a private. The lowest is a private. And when we went overseas, we were all given one stripe to be private first class. But then that was it, as far as I was concerned. My whole future was to be a private first class. In the infantry and on the battlefield you have to show you are capable and strong in terms of self-preservation. I got up to 134 pounds, but that's still very, very slight. Yet I endured all the hardships—there were many, both mental and physical. Some guys who were 180-pounders couldn't. They broke down emotionally. Or they didn't know how to take care of themselves, so they became ill.

One of the worst things for infantrymen is to have something wrong with your feet. If you get a severe case of athlete's foot or you can't hike, you can't march. You're a sitting duck. So I learned how to survive. I usually carried an extra set of woolen socks. When night came I would put one pair next to my body to stay dry. In the morning I would put on the new dry socks. Then at night I would take the moist or wet ones off, put on the dry set, and put the wet ones next to my body and let my body heat dry them up for the morning. So I never had any problem with my feet.

There's a lot of attrition going on in the front lines. I didn't have what they called the GI runs because I kept my utensils clean and took care of myself. So I reacted well, at least in the sense that I seemed to have a sixth sense for danger and how to avoid it and for self-preservation. Because of that the captain said, Well why don't we make Chin a squad leader? So they entrusted ten to eleven people to me for my leadership in survival.

I always felt, certainly in the younger days, that I had to do more, be better, because of being Chinese. For instance, they were more demanding in basic training. I don't know if they intended to break you down or not. Besides the basic training games, we also had physical games. One of the games we played was called the

Red Dog. The whole platoon stood facing inward in a circle and held their hands behind them. Then the sergeant would go along and hand this webbing in his belt to the person on your left and he had the right to whip your butt, whip you in the back as hard as he wanted. And if you didn't run fast enough you'd get hurt. And if you fell down they would still beat you until the sergeant yelled to stop. So I suffered through those things. I felt it was racial because, more frequently than most, I was the target.

Then there was being put on KP. Kitchen Police. To wash dishes. Actually, they gave me a promotion when they knew I could cook. So I became a cook. Infantrymen get assigned to those menial tasks and I felt I was given more than my share.

Has my life as a Chinese person affected the way I think about things as an American? Very much so. After one particularly horrendous battle I was asked to go back and help the burial detail, to identify the bodies. After that I was literally sick to my stomach; I didn't throw up or anything, but I felt terrible. And I thought, What is it that you didn't break down like many of those your age? Because we were all college-aged kids when we went in. And I thought there were two things. One was my father's toughness on me growing up. He knew what the world was like; he was tough and he wanted me to be mentally tough. And the other thing was the sense of pride in being a Chinese. They think of the yellow man as being less than courageous. But I felt that I would not let my race down. Of course, in terms of our culture, what it imparts to you is very important—the reverence for your family and your elders. So therefore I always had a sense that I was privileged to have grown up in a civilization like that.

Life as an Engineer: Engineers are practical people. They're results-oriented. What they want is to see results. They don't care what color you are. When I joined my firm it had twenty people. There was a senior partner and a junior partner who was the operations manager. He kind of kept an eye on the operation. I was the only structural engineer in the firm. I had a master's in structural engineering. They had had some problems with the structures they had designed before. There wasn't any problem with the stuff I worked on. The long and short of it was that the junior partner was forced to get to know me better.

One day after I was there for three years I asked for a raise. They had had an annual review and they were going to give me $25 a month more. Even in those days that's a meager amount. I told my manager I couldn't continue on with the kind of prospect that this showed. I said I would like to see the junior partner, the operations manager, and have a conversation with him. Then I asked him, "Have you really reviewed my work?" And he said, "Oh yeah." I said, "This is what you really think I deserve?" He said, "Well, yes." I said, "Well, I'm giving you two weeks' notice right now; I'm leaving." He said, "What?!" I think he had a stereotypical sense that a Chinese person wouldn't do that. He said, "You got a job lined up?" I said no. I never put a gun to people's heads to negotiate, so I said, "I'm going to look for a new job." He was kind of shocked. One day he asked me if I had a new job, and I said, "I have several leads, one potentially can lead to being a junior partner." So a day or two later he came and talked to me about a new assignment for the firm, my part in it, and how important it would be. So he said, "If I give you $175 more a month, would you stay?" It had jumped from $25 to $175. The challenge was that the new job was the design of a new dam for the city of Seattle. It's one thing I'd always wanted to do, design a dam. He said, "You take care of your end of the bargain and I'll take care of you," and he was true to his word. A few years later when the senior partner retired, he made me a junior partner. When I was made junior partner, three of the senior managers left the firm. This was in 1961. Part of it was because I was Chinese; the other part was the resentment of having a young person promoted over them.

I worked on numerous projects. One was a preliminary design of a dry dock designed to take the biggest aircraft carrier—the *Eisenhower*—and then repair it. I did the preliminary design on the caisson that sits on the open end of the dry dock. The Navy thought well enough of that to compliment the partner. I was also chief structural engineer for the cleanup of Lake Washington in the early sixties. It was a $125 million project—I don't know how many billions that would be now. I had to develop all the design criteria for the structural work. The structural engineer's work is tested by nature, earthquakes. We have gone through several earthquakes and the projects did not suffer any damage.

I always said that if I were to have gone through adult life in any other country—even China as it is now constituted or in the old days—I would not have had the kinds of opportunities that I did in this country: to become president of a firm with 95 percent *lo fans* (Caucasians), to be elected president of the engineering association, and to be honored as engineer of the year a couple of times, here in Seattle.

Looking back, it was a plus to be a Chinese because it provided me with the inner strength, a pride in our culture and civilization, that I tried to apply in my business life. I tried to develop a sense of honor and trust in people. I would incorporate a culture that is based on integrity and competency and the public good. As long as you use those factors in making decisions, you don't have to consult with me. I will stand up behind you. The most rewarding thing was about three years ago when the company hosted its annual Christmas party. They were giving out twenty-five-year pins, and a number of those people were my hires and had risen to important positions. They came up to Winnie (my wife) and me and said, "Ark, you really left a legacy that we're so very proud of."

The Promise of America

Hoan Dang

Hoan Dang, who is in his forties, is an auditor for a major defense contractor in Washington, D.C. He was born in Saigon in 1966 and came to the United States with his family. He is also president of the Maryland Vietnamese Mutual Association (MVMA).

It was 1975. The Americans were evacuating people from Saigon—it was part of that whole thing where they evacuated 130,000 people by plane and also by helicopter and by boat; there were aircraft carriers parked off the coast. They took us all to the Philippines and from there on to Guam, and that's where we were processed. I remember our family was typical of other families there. We stayed for about two weeks before we got permission to come to the United States.

My dad's cousin was one of the colonels in the Vietnamese Air Force and I think he had some connections; he worked at the airport. So I think he was able to arrange for all of us to go on a transport plane. There were nineteen of us, from my dad's side of the family. In my immediate family we had five people: my parents, myself, and two younger sisters.

When we came to the States we stayed in one of the refugee camps, which was at Camp Pendleton, California. It was a Marine base that they converted. We lived in tents. I remember sitting in this giant tent that was designed for twenty people. It was basically a Marine training tent, where they just had straw on the bare ground and cots. It was interesting. It was cold at night and hot during the day because it was in the desert.

We stayed there for about six weeks because we had to get a sponsor before we could go out. My grandfather had a good friend in Annapolis, Maryland—a Vietnamese American who had come over in the sixties—so his family sponsored all nineteen of us. But it took a little bit of time for them to arrange all of that paperwork. We flew from California to Annapolis and all lived the first few months in a three-bedroom apartment.

Arrival: Annapolis. I didn't know it at the time, but it was the state capital. It's a neat little town. I didn't appreciate that at the time because we were living in an apartment complex.

I was eight, going on nine. We left Saigon in April 1975 and we must have arrived in Maryland at the end of June 1975. It seemed like a lot longer than that. It was exciting. I was just a kid and I didn't have any fear. It was kind of the exploration phase for me. I was with my family, my parents, and I was happy about that. I knew they went through some hardships but somehow I figured that might be temporary, that things would work out. My grandfather is kind of the patriarch and took us all out of Vietnam and he was able to transfer some of his money out of the country, so we had some of that to live on for awhile until we could all get on our feet.

My image of America was very different than what it [really] was. For some reason it just didn't occur to me that it was a normal place like Vietnam. It was a lot cleaner. I remember getting to the airport, I think it was Dulles International, and the sponsors came and picked us up. Just driving home on the highway, I was just amazed at how straight and smooth the roads were, and everything was so new and exciting. We landed at night so you could see all the lights on the runway, and the airport was just thousands of lights and that was quite a sight. So it was kind of exciting.

I was in the third grade. Actually I had been sent away to a French boarding school in Vietnam the year before we left. It was up north, a good day's drive from Saigon. I got to live with my aunt and uncle. I ended up not finishing the school year. Around February or March they had to go back to Saigon because of the news

**Hoan Dang and family, in Maryland, 1977,
two years after escaping from Vietnam**

that things were getting bad and communists were advancing toward the South. My uncle and aunt were French citizens so I think they had some kind of diplomatic immunity, but they weren't going to take a chance.

My uncle actually worked for the French government as a teacher or superintendent of the school I was going to. I think the French government called him back to France, so they arranged for all that, and of course they took me back to Saigon before they left. I found out later that he and another uncle of mine from a fairly wealthy family up there happened to have chartered the last airplane out of Dalat. It's actually kind of a special resort place. The French used to live there and now it's kind of a resort, a honeymoon destination.

Settling In: I was placed into second grade in Annapolis because I didn't speak any English; but I did speak French. I picked up English fairly quickly, as I could recognize some of the French vocabulary in the English language. We had a special teacher and she would come and get all the Vietnamese kids from the different grades. There were only a handful of students—about seven or eight of us, all in different grades—and she would teach us English one hour a week, twice a week.

After about six months they moved me back to the fourth grade. One day the teacher walked me out of my classroom and into another classroom. I said, "Where are we going?" She said, "Well, what grade are you supposed to be in?" I said, "I think I'm supposed to be in the fourth grade," and she said, "That's where you're going."

I think I had a facility with languages. Even when I was in Dalat, I remember translating for my uncle because he's French and there were people coming who wanted to rent the house and he couldn't speak Vietnamese. He would call me, this eight-year-old kid, to come out and interpret for him.

I still speak Vietnamese fairly fluently and keep up with my French. I actually studied French from fourth all the way to twelfth grade.

Moving Out: We only lived in Annapolis for a little over a year because my grandfather bought a liquor store in Washington, D.C., and the family started moving out to their own apartment. How can nineteen people fit in a three-bedroom apartment? My family occupied the dining room, the big family slept in the living room, my grandparents, one bedroom. Another room was for my aunt because she had a two-month-old baby. He was two weeks old when we left Vietnam. Now he's getting married in a few months.

The big family eventually moved to another apartment and when my grandfather bought the liquor store, we moved to the D.C. area to work there. My family moved to suburban Bethesda, which was great. We were lucky that my parents wanted a good school district and that they were able to get a loan to buy a house.

The high school I went to was named by a trade magazine as one of the top ten high schools in the country. But the funny thing was I didn't know many Asians. There was one other Vietnamese family in my school and the other Asians were mostly kids of diplomats, because in Bethesda we lived near all the embassies. I knew a couple of kids from Japan.

When we first arrived my dad worked as a bartender at a French restaurant in Annapolis because he spoke French. He went to high school in France. My mother started working at first as kind of a maid and then soon after that she got a job working at a drugstore. After my grandfather bought the liquor store, my dad worked there as manager and my mother worked as a salesperson.

That was basically how my family made a living, at least until 1984—about nine years. It seemed a lot longer than that. My grandfather decided to sell the liquor store at that point, so my dad and mom were out of jobs. Fortunately my mom had been working part time and going to school part time. She got her associate's degree as a laboratory technician. My dad went to what was a computer learning center. Back then they were just teaching people how to get into the computer industry, and he got into a six-month training program as a computer operator. He's been working with the same company since 1985.

One sad note was that my parents separated in 1984 and eventually divorced a year later. That was kind of an unusual thing at the time for a Vietnamese family, to go through a divorce. It wasn't completely foreign but more like an American thing.

Two "institutions" had a big influence in shaping my character while growing up: the Boy Scouts and Tae Kwon Do. I joined the Boy Scouts at the age of twelve and became an Eagle Scout just before my eighteenth birthday.

College: I went to college at Vanderbilt University in Nashville,

Tennessee. I really wanted to see another part of the country and I thought college was the best opportunity to do it. I wanted to study biomedical engineering and I narrowed my choices down to the South. I was at Vanderbilt from 1984–1988.

It was a very eye-opening experience. Growing up in suburban Bethesda, I thought I was like everyone else. But after my Vanderbilt experience I discovered—myself. So if I had to, I would do the same thing over again. It really gave me an opportunity to really discover my heritage as an American of Asian descent and to understand what it meant to be an Asian American.

It means you are not always treated as an equal. It means you stand out and you do face discrimination even though it may not be open discrimination and it may not be intentional. It really hit me one time when the girl I dated from Alabama said, "You want to come home and visit my parents?" I said, "Sure, but I'm kind of busy," as I was actually in the middle of my summer school sessions, and she mentioned something like, "Yeah, my dad might get out his shotgun." She was joking but I kind of knew what she meant. So being in that environment in the South—I know it's different in the North—I saw that racism is still alive and you need to be aware of it.

At times you could sense you were different; people looked at you funny. I remember just driving down during the Thanksgiving break, Christmas break. We would stop at restaurants or one of those convenience stores and people would just look at me like they hadn't seen an Asian person before—people just staring at me. I knew what they were thinking, The Chinese man, or something.

Vanderbilt was known as a southern school where a lot of the southern students who couldn't get into the Ivy Leagues went. So I think the majority were from the southern states like Alabama, Mississippi, Georgia, the Carolinas, Texas, those regions of the country. They were very proud southern kids, proud of their southern heritage.

So at Vanderbilt the big shock was the racism. One time there was an incident where someone called me a chink and I knew what that meant. But it didn't surprise me because you were in that environment and you heard them calling other people the n-word, so you figured people were calling you names even if they didn't say it to your face. So I wasn't completely naïve, and overall, it wasn't blatant.

In my freshman year of college, I joined the Vanderbilt Tae Kwon Do club and met Mr. Tae W. Haw, who was an eighth dan Tae Kwon Do master who immigrated from Korea about 1970. Mr. Haw became one of my mentors, who not only taught me the martial art, but also taught me about "sweating" (hard work), dedication, and commitment. He served as a role model for me because he was one of the few Asian American males that I knew who was a leader in the "dominant culture." He was also a nontypical Asian American because his leadership style was more like John Wayne's "Let's take the hill and take no prisoners" approach. I would say that this experience, along with my experience with the Asian American Students Association (AASA) at Vanderbilt, helped form my identity as an American of Asian heritage and as a community activist.

Politics and Aspirations: Our group, MVMA [Maryland Vietnamese Mutual Association], was started in 1979. Back then the government gave grants to mutual assistance agencies [MAA] and we are one of the few surviving MAAs. Today we probably have about fifty active members. We do some immigration work, which is one of the three programs we offer. We have served in the past twenty-five years over 20,000 refugees and immigrants. Not just Vietnamese—probably 80 percent Vietnamese—but we also serve a lot of Russians, eastern Europeans, and Africans, like Ethiopians.

We help them with the paperwork to apply for their green cards. The migration from Vietnam today is different from the past. It's no longer refugees, it's immigrants. They have to go through the same process as everyone else. Now it's mostly family sponsoring, bringing relatives over. So we do a lot of family petitions for mothers, brothers, sisters, or spouses.

As a result of being president of MVMA, I'm also pulled into a lot of the more political events. Elected officials during election year want you to get involved—council members, state delegates, gubernatorial candidates, county executives.

Since I've been doing it for a long time as president of MVMA, they just kind of automatically go to me to get the votes of the community. Montgomery County is overwhelmingly Democratic. I've been involved with a lot of initiatives and collaborations with other leaders. For example, we helped pass legislation last year to recognize Asian New Year in the state of Maryland.

Might I run for office? A lot of people have been asking me that in the past couple of years and I have been seriously considering it. I think it's not a matter of if, but a matter of when. What position? I would be interested in running for the state legislature. They're in session for only three months out of the year, so I could handle that. I actually have a separate career at a private company as an auditor.

How high do I think I can go up the political ladder as a Vietnamese American? As high as I want to go. And I would aspire to become the first Vietnamese American voted to Congress.

SETTLING IN

It's About More Than Hitting the Books

Susim Chen

Susim Chen is an artist living in Seattle, Washington. She speaks about life as a Chinese American woman in the 1950s and 1960s.

I came to the United States in 1951, at sixteen, with my brother and cousin. My dad was already here in the United States; he was an American citizen when I was born, so I was an American citizen as well.

Before I came to this country, my only contact with it was from magazines and movies. In my mind the country is happening, everyone goes to parties all the time, wears beautiful clothes—no poverty in this country, everyone's rich. But after I came here I realized that wasn't the case.

I first lived in Washington, D.C. My uncle owned a restaurant, and I stayed in a little room in the back of it. In the front of the building there was lots of gambling going on. It was dangerous. What would happen if people got drunk and did something terrible to me?

My dad felt it wasn't very safe for me to stay there, so I went to New York to be with my brother and his wife and family. But I just didn't feel comfortable living with them, so I begged my dad to let me come back to Washington, D.C.

When I observed people, they were not treated equally. Sometimes black people, customers, would come to the restaurant, and people would not welcome them. I felt it wasn't fair, but I didn't say anything.

D.C. is a beautiful city, with trees. I went to stay with a cousin on my mother's side; they owned a Chinese laundry. A lot more black people lived in the area. I just felt they weren't treated right. Sometimes they did white people's laundry first before the black people's laundry. Somehow they can tell, because they are old customers. Then I saw that not everybody was wealthy. I saw more poor people than rich people.

My dad was working for the U.S. Navy then. He just didn't feel comfortable that I stayed in that little room so he asked his friend in Ann Arbor if I could go live with his family. My dad used to own a restaurant near the University of Michigan. He hired an American guy (who was going to the university at the time) to do the dishes. They kept in contact. The guy became a dentist. Dad asked whether I could go there and do some housework for them and earn my room and board. My dad thought, Maybe if she goes to stay with them, that would help her learn English.

After six months in Michigan I returned to live with my father in New York, as the dentist died and I didn't want to stay with the family. In China I lived in a missionary school and I had lots and lots of friends. But after I left China there wasn't one day that I didn't cry. I didn't have many friends, only one; her name was Andrea. She walked me to school because when I came to New York I didn't know how to take the subway and things like that; one friend that took me to school.

Eventually I was accepted to the University of Michigan for college. But we didn't have that much money, and the school was expensive. I worked in a cafeteria to make ends meet.

College was hard. When I studied I had to take a long time to learn a little. The University of Michigan has the Burton Tower clock, which would strike three before I got to bed every night. I never thought about going out or having fun because I had to work and study very hard; that's my life.

Susim Chen, Seattle, Washington

My roommate was an exchange student from Germany. Her name was Brigita. Brigita was a beautiful blonde; she was always made up and dressed very well. She was very popular. Always had many calls. One day there was this Chinese student club New Year's party that I was invited to. So Brigita said, "Are you going?" And I said no. She asked why. I said, "I don't have anything to wear except some Chinese dresses." And she said, "That's good, you can wear a Chinese dress." She talked me into to it. At that time I was a sophomore already, no partying, no boyfriend, nothing. So she helped me; that's the first time she put makeup on me and I wore a pink Chinese dress and I went to the party. Before that nobody called me, but after that people called me, even the man I ulti- mately married—so I believe if you don't have any makeup on, and you cut your hair short, people think you are not interested. Only when you use some makeup, dress a little bit better, they think, Oh, this is a girl. They probably thought I was a boy. I always wore short hair and just didn't care about things like that. All I thought about was how to do well in school. So after that I was happy. I lived at school and met some students from China. But still, at that time I did not have that many friends.

It wasn't that I felt people were against me. I felt so inferior. I didn't want to talk to people because if I did, then I might be bothering them. I had that feeling—that I have nothing, so why would people want to be my friend.

I remember there was in my botany class a black guy, and he talked to me and said, "Do you mind if I asked you to go see a movie with me?" I said I didn't mind. He said, "How about your parents?" I thought my parents would mind. We never did go to a movie, but in the class he would talk to me. Other than him, the white students were very cooperative. If I didn't have anything, I asked them, and they would share things with me, but never socialize.

At that time there weren't that many Chinese girls in Michigan, probably a handful, but there were lots and lots of Chinese boys. If I knew a Chinese girl in the same class, I would talk to her. I was afraid to talk to others, first because my English was so poor, and second, I had the feeling that if I talked to them I might bother them. That's how I felt, culturally inferior. Maybe if I talked to them they might be friendly to me.

But they were very nice. One day I took a test in history class; there were two teaching assistants, and because I needed much more time to read the questions before answering, those two girls took me back to their apartment and they let me finish my test. Not only that, they fixed me dinner. People are like that. But yet I just felt afraid to talk to them, because I was afraid I'd bother them. All of my life, even up to this day, I still feel like I'm an outsider. I just cannot get to feel like one of the members.

Changes Over Fifty Years: I think things are improving. A long time ago, when we first went to buy a house, they'd say "It's sold" as soon as they saw a Chinese face. Then we'd drive by and the For Sale sign would still be there. We came to Seattle in 1960 and at that time they were still pretty much against selling things to the Chinese. But now I think it's much easier. Now they will talk to you. My friend Brigita from Europe married a Chinese and they moved to Seattle. Back then, she saw a house for sale and called up. They were nice to her and said, "Come on over, we are a very friendly neighborhood." As soon as she said, "My husband is Chinese," they hung up the phone.

Work: Things have gotten better but I feel that it's still not equal. I was working at a laboratory as medical technologist in the nineties. There was a promotion and they didn't give it to me. I was kind of upset. I was there longer, knew more things than my co-workers. At the time there were a couple of people to draw blood and even insert balloons into the esophagus. Those were difficult tests. The supervisor always wanted me to do them instead of the other workers; he just tried to do them a favor and give them the easy tests.

I left and went to work for another hospital. But the medical director at the old job called and begged me to come back. That's how I got to become a manager. They promoted me right away because they couldn't handle it.

The glass ceiling—my husband encountered it in his career, much more so than I. The company he worked for sold planes to China. He worked for years, making connections within China. When the promotion came, they gave it to someone else, someone tall, handsome, white. This was in 1994. After he quit, several companies, including airlines, approached him to work for them. That's how we went to China; we were there for eight years. That's when I started painting.

Art: It started with a gift to a friend. I learned flower arrangements, and when I was in China, I gave an arrangement to my husband's friend. His wife reciprocated with a painting of hers. She said she had taken two years of painting lessons, and that got me thinking. That's how I started. I feel people enjoy my art. I feel very good about it. The teacher would give me a project title, and I would think, It's October 1 (Chinese Independence Day), so how can I connect the two? I would paint five chrysanthemums to represent a star; I'd call the painting *Long life to my motherland*. That's how I would begin to approach it. I often go to museums, travel; whatever inspires me, I print it in my mind. When I paint, it pops into my head. It tells me what and how to use it, just like vocabulary when we write. My paintings are my sincerest efforts to share feelings with my audience.

Do I think this feeling of being a little bit outside of mainstream white America is ever going to change for me? I don't think in my lifetime, maybe because I came from China. When I talk to my children, they say, "Mom, you just feel that way because you feel different, that's why they treat you different." My children don't feel that. I'm happy they don't, because it's their life.

No Dating, Just Get Married

Qing Shan Liang

Qing Shan Liang is in her early thirties and is from Kwangtung, China. She works in a jewelry store in New York City's Chinatown. (Interview conducted in Toishanese.)

I came to the United States in 1997. My husband applied for me to come. I lived in Toi Shan, Canton. I really didn't know him well. His uncle knew my uncle. He went back to get a wife, so they asked me if I was married yet, and I said, no, not yet. They said they knew of this young man, and asked whether I would like to meet and marry him.

So he came to the village to meet me, and once we agreed to get married, it was settled. I saw him only once. In the village, that is the way it happens, you see the man one time and decide. When I first met him, I had just finished high school; I was eighteen years old. We were both very young. Then he came to the United States. Three years later he applied for me to join him. In China, I was a teacher—of young children—and an accountant. But once I registered for marriage with my husband, I stopped working. And I went to study English. I waited four years.

Many immigrants who come to the United States to work in restaurants or as laborers don't know much English, so it is hard for them to meet girls and to find wives. So they go back to China. Think about it—you don't have a great job, you can't speak English, how are you going to find a wife in the United States? American-born Chinese girls—they speak English, so it would be hard to find one to be interested, so men basically have no choice but to go back to China to find a wife.

Do the girls in China like men who come back to get a wife? Yes, of course [chuckles]. These men who go back—they want, first, someone who is pretty. Then they want someone who is smart. They certainly have high expectations and standards in selecting whom they want. But it is only the man who selects the woman. Women aren't in the position to select. For instance, a man comes to the United States, his situation isn't great, he has only a so-so job, and isn't very good-looking. But he goes back to China and can pick a very pretty girl from a good family background. The man certainly wouldn't go for an average or subaverage girl.

That was more than ten years ago. The conditions in China weren't that good; it was hard to make a living, so everyone wanted to come to the United States. Some people were basically peasants working the land, with no house to live in, enough to eat, or a job. So the dream, of course, was to come to the United States. This is the land of plenty. At that time, even if the guy wasn't physically perfect, he could go to China and get a beautiful wife. It was always the man's choice.

Most of the introductions were done by connections—friends, matchmakers. Word gets out—oh, a single guy is back to get married! All these girls would line up, basically for his selection, to be looked at and to be picked by him. Sometimes these men would be visiting a teahouse and would see a pretty waitress—most of the restaurant help are women—and they might ask about that woman, get an introduction, find out if she's married, and that's how it's done.

Then they would both register for marriage, to make it official. It's all connections—someone has a friend who knows a matchmaker, or a fellow student knows of so-and-so who is looking. So it is very much connections—one person to another—a string of introductions, until the match is made. A lot of people did it that way in the nineties . . . even today, some people still do it. They go all over—back to the village, to the big city—it's wherever they know people and have connections.

Dating: I never had a real date with my husband, like dinner or the movies. Basically, the way it works is that the man and woman meet each other, and if they agree, they register to make the marriage official. The idea is that understanding and feelings will come, with time. Most people who get married this way don't really know each other; as for dating, forget about it—it doesn't happen. The practice for most marriages is for the couple to go out, get to know each other, and decide over a few years. But that is definitely not how it happens if the man goes to China to get a wife.

Once the decision is made, the couple goes to register, makes it official, and the man returns to the United States to apply for his wife to come. I basically waited four years before I got to the United States as my husband had a green card but wasn't a citizen yet.

Life in the United States: My husband works in a bakery in Brooklyn. When I first came to the United States, it was hard to adjust. I couldn't get used to the food, and I wasn't able to communicate. I spoke no English. I was here without any of my family; I didn't have any friends. It was scary. I wanted to go home.

Gradually I got used to things. I got a job, met new friends, was able slowly to acquaint myself with new people. I'm earning money, I can buy things and send money home to my family in China. In China, there was no way to earn money. Working one day here is like working a whole month in China. So slowly my heart got less heavy, and now I like it better here than in China. I have two children, a six-year-old daughter and a four-month-old son.

First Job: When I first came to the United States, my mother-in-law took me to the sewing factory to work. But I didn't know anything about sewing, and most of the women there were older. I thought, here I was a young woman, and I would have to spend the rest of my life laboring in a factory with all these older women. I was young; I wanted to learn English. I wanted to do something else. But things were very hard. I had no money of my own, and the prospects were not good. Fortunately, my husband's friend saw me in the street with him. She said to him, "Your wife is so young and pretty, what a waste it would be for her to spend the rest of her life in a sewing factory." So she said to me, "Don't go to work in a factory. Go home, and in a week, I will take you to a jewelry store and they will give you a job." I said, "Really?" And she said, "Yes, just go home and wait for my good news." So sure enough, in a week she called. At first I was a bit scared. Here I am from China and had not seen anything as grand as a jewelry store in the United States. I never bought anything elegant, and certainly didn't have the money to be near gold jewelry. I didn't have much confidence that I would be good at it. But I listened very carefully to others when they instructed me as to how to talk to customers, how to make a sale, and so they kept me on after the trial period. That is how I got started. I've been working there ever since—nine years. I am very happy about the work.

I work six days a week, ten to six-thirty. I take the subway into Manhattan every day. In the beginning, I took care of my daughter for the first nine months, then I took her back to China for my mother to raise so that I could continue working. I really didn't have much of a choice. We needed to pay the rent, and I had to find a way to work so I could send money home to my mother. So I left my daughter with my mother until she was four years old, and I was able to bring them both over to the United States. When my daughter could attend preschool, and I got my citizenship, I applied for my mother to come to the United States. With my mother here, I could have a second child; she would take care of him, and I could continue to work.

That's very common—many immigrants, husband and wife, work, so they send their young children back to China for parents to take care of until they are school age. This way, the family in China can also be helped out financially. Right now my mother is here, but my brother is still in China. It will probably take another ten years or so before he can come to the United States.

I think living in the United States is definitely better than living in China. Here, if you work hard, you can earn money and buy the things you want. In China, if you can't get work, you can't buy the things you want, so of course the United States is better. Here, I can earn enough to buy a car. In China, you can work as hard as possible but still can't afford expensive things.

We lived in Queens with my husband's family when I first arrived. They came in 1986. Last year we moved to Brooklyn. We rent. We would like to own a home, but right now I can't think that far. Perhaps if we can find a way to buy through government-supported housing, that would make things easier. Houses are so expensive now.

I used to go to English classes from seven to nine at night, after work. That was for a few months. Once I got pregnant with my first child, it was just too hard to keep going to classes after work. Now with my job and two children, there is no way.

What is the best thing about the United States? The ability to earn money, to know that when you work, it is worth something. The worst thing for me is that I can't speak English, and so there is so much that is closed to me. Even when I go to buy something, and it isn't right, there is no way I can explain it to people. If I need to go to a doctor, I can't communicate my problem. So I go to a Chinese-speaking doctor for everything.

I haven't seen anything in the United States. I haven't gone anywhere for leisure or vacation. First, you need the time, then you need to have some money. For immigrants like me, I need to earn money to support myself, and support my family in China. That's the expectation. So I have to save what little money I make, and support my family and relatives in the village. It's basically unheard of for me to think about taking a vacation or going somewhere for fun.

Eventually, we might do that, but I don't know when. The thing is, immigrants like me who have a chance to take a vacation will choose to go back to China rather than see the United States. They want to visit home and family.

Growing Up in China: When I was growing up and a student in China, I was very smart. I wanted to go to college and get a good job afterward. My father was a teacher, so he was proud that he had such a smart daughter who wanted to do well in school. The hope was that I would earn lots of money and support my parents. That was my dream. And then to marry into a well-to-do door [household]. That was essentially the dream, because relations between the United States and China had not really thawed, so it was hard to think in terms of coming to America. When I was little, there wasn't much hope or thought of coming to the United States.

My village was about a two-hour ride from Guangzhou. There were about three hundred families in the village. When I was ten, my maternal grandparents lived in Hong Kong and had some money, so they bought a building for us in the city. So I was raised in the city.

When I was little, in the village, my father was a teacher and my mother should have farmed, but there was enough money sent home from her parents who lived in Hong Kong, so she didn't have to do that. In those days, farming meant growing and harvesting rice, cutting firewood, raising hogs, chickens. As my grandparents were in Hong Kong and they sent money to the village, my mother didn't have to work in the rice paddies. There were no jobs to be had.

My grandparents sent money back for schooling, and that meant a better education and better opportunities for work and earning money. That's why they bought a building and moved my family out to the city.

Getting a Wife from China Today: Many of my current friends also came to the United States by marriage, or their parents were citizens and brought them over. Those are the two ways they enter the country. But today, not everyone wants to come to the United States. It is sort of half and half. There are jobs now in China, people have money, and life is even better than in the United States—there is a chance to live in a nice place, earn money, and have a good job, so coming to America isn't what it used to be in terms of demand.

Now, when someone goes back to China to get a wife—well, women have to think twice about it: what kind of job does this person have, what are his prospects? Is he a good catch? That's what people are thinking before they accept a proposal. That's different than when I got married ten years ago.

When I was going to learn English in Guangzhou before I came to the United States, I met many women who were also waiting. They too had registered for marriage. Some of these women were marrying men who were a lot older, or men who had children and a previous family. They were willing to do it to come to the United States, for a chance to improve their lives. The idea is one person's sacrifice will lead to honor and a bright future for the whole family. It's a way to sacrifice yourself to save your whole family.

Today, when someone goes back to China, the people in China are doing the selecting—deciding whether you would be a good match. It's not just about coming to the United States anymore.

Making a New Life

Frank Bai

Frank Bai, in his mid-forties, arrived in the United States in 1997. He lives with his family in Brooklyn, New York. (Interview conducted in Cantonese.)

I met my wife through family connections. We were introduced through distant relatives. She passed through China on her way to a business trip in Japan, and that's how we met. She applied for me to come to the United States as her fiancé. We've been married ten years.

Ten days before I was to come to the United States, the retailer Nine West contacted me, offering me a position to open their shoe stores in China. After getting my green card, I did in fact, go to work for them. I would spend six months a year in China, and then return to the United States while continuing to help them monitor their business in China. I did that for three years. But it was probably difficult for them to run their operation under such circumstances, so once they opened twenty-eight stores, I left the company. I had also brought my parents to the United States by then. I am an only son.

How do I describe my life? I worked for a large Hong Kong shoe manufacturer, overseeing all their China operations—basically I was their highest executive in Mainland. They had over 20 stores, with 280 people under my management. I had a chauffeur to take me to work and bring me home. I was paid in the tens of thousands each month [local money]; by comparison, the average worker got about a thousand a month. The shoes were sold in China and Hong Kong, but they also distributed to Italy and other parts of Europe as well. So essentially it was my ability to get things done in China that Nine West was interested in when they hired me.

I've had many jobs since coming to the United States. I've done picture framing. Then I had my own jewelry business in China-town; that was for two years. But the rents were very high, and it's a risky business. Now I am a delivery man, six days a week, for a Chinese dry cleaning business. I drive all over Brooklyn. I leave the house at 8 A.M. and get home by 8 at night; been doing it for over a year. Got the job from the newspaper want ads. It's a rather low-skilled job, but in many ways it is very comfortable, because I don't have to think much. At the end of the workday I just park the truck and go home.

Maybe on Sunday I get a chance to play with my children, or go for a tea lunch. On long weekends, a few times a year, we try to go camping—pitch a tent, cook over an open fire. Not much else in the way of recreation.

Compared to my past, it's a 180-degree difference. Every month I would travel, take a plane trip to Beijing, check out our store. The next month I would go to Shanghai; it would be an easy visit, with drivers picking me up and seeing me off. There was no set time for me to show up at work, or to leave. I would probably eat out six days a week for business meetings and have late evenings. That was great, as I wasn't married. Now, things are more settled, not as exciting. I can see my children, my parents, my wife. My responsibilities are to my family.

I have two children; my daughter is eight and my son is three. My wife works in Midtown Manhattan for a clothing manufacturer. It's fairly easy for her to find employment. She grew up in the United States and has been here almost thirty years, so English is not a barrier.

I think going back to China would make things easier professionally. With my experience, I can get a position fairly quickly. But as my children were born here, I wouldn't think of moving them away. My dad doesn't want to be in the United States. There isn't much for him to do. My mother is okay with it, because she is with her grandchildren.

I did bring my wife back to China to live for six months, but she didn't feel she could live there permanently. She had a very leisurely life, with maids to clean and cook and not much to do. On my days off, we might have the driver take us somewhere. Her friends who visited us kept telling her what a great life she had. But she found it boring. Plus, her family is all in the United States.

Sure, in the past, I was very highly paid and had a very exciting, different sort of lifestyle—a big life. But I was going 24/7, nonstop. Now things are much calmer, and I am comfortable—sort of a time for me to rest.

My parents live with us. We have a co-op. With maintenance, it comes to over $1,000 a month. We've looked at houses, but the mortgage was over $2,000 to $3,000 a month. We thought it would be too much pressure to do this. So we figured a co-op for now would be fine.

Growing Up: When I was little, about five or six years old—in my parents' time—it was hard in China to live well. Every month, we were limited in the amount of food or cooking oil we could have. But I didn't really encounter a difficult life, politically or socially. Today, I think there is little difference in terms of doing business in China. If you are capable, you can have a good life. It's pretty much like the United States.

In the past in China, it was hard to get information; things were closed. But now with the Internet, it is much harder to keep things from the people. The politics of running a communist country is one thing, but doing business, that is another. They basically won't stop you as long as you conform.

My children speak Chinese at home. With my daughter, it's 70 percent English, 30 percent Chinese. But when she speaks to her grandparents, it's definitely all in Chinese; this forces the children to retain the language. When they were very little we took them to Chinese school, but now they've stopped. I figure that if they want to learn it as they get older, they can do so on their own. My daughter learned to write and read some Mandarin, but as she seldom used it, it was easy to forget.

I came to this country late in life—thirty-six years old. If I had come ten years earlier, I think my life situation would be much better; I would have better language skills. I am between cultures, and can't compare my career and professional standing with what I had in China. But there are definitely positives about being in the United States.

Interestingly, last month I was contacted by one of the largest diamond jewelry dealers from China—they have over one hundred stores. They were interested in setting up a wholesale business in the United States. So they want me to get involved with that. But I think even here, English fluency may be an issue.

Right now, it is difficult for me to think in terms of being able to control my professional growth—my language skills are basic, and I have small children, so there are limitations. Even the things that I believe I can accomplish, I hesitate to consider.

I see this diamond contact as an opportunity on the horizon, so I will probably pick up my professional life again when the time is right.

II. Aspects of Americanization

ANSWERING THE CALL

Changing the Tide of History
Dale Minami

Dale Minami was lead attorney for the plaintiff in Korematsu v. United States, *1984,[1] a landmark decision overturning a forty-year-old federal conviction for refusal to obey exclusion orders aimed at Japanese Americans during World War II.*

Getting Started on the Korematsu Case: I had been involved in civil rights in the seventies, suing institutions, a lot of institutions. I had just finished a case against Washington State University about creating an Asian American studies program because they didn't have one there. At about that time the redress movement was heating up and I had been involved in the earlier resolutions of the JCL—the national Japanese American Citizens League—to promote redress, and that was in 1972, 1974. But it didn't really get on track to moving until the late seventies and early eighties.

At about that time, the U.S. Congress decided to create a commission on wartime relocation and internment of civilians and had hearings throughout the country. I felt we should be a part of those hearings because what happened to Japanese Americans was so contrary to the Bill of Rights—to the first ten amendments of the Constitution. I helped organize a group of lawyers to put together a brief. It looked like a formal brief to the commission, arguing the depravation of a number of the Bill of Rights issues that occurred in 1942 when Japanese Americans were taken away: loss of First Amendment rights to assembly, no government rights to redress, loss of Fourth Amendment rights against illegal search and seizure, Fifth Amendment rights to due process, Sixth Amendment right to counsel, Eighth Amendment rights against cruel and unusual punishment, on and on.

What happened was another gentleman, named Peter Irons, a professor at the University of Massachusetts, Amherst, was writing a book at the time and he was given my name by people that knew I was doing civil rights work. He called me up. He had discovered evidence that the Supreme Court was defrauded—was lied to—by high officials during the Supreme Court cases of three Japanese men who refused the internment orders. He said that we may be able to open the case based on newly discovered evidence of a fundamental injustice, and he asked me if I wanted to participate. I was totally floored, shocked. I thought, Man, this guy must be crazy. I had wondered about it all this time and now I find that he has this actual evidence, so I looked at the evidence and it was remarkable. Memoranda from government lawyers saying, We are lying to the Supreme Court in these cases; we have evidence contrary to what we are arguing—now if we don't reveal this we will be breaching our ethical duties as lawyers.

There was also some additional evidence that showed that they deliberately falsified some of the rationales in writing and they changed the wording and destroyed the originals so no one would know they changed the original justifications and submitted the revised, more palatable justifications to the Supreme Court. That was the proverbial smoking gun that lawyers dream about.

So I assembled the original pro bono team that had submitted the brief to the commission and contacted the only Japanese American lawyer I knew in Portland (because we had to bring the case to Portland), and two Japanese American attorneys in Seattle. We developed this great young work team and that's how we started it.

Through the people I've talked to, people I've seen and observed, I think the case made a difference in terms of understanding the legal system and its failure in 1943–1944. It's helped people understand the injustice that happened to Japanese Americans in

1942 when they were taken away to camps. It's helped to inform the history of American racism, which has been an undercurrent, and sometimes overflowing to overt racism, in our history. So I think to the degree that we've educated people, I think we've made a difference.

An American of Japanese Descent: I'm third-generation Japanese American and was born right after the camps. It informs your sensibility of how you look at this country when your brother, who is one or two years older, was taken away to camps without due process. That type of injustice occurs and the Congress acquiesces, the president issues the order, and the Supreme Court blindly accepts the judgment of the military that there was some necessity to imprison these potential spies and saboteurs. When we were able to show later on that in fact there is no good cause to intern Japanese Americans, that definitely has an impact on how you see the world.

To that extent it propelled me into doing more types of civil rights work and speaking out about racism or discrimination. But that actually is a lesser part of my law practice today, since I mostly do personal injury work, which in the earlier period sustained the civil rights work that I was mainly doing pro bono.

When I was doing civil rights work, it was a major factor in getting me involved and helping create a firm that emphasized civil rights cases along with other types of practices. I also do some entertainment law, representing journalists.

Growing Up: I grew up in a city called Gardena, south of Los Angeles. It was a mixed, lower-middle-class community at that time. Kind of a balance of mostly Caucasian but also a large number of Japanese Americans, Latino Americans, Mexican Americans, and African Americans who lived in mostly the border areas, but we all went to school together.

It was a time of innocence—when the nation's race problems hadn't exploded yet. It was a time of blissful ignorance, perhaps partly because we accepted the principles of the majority society—the melting pot theory.

Then too, in Gardena, going to school, a high proportion of the student leaders and athletes were Japanese. Student government had the highest academic achievers. So there was visibility of achievement. You really didn't feel much different.

It was only when I went to USC that I discovered—USC at that time was kind of a microcosm of this country—that rich white males dominated the fraternities that essentially ruled the campus. It was there that I first discovered social ostracism, class differences, race differences. It was only after I watched Watts burn down from the freeway driving home from a volleyball game that I got to thinking about these race relations. My world had been very Pollyannish. It was very simple until I started going to college. I started to learn a lot more growing up.

Family and Values: Being Japanese Americans, we were taught to be very achievement oriented. We were taught to succeed. It wasn't whether you *wanted* to go to college, it was that you *had* to go to college or grad school. Those values of education were Japanese definitely, no question about it. But they're also influenced by the depravations my parents suffered. My older brother told a story a few years ago—it was the first time I'd heard it. My dad had wanted him to go to grad school and he wasn't sure what he was going to do. So my dad looked at him and said, "They can take away your freedom but they cannot take away your education. You're going."

My dad was a gardener, my grandfather, a farmer. My dad was born in Riverside, my mother in Oxnard. My father started out farming. Coming back from the war he repaired appliances then he became a gardener just to make a living, but his passion was sporting goods. He was a really good athlete. He sold golf clubs, taught people how to play golf and tennis, and eventually he opened a small sporting goods store in Gardena. My mother's father was an insurance salesman. He was actually pretty well-off, at New York Life, one of the few companies that accepted Asian American agents. So he became pretty successful.

When I was growing up, my parents only talked about internment in bits and pieces. Until the redress movement started they didn't really want to talk about it. They told stories that were harmless little anecdotes. There was kind of a bitterness; the stories of depravation—we didn't begin to hear them until much later on in our lives.

They were taken to Santa Anita at first, a famous racetrack in Los Angeles. That's where Japanese Americans were first sent in Los Angeles. They were put in horse stalls. My mom says when my aunt got into the stall, there was horse shit on the walls, on the ground. They had to sleep on old hay; it smelled. They had no privacy because it was like horse doors—the wind came through. It was freezing. It was the first time I saw her cry when she talked about that experience.

Then they were sent to Rohwer, Arkansas, which is a swampland in the south of Arkansas where they lived for years. The conditions were bad. They talked a lot about how hot and humid it was, something they had never experienced, and about these bugs, these mosquitoes and these certain kind of gnats that they had never heard of. They had to build a lot of their own furniture.

In the camp they had to use latrines that were open-door, and they had to share barracks with another family, so they had no privacy. My brother was only one year old at the time.

Identity: I think so many of us in our generation have gone through points where we rejected all things Japanese. We disliked Japanese for their cheap products, for the fact that they started the war and put people in camps. From the way they looked, the way they dressed, to making fun of FOBs (fresh off the boats; now they're fresh off the planes), and so we were filled with self-hatred that was partly induced by the fact that Japan went to war with the United States. Also, the Japanese in Japan disowned the Japanese that came to America—treated them as second-class citizens who weren't good enough to make it in Japan. I think that's changed quite a bit. Japan is much more embracing of Japanese Americans now.

So at one point I would have preferred not to have been Japanese. If someone granted me a wish, of course I would've said I want to be Caucasian.

Moving out of that mind-set was pretty evolutionary at one level and revolutionary at another, in the sense that without the civil rights movement, without being able to read the autobiography of Malcolm X or Richard Wright's *Native Son* or Ralph Ellison's *Invisible Man*, without those kind of guidebooks for me and my generation, it would have been very difficult for us. I think we would have never seen the similarities between the Japanese American and African American experience of racism, which essentially colonizes your mind and makes you inculcate feelings of inferiority. Without black Americans essentially throwing off the psychological shackles of a colonialization process, we would have never understood—I would have married somebody, moved out into the suburbs, and tried not to be Japanese.

I think that black pride and all of what happened afterward in terms of understanding your history made it possible for us as Asian Americans to feel that we had self-worth. Without Latinos and Brown Power and Black Power I don't think we would have had the same kind of stability in regard to our identity as we do now.

I just got back from Japan two months ago and I loved it. But I know I'll never be Japanese like them and they know it too. Yet I have a number of friends from Japan and we operate on a level of affection and affinity which is unlike anywhere else. So that part of it makes no difference at all. The fact that I don't speak the language at all and that I don't understand the culture quite as well as the people from Japan doesn't bother me all that much.

Can Internment Happen Again? Absolutely; it's not a foregone conclusion that everybody or a lot of people thought it was the wrong thing to do back in 1942, or that it can't happen again.

You still find a great number of Americans who have never known about internment. I think it depends on where you live. If you live in the San Francisco area, which is very liberal and progressive, most people I know are taught about it. I think if you live somewhere else, there is a great deal of ignorance, despite all the publicity, all the educational work and materials that have been created, and the books that have been written.

During the most recent Persian Gulf War there had been talk about imprisoning Palestinians, Arabs en masse. We almost saw a recurrence of that after September 11, when hysteria led to the curtailment of civil rights in a great way. I think the fact that Japanese Americans have gone through that experience—the fact that they have resurrected the notion of injustice and that they institutionalized that injustice and the reclaiming of their citizenship and birthright through the redress movement—has done a lot to educate this country. It's done a lot to deter people from making that same mistake. So, politically, if there's enough of a crisis or hysteria, absolutely it can happen again. I don't have as much faith that the simple strength of people's morality in this country is going to prevent this from happening. I believe the political and economic circumstances will dictate whether this will happen again.

I think it's an absolute principle that international tensions affect the minority groups in this country. That's why in the 1980s, when Japan destroyed the competition in cars, people mistaken for Japanese got killed. I think it's a natural phenomenon and it should be reversed; it shouldn't be natural. But I think people tend to take out their hostilities because they can't distinguish between people from other countries and American citizens—especially in the racial context, like Japanese Americans. I think that's going to happen to Chinese Americans when China becomes even a greater power. I think you're going to find more backlash against Asian Americans because they can't distinguish between us. In terms of either hate crimes or legislation, it's going to take a different kind of manifestation, but it will reflect, I think, an anti-Chinese viewpoint whether you're Chinese American or Chinese from China.

You can always catch or always feel hysteria in this country, and, given the underpinnings of racism in this country, those feelings really come out. They haven't been eradicated and I don't think you can legislate how people feel.

I wish I was more optimistic. I do feel that you need great leadership on racial issues and people who speak out—people who lead by showing that the terrible results of racism are important. Continued education is very important, to teach people to value diversity. So I think this is a kind of phenomenon, racism, that has to be fought on all fronts.

The political power of racial minority groups is important because without political power you don't get respect. People of color need to organize and be strong. They can't do it alone. They have to rally with people of goodwill of all races and all colors so that the leaders that you respond to and elect, the people you vote for, will be on your side if there is a crisis or hysteria.

Into the Governor's Mansion

Gary Locke

Gary Locke is the first Asian American governor to be elected in the continental United States. He took office in Washington State in 1996 and served two terms.

I'm first generation born in the United States. My dad came over to the United States when he was about twelve or thirteen, in the late 1920s. My mom was born in Hong Kong and they got married after the war. My dad was in the U.S. Army during World War II. My grandfather actually came to the United States as a teenager and worked as a servant for a family in the [Washington] state capital. We joke that it was a house that was literally a mile from the governor's residence—that it took the Locke clan one hundred years to travel one mile.

When I was growing up I never thought of politics. I went off to college thinking maybe I'd be an urban planner, maybe a forester. Then I attended Yale undergrad. It was during a tumultuous era of antiwar protests. With *Doonesbury* cartoons and things like that, I realized that perhaps I was more inclined toward government and had a fascination with government. I felt I could be more instrumental by being a lawyer and making change through the legal system than by simply protesting and burning buildings and things that other people were doing. I never even thought that I would be in government.

I thought I'd come back to Seattle and open up a law office in the international Chinatown district of Seattle and be involved in community work. I ended up being in the prosecutor's office, as a prosecutor of felonies. And then I started helping people run for office, and I just loved it so much—Ruby Chow for reelection, for instance. Then I was involved in some political activities on affirmative action issues.

I was encouraged by people to consider running for office myself. It was just so foreign to me. But I got involved in other people's campaigns and I had an opportunity to work in the state capital as a lawyer for one of the committees in the state senate. From there I got to see that the legislature was made up of everyday people from all walks of life—from hairdressers to Christmas tree growers to travel agents to car salesmen to dentists and lawyers. I said, Hey, if they can do it, why not me?

Running for Office: Working with some people in the community, I ran as a Democrat against a Democratic incumbent in the state legislature. There were many challengers, and traditional wisdom is that the challengers will kill each other off, basically, and the incumbent will waltz on through. The incumbent was supported by all the traditional interest groups and so we had really very little money. We were just doorbelling like crazy, and we won. We won the primary with 52 percent of the vote. The other two challengers got about 10 or 12 percent of the vote and I think the incumbent got 28 percent. It's a solidly Democratic district so we were home free. I came up with about 85 percent of the vote in the general election.

I was in the state legislature for about eleven years. I always wanted to do management. I had considered running for governor at the end of that legislative career, but a very respected past congressman decided to run for governor and I decided that there was no way I was going to beat him. Still, that's when people started to approach me and say, Hey, you should run for governor.

I did not run for governor then, but a year later I was the first runner-up for county executive. I ran against a Republican incumbent. Our primaries are in mid-September, so that when you come

Gary Locke

out of the primary you only have seven weeks to go before the general election. It was a very hotly contested primary which I won—it was against a lot of good friends of mine on the Democratic side. A day after the primary we had zero money in the bank with seven weeks to go and the incumbent was sitting on a huge war chest because he had been basically unopposed.

I really enjoyed that. Then the opportunity to run for governor came. It was out of the blue. I had just been married about a year, and our governor suddenly announced that he would not seek reelection. I never thought the opportunity to run for governor would really present itself. I figured in a few years my wife and I would have kids, and who knows what we would want to be doing in our lives. I felt that in a few years there would be a new rising star, and that person would run for governor and would probably win or something.

So when our governor suddenly announced that he would not seek a second term, I was encouraged by a lot of people to throw my hat in. We came to the conclusion that this was a great time to do it. So this was kind of a dream that materialized over the years of working in government. We didn't have kids yet, and my wife would be very active on the campaign.

The Asian American Factor: We knew that would hurt us among a certain percentage of the population.[2] When I ran for county executive, that came up in some of the polling. We also saw in some of the polling for governor that it could hurt us.

I'm very proud that the state of Washington at that time had an open primary system where you're not registered by party. You do not ask for a Republican or Democratic ballot in the primary. All the candidates running for office—Democrat, Socialist, Communist, Independent—are on the ballot; you just vote for one. You flip the page and there are all the candidates for lieutenant governor and you could vote for somebody of a totally different party. There's no registration by party whatsoever. You can vote for one candidate of one party and vote for another political party's candidate for a different office and just keep switching back and forth.

There were some fourteen candidates on the ballot for governor when I ran in the primary: four main credible Democratic candidates and about eight to nine Republican candidates—senators, lawyers. The mayor of Seattle was my main competitor, along with a former member of Congress that I helped and who served with me in the state legislature. I'm really proud of the fact that of those fourteen candidates, the mayor and I—an African American and an Asian American—got virtually 41 percent of the total votes cast in the state of Washington. I got 28 percent of the vote and he got 13 or 14 percent of the vote. And because I got the most votes of all the Democrats, I went to the final as the Democratic candidate. The top Republican only had 12 or 13 percent of the vote. She moved to the final as the Republican with the most votes. So here we are in a state where roughly over 40 percent of the total votes cast in that election were for two people of color.

Changing Prominence of Asian Americans: I think that Asian Americans have changed. There are more Asian Americans in key positions of government, in business, in academia, and I think that's great. The greater attention to names, whether it's Yo Yo Ma or Michelle Kwan or Jerry Yang of Yahoo, means people are aware of more Asian Americans of prominence in a variety of fields. And whether they were born in the United States or came here, like Yao Ming, that creates positive role models and images and allows people to have higher dreams and aspirations.

While I was governor, there were all these requests to go to these Asian American conferences and events all across the country. We were very selective. We did not want any publicity on being constantly out of state or focusing on Asian American communities around the country. I really wanted to be successful and respected as a governor in Washington. I felt if I could do a really great job as governor I could raise the glass ceiling for others to go into politics and make it possible for them to succeed and win. I mean, if there's a lot of criticism about me, if the voters in the state of Washington have a negative image about me, then that can hamper other Asian Americans who want to run for office. Is there a glass ceiling? I don't think so. Obviously I think there's a glass ceiling for very high offices like the presidency, maybe vice presidency. But look how Asian Americans have succeeded. There is a governor, other Asian Americans or Pacific Islanders running for office in Illinois or governor in Louisiana, and members of Congress from California.

To people who want to go into politics, I would say that, rather than numbers, you should look at how successful you have been and how you've distinguished yourself in your particular field, whether it's in local politics or the state legislature—and if you have a good reputation, or if you've accomplished that in business.

We have people from the private sector that run for office—that's how most people run for office in the Senate. There's the city council, the mayor's office—they come from the business sector or they come from academia. A few come from local politics. There's no reason why Asian Americans can't do exactly the same thing that others have done. But the secret is, were you a successful CEO or a well-known sports figure? Even people in Hollywood have gone on to politics. And so, really, race should not enter into the equation.

Asian American or American? I think the question pops up more among us as Asian Americans and Chinese Americans than in the voting public. I'm all. I'm very much Chinese American, I'm also Asian American, and I'm also American. I'm also very proud of my Chinese ancestry. I used to speak much better Chinese. I didn't really learn English until I went to kindergarten. And then I kind of lost it all. I went back to Hong Kong when I was about ten years old and picked it all back up.

Who is Gary Locke? A person of different upbringings with different cultures. A person who's bridged different eras of technology. I'm not very conversant with the computer but very much believe in the power of technology. I grew up in the time of *Ozzie and Harriet* and *Father Knows Best* and the *Donna Reid Show* and wondered why my mom didn't wear a dress and pearls and high heels. How come our dad didn't sit down with a tie and sport coat or suit at dinnertime? And yet I really rebelled. I had a hard time. I rejected a lot of Chinese customs and traditions. But I think I understood them, and had a greater appreciation for the trials and tribulations and challenges that my friends faced, so I'm a product of that tension.

I've gone back to China and I've seen. I went back again in the late eighties. I was really sad and kind of emotional about the poor state of the Chinese people at that time. I'm a person with a lot of mixed emotions and inputs, I suppose. But I think I have used those experiences and remembered those experiences throughout my political life in terms of policy; for example, trying to enact greater information availability for noncitizens when they plead guilty to crimes which could be grounds for deportation—insisting on interpretation and bilingual information for people in the criminal justice system.

When as governor I did welfare reform, it was a time when Newt Gingrich and Congress had eliminated food stamps for immigrants. I had a totally different notion of welfare reform. I threatened to veto the proposed bills from our entire Republican-controlled legislature, even though I negotiated every point of them, unless we came up with our own food stamp program for immigrants and made sure that our welfare program was also eligible to immigrants after they had been in the country for a few years. So I think I have been very sensitive to our immigrant history and the immigrant story of all of America as we put together our policies.

Even when I first was elected to the state legislature, I never plotted a plan or a political career. I never said I wanted to be chair of this committee. Surely after I joined the legislature I knew that if you wanted power you had to be part of the budget committee, so I joined the budget writing committee. Then I realized there was a chairman who wrote the entire budget and left a little bit of extra money on the table for committee members here and there, but that really it was dictated by the chairman of the budget writing committee. He or she would negotiate with the Senate with or against the governor's office and put together a budget for the state. I said, Oh, I want to be chair of the budget writing committee. But other than that, I never planned or plotted a political career. Some people in the legislature have said, I'm going to do this for so many years and then run for governor, then run for U.S. Senate, and then I'm going to run for president. I never believed in that. It's a matter of luck and timing, being prepared, having a database, keeping your files up to date in case the opportunities present themselves to run for higher office.

Who knows what your kids will want to do? Maybe they're training for the Olympics; my daughter really likes swimming, but she may also want to be an Olympic athlete in swimming and your whole life changes. Politics may take a different turn. Who knows when we will have another Democratic administration in D.C. and whether or not an opportunity will present itself to go back and work in D.C.? Then it also depends on what my wife is doing with her career as a journalist and what our kids are doing and the health of my mom and dad, who are getting on in age, and if the sacrifice is worth it and in what stage of life we are. So do I want to plan and plot a career in politics? Do I want to stay active in politics? I miss the debates, the discussions of public policy, and being able to help shape public policy. I don't miss the grind of Olympia, our state capital, but I'm very proud of what we were able to accomplish. And so that's how I see it.

Growing Up: The whole Locke clan from the village settled in the Olympia area. I remember our family not taking very many vacations but a lot of uncles hanging around, and Mom and Dad always involved in big family, uncles, grandmother, and grandfather.

My grandfather went to work as a chef in one of the hospitals and so did all of the other uncles. My dad and his brothers also worked, helped my grandfather in the restaurant, and learned to cook, and we got leftovers at home. My grandfather and then my father were cooks. It was a restaurant at the Pike Place Market, a Chinese American café, a "Happy Days" type restaurant with the U-shaped counters and booths and spinning chairs and things like that. Then he sold that because the kitchen was too hot, and opened up a grocery store, which was open 7 days a week, 365 days a year.

I worked in the grocery store and helped stock the shelves, made deliveries, and worked behind the counter; I put the milk back in the milk case and put the bottles of Coke and Pepsi back in the coolers. Back in those days, at ten or eleven years old, you could grab a bus to south Seattle, and it was about a forty-minute bus ride up to the north part of Seattle to work in a store after school or on weekends. Nowadays I wouldn't dream of having my little nine-year-old grab a bus. Back then, at ten, eleven years old, I grabbed a bus down to the YMCA and learned how to swim; I made my own breakfast and hopped on the bus to go get my swimming lesson. It was at 7:30 in the morning, so I'd catch the bus at about 7:15.

I know that I was eleven years old because when I joined the Boy Scouts I didn't really know how to swim. To become an Eagle Scout you had to get a swimming merit badge, so I had to learn how to swim. By twelve years old I was in the advanced class; I had to do that on Saturdays.

I had no idea what the future held—other than it was expected that we would go off to college. Mom and Dad would write out multiplication, addition, subtraction, and division problems and we would do that at the kitchen table or at the back of the grocery store. I really had no idea when I was in high school what college was like or what colleges were out there. It wasn't until my junior year that my counselor encouraged us in the inner city to think of private schools outside of the state of Washington; things like scholarships and financial aid packages were available. That was at a time when Harvard and Yale had alumni that came out and recruited us and were actually assigned to the different schools to tell us about the different opportunities that were available. I had no idea. Many of the schools I had never even heard of until that junior year.

There are actually five kids in my family. My older sister went off to community college; she's a year and a half older than I am. Then I have a sister who is one year behind me and I have a younger brother who's eleven years behind me. Another sister is thirteen years behind me—so three of us, and then kind of a break.

Education: I ran for the state legislature because I was concerned about the policy of the schools. I was not happy with the education my little brother and sister had received and how the school system was not helping them realize their potential—how we at home had to help them and guide them and encourage them. So I really tried to focus on that as governor. And even right now as a private citizen I'm just as concerned about the education system. These are values that Asian Americans and Chinese Americans have always instilled and focused on. Our cultures have always emphasized education, and that's what our family, our clan, has always talked about. Work hard, get a good education, and we take care of each other. Take care of your elders: my brothers and sisters are all talking about it—Okay, which one does Mom and Dad come live with—and it's expected that we're going to take care of Mom and Dad.

Role Models: It's hard to believe that I'm a role model. I think of the real trailblazers as people like Ruby Chow and Dolores Sibonga, who was the first Asian American woman city council member in Seattle and the first Filipino American to be elected to the council.

When I was about thirteen or fourteen years old, a teacher took us to a musical and Wing Luke came in. I had heard about him, a Seattle city councilman. [He was elected in 1962 and became the first Chinese American from a large mainland city to hold such an office.] He died tragically a few years later in a plane crash coming back from eastern Washington; they did not find his body until ten years later. He was an assistant attorney general, incredibly well respected, and everyone said he had a huge political future. And so I think of people like that. When I ran for office, whether it was for county executive or state legislature, I owed my success to all these other trailblazers who did a great job and who were respected, admired. Because they did a great job, it made it easier for me then to move into office. I have great thoughts and great feelings about these other trailblazers, and that's why I felt too that I need to devote my time to the state of Washington, to be as successful, as effective, and as respected as I could be, so I could make it possible for others to run for office and win.

I've always admired public officials who are articulate, who have a sense of the public, who don't talk down to people. That's why Bill Clinton is so incredible. When you listen to him you feel like he understands your angst, your trials and tribulations, your concerns, and is speaking to you about those things. There are some politicians who are smart but kind of condescending. I've always tried to talk to people in everyday terms; terms they can understand. I always try to condense government policy in a way that relates to them, because you care about the issue and what it means to them. I really believe in getting results. You can make a difference by focusing on key areas that the public can feel, touch, and hear, instead of government trying to do everything in a mediocre fashion. Let's maybe not do a whole bunch of things but focus on some things and do them really well. I really believe in performance and results, and I admire those public officials who can really speak well.

Would I run for governor again? I don't know; I'm happy where I am now and it was a great, incredible opportunity and a great experience, and in some ways I wish our children were a little bit older so they would have good memories of that. I think perhaps as they grow up it will just be a glimmer of, or very few or faint memories of, Olympia.

We took a lot of pictures, a lot of videos, and I bring them back occasionally and we talk about it so they don't forget. We have three trees planted outside the governor's mansion—one for each of the children planted on Arbor Day shortly after they were born. We had them moved to a location where you can see them so that in the future they can bring their friends and family and say, This is the governor's place, where I was born. We lived here and this is a tree he planted for me. All three children were born while I was governor. I was the only governor who had more than one child born in office.

My parents never understood politics; they never understood the state legislature, or what their state representative did. They never wanted me to be a lawyer; as a Chinese family, they said, Be a doctor, be an engineer. But once I did run for office they were just so supportive, so helpful making those yard signs and lots of food for the campaign workers. They were very, very proud and I just owe so much to them. And to my wife Mona, who, when I ran for governor, quit her job as a TV broadcaster (she had a great future in front of her) and completely sacrificed it and threw herself into the campaign. Emily was born two months after I was sworn in as governor. I just cannot thank all those thousands and thousands of people who worked so hard on our campaign and contributed. And there are people outside of the state of Washington who donated anonymously, people who I never met just sending in contributions, $5, $10, $100. And people at the Great Wall of China saying, Are you Gary Locke? They'd heard of me as somebody from America—not even of the state of Washington.

I just feel like an everyday person and I'm very lucky and had incredible support.

Restaurant, Public Office, Even Bruce Lee

Ruby Chow

Ruby Chow was born in Seattle in 1920 and became the first Asian American elected to King County Council.

My family has always been in the restaurant business. I'm not ashamed to say it—I've always had to wait on tables for a living. My father came to this country to help build the railroads. He came when he was very young. In those days they match married. He already had a wife in China. But wives couldn't be brought over, so he married my mother. She was from Victoria, Canada. My father was quite a bit older than my mother. They had ten children together.

I was twelve years old when my father went back to China to see his first wife. He passed away in China and left my mother with ten children to take care of. I was child number four. In those days there weren't many jobs available to the Chinese—restaurants and menial work, mostly. After they finished the railroad there was no work for them.

My mom spoke both English and Chinese. But she couldn't read and write very well. She couldn't go out and work, so she ran a laundry and had this little lottery place where white people would go up and buy their tickets. She made a living that way—that's how she raised us, with a little help from welfare.

After school and on weekends I would get a job waiting on tables to help my mom. I dropped out of school when I was a sophomore or junior in high school.

I eventually got married; but my first husband . . . in those days there was no such thing as domestic violence. It wasn't easy being in New York with two small sons and having a husband desert you and dealing with domestic violence. And in New York you could not get a divorce unless you could prove adultery. I met my current husband, Ping, a Chinese opera singer, in New York. After he got out of the army, we both came back to Seattle. It was very difficult. We got back here in 1942 after he got out of the army. When we came back it was already bad enough that they looked down on our family because we were so poor—and then for me to come back a divorced woman and with an actor? Being a Chinese opera person is the lowest wrung in the ladder. They have no respect for that. But what are you going to do about it? Cry about it? No—just have to say, To hell with them. In those days, Chinese women didn't get divorced. But on top of that, to marry a person in Chinese opera—that's a no-no. It was okay if men went out and courted the actresses, but not for the actors to court us. But it's changed since then.

Ruby Chow's: I was in the restaurant business for thirty-one years. We owned our own place, Ruby Chow's—built up a clientele. Being in the restaurant business is not easy. It's very difficult, very hard to raise children. You make the money at nighttime and on weekends. You want to spend time with your children, but you can't because of the restaurant. And so I thought that I would like to make a change in my career. I didn't want my husband to be working so hard, because it's a twenty-four-hour job.

Things seemed to happen. I remember going to Chong Wa (the Chinese Benevolent Association in Seattle) and saying we needed to have better public relations. My sister was pushed out of her seat on a bus—a white male ordered her out so he could sit, thinking she was Japanese. Those incidents happened and some of the Chinese were worried, so they would say, But I'm Chinese. I

The Chows (front row: Ruby Chow with her husband Ping Chow; back row: Roy S. Mar, Ruby's younger brother, and Cheryl Chow)

thought at that time, That's why we need public relations. I never said anything about the Japanese or internment; I just brought it to the newspapers' attention about the Chinese people—how they eat, and how they would participate in the Sea Fair Parade, which is going on fifty-five years now. I started the girl's drill team in Chinatown in 1952.

Fortune Cookies and Politics: In the sixties a man called Wing Luke came and asked for my help. He wanted to run for city council. I thought of the idea of putting Wing Luke's name in fortune cookies. We had to call all the restaurants to get their permission, then find out which cookie factory they patronized. Instead of "Confucius says," we would write, "Wing Luke says this, says that. . . ." The cookies went all over the whole city—over two hundred restaurants—and in all the Chinese restaurants at the same time. I don't say that's the only thing that got him elected, but I think it helped him. He was a city councilman for less than a term. He died in a plane crash. But we remember him as the first Chinese to run and win office in Seattle.

In 1972 I was appointed to the county's Equalization Board. When I looked around to see what they were doing there, people encouraged me to run for office. King County, the largest county in the state of Washington, had an open seat in the county council. The then-governor, Dan Evans, called me and told me to please run, and as a Republican. He said, "I will get you support and financing." That's two things you need to have, support and financing. And so I decided to run—but as a Democrat, as the district was Democratic. There was no other Chinese, or Chinese woman, who had done this in Seattle.

King County Councilwoman: I was a councilwoman for twelve years—three terms. I considered myself more as an Independent in some ways. This was from 1973–1985. I learned how to campaign, how to raise money. I had joined Chong Wa, and the association always needed money for the Chinese school, so I just got the knack of asking people for money. I don't think being a Chinese woman hurt me.

Three Democrats—men—ran against me, or I ran against them. And I wasn't a Democrat who went to the meetings and all that. They have meetings and you have to pay your dues to become a Democrat. But I still got elected. The man that vacated the seat was Johnny O'Brian. I went to ask him, "Hey, how do you get elected? I would like to run for the open seat."

At that time anyone could run for an open seat. He said, "Ruby, there are only four things you need to have. You need someone to endorse you, you need to have endorsements, you have to have places to put your signs up, and you have to raise some money—things like that." So I thought to myself, I've connected with a lot of people in running my restaurant, so I can do this. Seattle only had like seven thousand Chinese in the city. I wasn't even confident I would win or not. I was just doing it because I thought I'd better change my career, because it's hard working in a restaurant and I didn't want my husband to be working so hard. Most of those who voted for me were non-Chinese. I don't know how I got their vote. It's just that I was in the restaurant business and people knew me. Just like when I started Ruby Chow's. I placed a $20 ad in the beginning, and the place was filled. People were coming and I was getting a lot of press. People in the area knew me, I guess.

Bruce Lee Called Me Auntie Ruby: Bruce Lee wasn't easy to handle; he lived with us for four years. He was a houseguest. His father knew my husband; they were Chinese opera people. The story got out that Bruce Lee worked for us, but he never worked a day in his life for us. How could I put him on the floor with his acne, with all that stuff running down his face—he wouldn't work for a living, anyway. He was there with my children. The restaurant was on the first floor, we lived on the second floor, and we had many rooms on the third floor. He came up here from San Francisco to study. His father said to him, You can never make it without me. So Bruce came and asked if he could stay with us to attend university. His mother wrote to me and asked us to please take care of him. She thanked us, saying if I needed anything, let her know. He created an image worldwide; people would call from England and ask if they could just come and look at the room that he slept in.

I have had lots of interviews. The last young lady that wrote about me gave the impression that I set my hat to do this and that. I thanked her, but that wasn't what happened to me. Circumstances happened and I had to deal with the situation as it was.

If you did a story on me, I'd say, I'm a high school dropout, mother of five, owned a restaurant. There was a big article about me on the front page of a weekly. In big letters, it read: High School Dropout Retiring, but Not From Controversy.

Grassroots Victories

Cheryl Chow

Cheryl Chow is a former Seattle city council member and daughter of Ruby Chow.

Running for Office: Being a Chow means you give back to the community. That's what I grew up with—that's what you're supposed to do. A couple of the people in the community helped my parents out, so because of that my parents have always given back.

When my mom was in politics I saw how dirty it was. I had done fieldwork during my mother's campaigns and I always said I would never run for office.

As my mother's term ended as King County Council member, people in the community said there's no woman running and basically no Asian running for the county council seat. I started feeling the community pressure. When I told my mom I wanted to run, she was very upset with me. Most people thought she was grooming me, but she was very upset because, she said, "You're in education, you're doing well. You're a principal already—the youngest secondary principal. If you become superintendent that would be the ultimate goal; I would love to have you in that career." I asked why, and she said, "Well, I don't mind people bad-mouthing me or being mean to me, but I don't want that to happen to you." But when she realized that I was determined to try, she and my dad supported me 110 percent.

In the field against five men, I came in second. This was the open seat for King County Council District 5. I lost by about three hundred votes. But what I learned in that process was that I didn't mind it. I enjoyed the campaigning part.

When I was working in the Seattle school district as a supervisor of principals, a position opened up at the state level in education. To make a long story short, I was appointed as state assistant superintendent for public instruction and really enjoyed that position.

During my second year there, a city councilman called me up and encouraged me to run; he was an African American gentlemen who had been on the Seattle city council for twenty some years. I talked to people and they said, Yeah, we haven't had a Chinese council person since Wing Luke days. (He's the first Chinese American to run for political office in this area. He broke open the door.)

Winning, Losing, and Winning: I ran against an incumbent who was in the office for twenty-four years. In that time, which was 1989, you didn't beat incumbents. But I did. So that was kind of fun. I was on the Seattle city council for two terms—eight years, from 1990–97.

When the mayor's position opened, I figured why not—put my credentials out there and if they like me, fine; if they don't, then fine. I was just coming off the city council in 1997, so I ran. Early on in the race, the polls showed my campaign as pretty strong.

But the daily newspapers had chosen their own candidate, so I started getting dinged about how I had no vision because all I talk about are children and family and education—I should run for the school board, they wrote. That was their big hit on me. Really, that's not a negative, but they used it as a negative. So I lost, which was okay.

Then in November 2005 I ran for the school board. Did they support me? No. But I won.

My mom, she's smarter than I am and she said, "Cheryl, don't worry about the editorials, they're not going to be for you." I'm thinking, How can they not be? I have thirty years in education—I'm running for the school board. Sure enough, she was right. Because she knows people. They didn't really go after me, but they weren't favorable.

The "king- and queen-makers" of the city—so-called editorial boards—don't ever admit that they're wrong. Both daily editorials supported the other person. The unions supported the other person. The Democratic organizations supported the other person; the business people. What was sweet about this victory was that I kicked their butts. Without organized support. Because the people voted for me. They recognized my name as a city council member. I figured if they'd voted for me, I must have done something right. My agenda has always been the same: children, families, and supporting them.

So my point is, this is really a small-town mentality that is still growing up into a big city. Our community is so small, still, that people can't get past saying, "I was wrong; I want to support you now."

Campaigning: Learning to Smile and Hug, and the Whammies: I'm not a natural smiler. I have to concentrate on having a smile. Hugging still drives me crazy. I am not a hugger and, at five-foot one-inch, I find that usually their armpits are on me because they're always taller than me. So whenever I get ready to campaign, I have to get myself mentally ready. Shaking hands, if you will, pressing the flesh. That was difficult, and because it was like I'm just saying hello and just keep on moving, it seemed so superficial. What I used to do more of was stand and talk and listen to somebody because I was trying to find out what was on their mind, but I would never get around. I found out people saw that I was being aloof, so I had to learn not to do that. I had to really push myself to say hi to as many people as possible and keep walking. That was a behavior change because it just didn't feel right. It just seemed like I didn't care about them. Talking about me, instead of we, was difficult.

It's tough running as an Asian American woman because, depending on people's experiences or stereotypes, they expect you to be a certain way. When you're not the smiling quiet Asian woman, then it breaks a number of stereotypes. It's like a double-edged sword. There's a lot of goodwill toward Asian Americans—in particular, within the Caucasian community. Their stereotype of us is that we're smart, artistic, law-abiding. But then the opposite side of it is that if you happen to take a stance that they don't agree with, all of a sudden it's, What's wrong with her? She's not like those other Asians.

One, I'm Asian and you're supposed to be humble, and two, I'm a woman, so it's a double whammy. When you're out there, you're not just representing what you think; you're representing your family, your whole community. So I think it's an extra burden. The support is there most of the time from the community, but at the same time (and I've learned this in my professional life), the ones that are closest to you are the most critical. So you can't be Chinese enough for some people or Asian enough for some people. It's a real difficult situation.

Our governor was Chinese American, Gary Locke. And he of course had the same dilemma. But the plus he had was that he was male. So taking a stance means he's a strong leader. A woman, especially an Asian woman, taking a strong stance is a dragon lady. So it was very interesting; it still is.

Making Decisions: Because the Chinese community has a continuous influx of immigrants, the scale of need and achievement goes from zero to one hundred. You have to be aware and sensitive and speak up for just the survival issues, bilingual issues. Then you have the other side of the scale, where people have assimilated, or they're third-generation American and they want you to talk about potholes just like everybody else. Their concern is not food stamps per se or survival or getting an entry-level job. They are just like any other citizen—interested in when the garbage gets picked up, quality-of-life issues.

Within any community there are groups, so if you go to this dinner, how come you didn't go to that dinner? If you went to the Mark Association, why didn't you go to the Wong Association? So you have to be all over the place as well as at city council events. It becomes very, very challenging to balance all those commitments and have a personal life or semipersonal life.

There are more layers to the decision-making process if you are a person of color because American societal institutions set communities of color up against each other. When you have the budget-funding pie, the institutions tend to give a small slice to the communities of color, low-income communities, whatever you want to say, and then they have to fight for it. So not only are you supposed to be representing the Asian community, within a community you have Vietnamese, Southeast Asian, Filipino, Chinese, Japanese, Pacific Islander, East Indian—it's all those expectations.

Some in the African American community see us as a threat, taking what is due to them. So you have that layer, and then the different political parties, although Seattle is basically a Democratic city. I guess what I found difficult was being able to make the big decisions and then figuring out what kind of ripple effect it would have on the community I come from.

I don't believe that for a white member that would be the case, generally speaking. For instance, on the school board I vote on policies that will affect all children, but just because the Asian children represent only a quarter of the population doesn't mean they should only get one-fourth. I mean, there are special needs.

We're in the middle of closing eleven schools. It was very interesting because the racial dynamics have shown their ugly heads. There's a school called Martin Luther King that we have voted to close. The name we will keep and give to a thriving school. But some parts of the African American community feel very strongly about it. Which they should. And it's their right to make sure the school district doesn't just throw that away. But when I was walking by somebody who happened to be of African American descent, he said snidely, "Is Wing Luke on the chopping board?" because we have a school named after Wing Luke. It's unfortunate that it gets to that type of snide racial remark, as if, because I'm

Asian, I don't care about the African American children. That's what I mean by complex.

Now, a Caucasian person on the board (I'm the only Asian person on the board; there are two African Americans, and the rest are white) won't get that said to him or her. That really has a racial tone to it and not necessarily a positive one.

Race: I grew up with the stuff that was very overt—like gestures of slanting the eyes. When I was in the girls' drill team back in the sixties we would march down the street and some people would yell out, "Ching Chong, go back to China" or Japan. They didn't even know what we were, and we got into a number of verbal confrontations.

Society is such now that people don't do that; it's more subtle. I think it's harder for our girls and boys to deal with it because it's so subtle sometimes. Kids in high school don't really get to be in leadership roles because it's all about being loud, getting out there saying, "I'm good"—being demonstrative, if you will.

If an Asian kid spoke out, he would get slammed right away, whereas somebody else could be outspoken and the teacher might give [him] a little bit of leeway. If a quiet model minority does something, then bam, he gets slammed right away. They don't consider that it's just his age or it's just her attitude because she's an adolescent. It's almost like, How dare you. So the Asian kids don't even have a breather to be an adolescent. As adults we should be aware that Asian kids have just as many emotions that they're going through as other kids. And for them to verbalize it really is better so that they don't keep it within.

Leadership Through Volunteering: For forty years I've been volunteering with the girls' drill team. In our culture I think girls get cheated because they mostly stay at home to watch their little siblings and do the ironing while their brothers can go out. I also volunteer to help Asian girls and boys in basketball. I've done this about thirty-five years, with Asian boys and girls in second grade through high school where there's a place they can feel good about themselves. It's not just about basketball or drill team; that's only the vehicle. It's giving children a safe and positive place to develop their leadership skills, their self-confidence, their bonding with each other; it's knowing there are people in the community that support them as well as have the same values as their parents. That just supports the Asian values you find in every Asian culture.

Role Model: My mom, definitely. A twenty-four hour mentor. My mother was very involved in Chinese community politics before she got into the greater community of politics. She started the girls' drill team in Chinatown fifty-four years ago. All this basically helped us, the Chinese community, build goodwill. That paved the way for lots of things to happen; she was the first woman to be elected president of Chong Wa—Seattle's Chinese Benevolent Association. In the old days that was the umbrella community organization that brought in the family associations. They had the cemetery for the Chinese who couldn't afford it, and the Chinese school, etc.

Currently, I'm a director of customized programs for our Girl Scout Council, which spans over ten counties. And that's specifically to reach at-risk low-income girls who have never had the opportunity to participate. I also oversee a program that takes care of foster girls, girls whose mothers are in prison. We take them to have meetings with their moms in prisons.

Having a Mom in Politics: What has been an interesting dynamic for me is having a mother that's been so out there in the public. And it's been okay because my first career is education, so that's totally different from hers. She was a very successful businesswoman as well as community person. She's been very supportive in everything I've wanted to do. I think the only thing my mom and I have bumped heads on or that I stood my ground with is my not getting directly involved in Chinese politics.

I tend to be direct and candid. That's why I'm not a politician. I can't talk out of both sides of my mouth. I can't say things unless

I believe I can deliver. So I've always seen myself as an elected public servant, not a politician.

Asians are not really that large a group in terms of the population,[3] but the percentage of elected Asian officials in Washington surpasses our percentage in the population. That's why people in California come up and ask how we do it. I think part of it is the goodwill that my mom built up over the years. She is in the Washington history books, for God's sake. Before she even got into politics she and my dad owned a restaurant for over thirty years, and anybody who wanted something special would go to Ruby Chow's. Sidney Poitier, senators, etc., would go there. So all that goodwill that my mom had as a restaurateur carried over into the community.

Marriage and the Green Card

Shamita Das Dasgupta

Shamita Das Dasgupta, born in Cuttack, Orissa, India, immigrated to the United States in 1969, at age nineteen. She is founder of Manavi, a group organized to end violence against South Asian women living in the United States.

I moved to New Jersey and with five other women formed Manavi, in 1985, an organization for South Asian women. Our mission was to find out what was happening with women in our community. We didn't know. At that time the South Asian community[4] was prosperous and the immigration pattern was educated people. Technically educated people were coming in and establishing themselves and prospering. So the idea of a model minority was forming. Yet we didn't know about women, what was going on in their lives. We were dissatisfied, so we figured other people were too. Then we started getting calls from other women, just word of mouth. The major issue was violence—violence within the family, from intimate partners—and they needed to know what was going to happen to them; so they needed help. We listened to their needs and changed the focus of our organization.

We could understand the issue of immigration as it affects women in domestic violence situations. The first case was of a young woman whose husband divorced her and she became undocumented and the immigration court deported her. Since the father wanted to keep the child and the child was an American citizen, the court said, You can't take the child out of the country. So she was being deported but the child was going to be kept in the country.

This was the first time we saw this intersection of women, immigration, violence, and women's status. All legal issues. We started to become more and more conscious of these situations.

We actually launched a campaign with this young woman who was very resourceful and strong. She was an adjunct at a university and the department immediately fired her when she became undocumented. So we launched a campaign to reinstate her, to get an attorney to help her stay her deportation and assert her custody rights to the child. It was pretty successful. She was able to stay, she was able to have custody, she was reinstated. And later on she did get a green card.

There are many, many such cases. This has become one of the most serious issues within immigrant communities, especially since 1986, when the Immigration Marriage Fraud Act[5] was passed. Men would go back to the home country and marry. The wife would be given a conditional green card, which means they have to be married for two years to prove that it's a bona fide marriage. Then both of them go back to an immigration official to have the temporary green card replaced, which means if the marriage is abusive within those first two years she's at his mercy. He can do anything by holding this kind of life or ax over her head.

Sometimes men, abusive men, won't apply for a green card for them. They can bring the wives over on tourist visas—on any visas—but they won't even apply for the conditional green card. Sometimes when the conditional green card expires in two years, they won't go back and apply for the permanent green card. So she ends up becoming undocumented, so again she's at his total mercy. And he says, "Well, you're undocumented; all I have to do is call the immigration authorities and you'll be deported. Unless you listen to everything I say." It's very common and happens a lot, not just in the South Asian community; in all immigrant communities. If you talk to domestic violence places they say this is one of the biggest issues in the immigrant community.

The Violence Against Women Act was passed in 1994 and has

been amended several times. It provides some relief for immigrant women. That is, if you're in an abusive relationship, the woman can apply for a conditional green card and removal of conditions. It's called self-petition. It needs a lot of documentation, a lot of help. So that's some of the relief we can provide for women.

Domestic violence is still the biggest issue facing South Asian women in our community, and of course the issues that crop up again and again in immigration are custody issues, abandonment issues, transnational issues, what's happening in their original country. All these issues are culturally tied.

Culture is what we live and breathe; this is how we are brought up, how we respond to any situation. For women in South Asia, keeping a marriage intact is very important, which means that women will go through all kinds of problems; they will tolerate so many things just to keep the marriage intact. A lot of times parents who live many thousands of miles away put enormous pressure on women to keep the marriage going. And women do try as much as they can. The issue of "I have to provide a father for my children; they cannot grow up without a father," is very important to them: "Doesn't matter what the father is like. I need to be responsive and be with my community." And the community looks kind of badly toward women who are single or divorced.

Women are afraid that if they are divorced or leave their abusive partners, the community will act negatively toward them. These are all such important issues. I don't think they're unique issues, but I think the degree of it is unique. A lot of times one of the things a South Asian abusive man says is, "If you leave me I'll ruin your reputation in the community or with your family."

I talk to larger communities who say, So what? Well, it's very important because it means she may lose her native community, her native family. And it's very much life and death for many women. So it may lead to killing or total isolation, including from her own family.

Building an Orphanage in China

Ark Chin

Ark Chin talks about the building of an orphanage. Closer to home, he ponders the future of his family association in Seattle.

On a trip back to China, I met up with one of my shirttail cousins. He was afraid that we were seeking revenge for the terrible treatment that my grandfather had received in the village. They "gonged" him, as a capitalist. They tied his hands behind his back and they lit incense sticks and let the ashes fall and burn his back. Right after the communists took over the whole of China in 1949, he was punished, and so was my grandmother. They had the equivalent of Red Guards going to their house and harassing them and at dinnertime seeing what they were eating. If they were eating anything good they would take it away. So my cousin was afraid I was going to seek revenge and counseled me not to. He said it's better to just let the past be bygone. So anyway, we had known each other fairly well through that process.

By the time I went to China on subsequent trips he was still there in county government. He wanted me to visit an orphanage. It was in an old building that they had adapted for that purpose and he said that they wanted help to not only rehab but reconfigure it.

Afterward they asked me to help raise the money in America to help them construct this. So I said, "Well, what do you figure it will cost?" They had an estimate and I said, "My God, for that kind of money what you're doing is you're still going to end up with a facility that is ill-suited for that purpose." So they said, "Well if that's the case we ought to think of a new one." I said, "Yeah, I'd like to see what your numbers are for a new one." And they came back to us and said, "This is what it would cost to build a new one; could you help us raise the money?"

I said, "If the number is such that we can do it ourselves we will do it ourselves. If not, then I will ask a few friends to join us instead of a long campaign. If you undertake the project and the amount of money is not enough, you have to finish it. We're not going to give you another penny."

We signed a contract, but it took us about two to three years before the construction actually started. We stipulated during negotiations that in case of dispute we had the right to review and approve the general design and construction. I was more concerned about the structure being adequately strong for earthquakes so we wouldn't kill a bunch of infants. So they agreed. I said, "Well, you know people have a way of changing their minds during the process of this thing. So here's what we're willing to do—we'll make progress payments based on the value of work in place minus 10 percent, which we will withhold until the construction is complete. The second part is that in case of a dispute we'll negotiate with you, and if a mediator can't help us resolve it, then either party has the right to walk away from the project." They finally agreed to that and signed an agreement. And it was a good thing, because they think they have control but the party really has the control.

Someone from Beijing went down in the middle of the construction and asked how come we didn't have this kind of design on the building. Well, we had a representative in Toi Shan and he's a shirttail relative, he's an attorney. So he agreed to serve as our on-site observer. He called me up—they always call at about eight o'clock at night because that's midday their time—and said they want to make the change, and of course he's Mister Big. So everyone there wants to change. I said, "This is crazy. What he's proposing actually has no value and it destroys the architectural design of the place." I said no absolutely not. This was one change we would not yield on. So they held meetings for four hours and finally called (by this time it was midnight here) and said they agreed not to change. The project was finished and actually it's more beautiful and better construction quality than most public buildings they have.

On the Future of the Family Association: I've been involved in the Chinese community in Seattle for most of my life, and in the early years my father belonged to the family association, Oak Tin. The total number of branches is well over twenty or twenty-five on the East and West Coasts. So every major city that has any Chinese population of consequence would have a family association. In the early days it was obvious that they needed to have something like that to protect the people from other predators within the community as well as from outside predators. It also served as an organization to resolve disputes between members without resorting to court.

It goes back to about 1910. That's how long our branch has been established. For many years our association has been run by powerful elders. They're not officers but they have served as officers before, so they've become counselors. They became the power. Over the years that sort of behavior or mind-set really hasn't changed.

I was elected president for a two-year term in the late sixties. What we tried to do, the younger guys like myself at the time, was to develop an organization more suited to the needs of a transitional time and for the young people that are born here, but we have not been very successful.

There are about 250 members now, but we still don't have a computer list of names. There are some younger people who are in their forties who are recent immigrants.

Part of the problem is there's more inertia against it. You've heard the Chinese phrase "the officials speak," meaning they speak a grandiose term but when it comes to execution they just do it in their arbitrary way and they try to yell people down. And the young people like our children—I practically dragged two of them into the organization, but they don't participate. They see it as a useless exercise. In their own way they are involved in the community—one of our sons coaches the Chinese basketball team and other things. I think a lot of the American-borns especially feel it's not worth the effort.

There are several of us, we kept tilting at windmills. . . .

We managed to establish a very solid financial base. The association owned an old building in Chinatown and we went to the U.S. government and said we'd like to convert this into low-income housing. So a bunch of us—one guy had the time to devote to seeking grants and loans from the federal, state, and city governments—got something on the order of over $900,000, and we put up some money. So we have the building with storefronts which provides a nice income and low-income housing.

Now, we who did this initially had to become palace guards against the raiding of the treasury. One of the presidents that was elected said, "If you got it, let's eat it up." So they have banquets and they don't charge anything. Well, who's a member? Anyone who shows up!

I am still one of the elders. But what I think is that we could lose an organization that was founded to help us preserve our culture and the Chinese moral way of life, one that could continue to develop this sense of family. You have to take into account that we are in this country and we are losing the ability to preserve and enhance and promulgate those values that have for a long time given us a sense of identity. The Chinese take great pride.

The people that are coming into the association are the ones that are the new immigrants. They see an organization that they understand, that they can participate in and to some degree influence, although it is just a few people who have that idea for power.

Ark Chin, Seattle, Washington

We have lost in that it's not making any progress in bringing in the American-born. And that's a considerable segment. It's these people who have capabilities of doing things that an organization can provide, such as financial help. We have a scholarship program, but it's not run properly. We have Tai Chi and we have ballroom dancing and a number of activities like that. But it's just like those all-you-can-eat restaurants, where people can pick and choose and not give any thought to how one can help and contribute. It needs to be relevant to our culture as well as to the society that we live in. What I'm saying is that you have to develop an organization that's responsive to the needs and at the same time promulgates the good elements of the Chinese way of life.

I feel very strongly that if you don't really have a sense of identity, you don't have this central focus, and the core values to a degree come from that. That gives elixir to your life. You don't have to constantly wonder, Who the hell am I?

Many of the kids don't know what value there is in being Chinese now. They're able to get great jobs and get an education, but to a degree some of them suffer from the lack of identity.

Social Responsibility: We who are fortunate to get to where we are have received a great deal of support and teaching from a lot of people and from society in general. Our society provides so much—for instance, in college education. The real cost of it is usually at least two to three times the tuition that the student pays. In life I have generally encountered a lot of good people that have encouraged me and helped me to move on, or drew me into enterprise that is worthwhile.

I begin to understand how contributing to the overall welfare of society has helped me establish my own sense of direction and core values. In a sense you are paying a debt and you are setting a good example.

PASSION FOR MUSIC

Cowboy from Japan

Hank Sasaki

Hank Sasaki is a country-and-western singer and songwriter from Nashville, Tennessee. Born and raised in Japan, he moved to the United States in 1988.

Tennessee Moon
I left home and family to follow a dream
With hundreds of long lonely nights in between
I swore when I left her I'd be coming come soon
But I fell in love with the Tennesee Moon
—Song and lyrics by Hank Sasaki

In Japan: The first time I heard Hank Williams's music I was about sixteen years old. Even though I couldn't understand any words, his music touched my heart and totally changed my life. He was on the radio station we call FEN—Far East Network. After World War II the American government came to Japan, took over things, and set up radio stations all over Japan. We had a big opportunity to listen to American radio, music, and movies. So my first country music love is Hank Williams.

After I heard his music, I told my mother, "When I grow up I want to sing just like him." I asked my mother if she would buy me a guitar and she bought me a cheap guitar and I started to train myself. I bought records and listened to them over and over again. I tried to sing like him and imitate him even though I still didn't know any words. But his music really touched my heart.

When I was in school I hated music class. No one in my family plays any music, but I listened to music and trained myself and tried to sing just like him. One day I heard this Japanese country music band on the radio, so I called the radio station and got the manager's address. I wrote a letter to him and said, "I want to join the band; could you give me an audition?" So I went to see them and sang a couple of songs. I think they liked me so they put me in their band. They were called Western Blue Rangers, all of them Japanese. Most of the gigs they did were on American military bases. At that time we had lots of American bases all over Japan. So that's where we played.

I joined the band after I finished high school, so I was with them maybe nine or ten years. Then most of the American bases left Japan, so I had to find another job.

By then I was twenty-nine years old. I got married, had three kids, and needed to take care of my family. I worked for a sales company for another ten years. But music never left my side; I always wanted to play more.

When I was forty I bought a small country music club in my hometown. The place had been in business for about ten years and the owner wanted to sell. Then I played music every night. Sometimes I sang by myself as a single act. But most of the time I played with my five-piece band, Nashville Chaps. We performed at some city events and played at the American navy base and army base, so we were quite busy.

But I always wanted to be writing country songs. Around that time I met my wife, Jean. She's from a small town, Defiance, Ohio. She was teaching English at a Japanese college. Foreigners would stop by my place, so Jean and her friends would come in; we met each other and became friends. She tried to help me write songs. In America if you want to be a movie star you have to go to California. If you want to be a basketball player you have to go to Chicago, and if you want to be a songwriter you have to go to Nashville. So I decided I wanted to go to Nashville and try to learn song writing.

At that time I was about fifty years old. So everybody thinks I'm crazy. They said, Hank, what are you doing? They said, You have good customers and a good business, so why are you going to throw everything away and move to Tennessee? They think a Japanese country singer can never make it in the United States. But I followed my dreams.

It's amazing—here I was, born in a small coal-mining town in the southern part of Japan, about one and a half hours from the city; population, thirty thousand people. It's a small city. I'm the only person there interested in country music. So it's amazing that I ended up in Nashville.

In Nashville: I've been here almost nineteen years. My wife and I moved here in 1988. My music business is expanding. These last couple of years I have been to a lot of countries and places. I've been to Europe, Denmark, Germany, Poland, and I started going to Australia about three years ago, each year. My songs really opened doors to overseas gigs. In the United States I got gigs up in Minnesota, Wisconsin, Iowa, and next year I go to Michigan and Kentucky. So it's been good to me.

Writing Country Music: For the past five, six years I started writing songs and most of them are about my life experiences since moving to Tennessee. If I didn't write songs and just tried to sing like Hank Williams or some other big artist in the United States, I don't think I could get any job. It's a hard business. But my songs are unique and that's why I get job offers. Country music is just ordinary people's life stories, everyday life stories where people can share the same feelings. No matter where you're from or what language you speak, we can share hoping and dreaming and loneliness, sadness; we all share the same feelings. Country music tells a story about an ordinary person's life. So one of the songs I wrote is "Tennessee Moon," almost thirteen years ago. I was so down and out and depressed. The song came to my mind and I wrote it with a good friend in Tennessee.

Another song, "Cowboy from Japan," really opened doors for

me all over the place. "Cowboy from Japan" is almost a true story about me: "I came from the land of the rising sun to Nashville, Tennesee / To be close to the music I feel inside of me. / Sometimes I know there's some of you who don't quite understand / The love of country music by this cowboy from Japan." That's a verse. The chorus is: "I'm not tall like Jackson; don't look at all like Brooks / But my soul is just as country, though I may have a different look." Basically, the boy came from the land of the rising sun and tried to make it in music and it's not so easy. After I sing the song they understand me.

Anyhow, if I didn't have any of my songs I never would have jobs in Tennessee, Minnesota, Wisconsin, or even another country. Fortunately I've got songs. And people can feel them. But English is my second language so I need a co-writer. Most of my songs, I wrote the music and the story. Writing the lyrics is the hardest.

Gigs: *In Nashville:* Most of the time I sing at songwriters' cafés. They set up a schedule a couple of months ahead of time so when I come back from overseas I perform and try to promote my songs to some publishing company or artist. It's so hard to make money here. Even if you are a favorite, you have to go out of Nashville and perform at other places. It's hard to break into country music, especially in Nashville. If you are playing steel guitar or the fiddle it's easier, but for a singer it's so hard to get a break.

Overseas gigs: In February I stay in Australia for two months. I am going to be in a festival and after the festival I travel all around Australia and play at country music clubs. When I get back from Australia, I have gigs in Japan for about five or six weeks, then I go to Minnesota, Wisconsin, and Michigan. In September I go back to Australia and stay about a month and come back and go to Japan again. The rest of the days I spend in Nashville.

I'm still not famous and I'm not a big artist, but where I go the people support my music and understand me. It seems like life is so hard. It took me a long time to accept it and the music industry and Nashville, but I'm still chasing the dream and I enjoy what I'm

Hank Sasaki

doing. Country music is really white people music, but music is a global language, so if you're writing good songs they can touch everybody in the world.

I really love living in Nashville. This is the best place. You can listen to good music and there are a lot of good musicians and singers and songwriters and they all live in Nashville. I think I'm fortunate to live in Nashville for the rest of my life.

As an Artist: If you do the same thing other people do, then I don't think it can be a success. It's gotta be unique and you have to continue to follow your dreams, no matter how hard the times. You've got to have a job and then continue to do business, so still every day I'm writing songs and continuing the dream.

I've written between sixty-five and seventy songs and recorded about twenty of them. I have four CDs on the market. I'm on a couple of small, independent labels. Now I've got my own label, called Haki Music. It's my publishing company, which is also an independent record label.

Everyone's looking for a major record deal. But it's so hard. There's strong competition and you need a lot of support and sponsors. You can get an independent record deal easily but you have to spend a lot of your money.

Most of my CDs sell in this country. About a month ago some radio station in Hawaii played my CD and a lot of people called the station. I sold about 80 CDs from there—some small island in Hawaii.

I also sold many, many CDs in Australia. It's hard for independent artists to get airplay on radio in the United States, but down in Australia and in Europe—especially Australia—they have community radio stations which are nonprofit. If you send a CD there and if the DJ likes your music, they pick it up and put it on the radio. Newcastle Radio played my song on the radio one day and eighty people called the radio station who wanted to buy the CD. So that's what happened in Australia. About four years ago some radio station called me and said, "Hank, you should come to Australia," so I started going. This year I have lots of gigs coming up so I really appreciate the people in Australia. They like more traditional country music. But most of my audiences are older people, like age fifty, sixty, and seventy. Not younger people. But they love my music.

Now I'm about sixty-eight. I'm pretty old! When I was deciding to come to the United States I was fifty. But it didn't matter to me. If you've got some kind of dream you have to follow it. People told me, Hank, you don't look your age. They think I don't look a day over forty. You know Asian people, they look so young.

Probably people who haven't heard my music think, A Japanese country singer—they're not going to take it very seriously. But after they hear my songs they take me seriously. That's what happened in many places. I'd never been to Wisconsin or Minnesota, but the promoter and the country music theater heard me sing the songs "Tennessee Moon" and "Cowboy from Japan," and those songs really opened the door for me.

In Nashville they listen to country music today and they're looking for guys that are age twenty or twenty-three and twenty-five. There are a lot of good country singers in Nashville. But if you are age forty or fifty they're not going to promote you the same way—no, never. I'm still writing songs. Maybe someday a big artist could come and pick up my song. It's never too late to write a country song; you're never too old to sing country songs.

When I first started my interest in music, I really wanted to be a cowboy. I just loved the western movies. Now they're all gone and it seems like cowboys are not big for everybody. But the cowboy is still in the mind.

The cowboy is so independent. He has his own life and can be just the way he is. He doesn't have to worry about high-tech. The cowboy life is so simple, and I really like things simple. That's the way of life I'm looking for.

No matter where you're from and what language you're speaking, music can relate to everybody in the world. Like my song "Tennessee Moon." When I wrote it I was thinking about my daughter—I left her in Japan. And I wrote many songs about Tennessee and about leaving home and trying to make money—the feeling of missing people. So it appeals not just to a musician, but maybe to a traveling salesman as well.

When I go to Japan I perform in fifteen to twenty places, live country music houses around Tokyo, Osaka, Hiroshima, Nagasaki, and my hometown. The places are small, probably fifty or sixty seats. It's a small business. Small music. Many in the audience are over forty; they're in their fifties, sixties, or seventies. They're the people who listened to country music through the American radio stations in the 1960s.

Country music isn't really played in Japan on commercial stations anymore. Most of the young people don't have any opportunity to listen to it or see a country performer. The big music is pop
rock, hard rock, rap music, and Japanese music. But people would
love country music if they gave it a chance.

Jimi Hendrix of the Ukulele

Jake Shimabukuro

"Jake Shimabukuro is the Jimi Hendrix of the ukulele" (FRETS *magazine, Fall* 2005).

When I started playing the ukulele at the age of four I had no idea that it was something that I wanted to get into as a career. My mom played, and in Hawaii everyone grows up learning how to play the ukulele, so it's a pretty common thing.

I describe my music as sound and notes that I kind of create from my instrument—they are things that I've heard that have inspired or influenced me, or just things that I've copied from listening to other artists or other instruments, just taking violin pieces or piano pieces and applying that to the ukulele.

I think for me it just so happened that I played the ukulele— but with any art it's basically what you hear and what you feel inside, so I feel like I can create the same kind of emotions through different instruments, whether it's my voice speaking or telling a story or if it's a piano or writing a poem or if I have a paintbrush in my hand. You kind of channel that same energy. It just so happened I had a ukulele, I didn't have any other instrument growing up. Just playing the ukulele didn't satisfy me because I was feeling and hearing many things; I needed to be more expressive, so that's why I was led to create new techniques—so I could fulfill those things that I wanted to express.

The Ukulele: In the past there's always been this stereotype that the ukulele has been like a toy or something or a novelty type of instrument. My theory is there are just a lot of bad ukuleles in circulation. You think of those $10–$20 ukuleles that people buy at the store in Waikiki. But my equivalent to that is that if the only piano you ever saw growing up was one you bought at a KB Toys store—you know, one of those pianos you bought as a four-year-old—then every time you saw a piano you'd think of that and you wouldn't have much respect for that instrument as well. But when you see a very well-handcrafted ukulele—the ones I play are made by a family who has been making them for almost a hundred years, and a custom ukulele from them costs $5,000—you're going to really respect it because it's going to sound like a real instrument and it's going to look like a real instrument. But there are not a lot of those types of ukuleles in circulation. It's not like a guitar, where there are hundreds of great, quality makers out there; there's just a few in the world.

Kamaka was the first Hawaiian family in the world to start manufacturing ukuleles. They were the original makers. The ukulele is very, very popular but in a more novel sense—you know, like on television—so that's why people are more knowledgeable about what a ukulele is, but as far as what it's supposed to sound like and what it's capable of, I think people are just not exposed to that.

Going on Tours: The crowds number anywhere—if I'm doing a solo show—from a few hundred to maybe a few thousand, and a lot of times I tour with other artists, other musicians, and then of course it gets really big. One of the biggest tours that I'm actually doing right now is with Jimmy Buffett. So his shows—the smaller shows—are probably twenty thousand. We just did a New Orleans show festival that was like 120,000 people.

Being a soloist, you have a lot of opportunities to play in a club; tonight I'm playing at Joe's Pub (in New York City). I can do that solo but I can also jump on with other bands. I've played with Bela Fleck and the Flecktones and Bobby McFerrin. It's great in the sense that you can get yourself into any sort of situation.

They usually hear me first, then they ask me to come on tour with them. Kind of small first—like they want to test me out and see what I do. And it's funny because everywhere I play people are like, "When I first heard about the show and thought ukulele, I thought what is this?" But after the show they are like, "Wow, I totally wasn't expecting that—that was great. That was very musical." So it's nice to have that kind of feedback, especially from other musicians.

Last year we went through thirty different states and Japan. This summer we're doing a twenty-one-city tour of Japan. We've played in Guam, we're going to Australia in October and Germany next year. We've toured through Canada, east side, west side. It's usually by myself. For Japan, sometimes I'll take a five-piece band with me because it's a bit more affordable since there's less flying and we have a record label backing us up.

How Would I Characterize My Music? New Age? Jazz? Yeah, but I never believed in styles or genres. When people break down music, like this is rock, this is pop or jazz, to me it's just really nonsense. Music is just an expression, and the only reason I think they categorize it is so retail stores have a way to sell the stuff and market the stuff. To me, music is just about expression and it doesn't matter what kind of music you play.

One of my heroes growing up was Bruce Lee, and he didn't believe in any one style of martial arts; he said they're all expressing the same thing so you have to study everything about martial arts. Then you have to see which ones speak to you and which ones you believe in and which ones represent who you are, and that's basically what he did. His whole style and philosophy and form on his art was Bruce Lee—it wasn't kung fu.

I'm still a very young artist and I'm trying to learn a lot about myself, so to me, everyone is an artist. The whole thing about art is just about discovering who you are and what you like, and digging deep inside yourself, learning about all the things you like and don't like about yourself and accepting those. And then you just express that.

So I think for me that's why the artists that move me the most are the ones that are a lot older because they have a lot more life experience and knowledge and they've experienced so many other things that they can creatively express.

I know that my music is still evolving because I'm evolving as a person and changing and learning new things. So that's going to be a process that keeps going until I die.

As Far as Being an Asian American Artist? I'm always optimistic. I think it's a great time to be an artist but a terrible time to be a record label right now. In the music industry, it's getting harder and harder to sell CDs. Downloading music illegally and legally, especially illegally, is so common right now.

Now with the Internet and digital music it's easy for any artist to be heard. You can listen to people all over the world, people who don't even have albums yet or a record label, they can just record something on their laptop and they can put it up on the Web. It's a time where people will learn and discover things a lot faster, because the information can be accessed quicker. You don't have to go to the library anymore, you don't have to research books at a bookstore. Anything you want to learn, it's right there at your fingertips if you have access to the World Wide Web.

In the past not everybody could be heard unless you had a big record label behind you that could play your stuff on the radio. Now you can do everything yourself, from writing the music to recording it to publishing it to getting it out on a CD to the artwork. You can put it all on the Web, you can do everything yourself. You don't need a distributor, you can cut out the middlemen.

I'm signed with a record label so I'm doing the old school way of it. But I'm also registered with iTunes and we sell our music through the Internet—we have a Web site and things like that. So I try to take advantage of both sides because I think the old school method is a great way, because it's real, it's tangible.

With the Internet, everybody is kind of building their own bubble, and all they want is their own little wire to hook up to the real

Jake Shimabukuro (photo by Nobuyuki Itoh)

world. It's kind of scary because it's unfamiliar. There's a lot less working together, getting a team together, because everything is now just geared toward me and this.

The thing that I don't like about that, though, is in this time of digital technology and instant gratification the younger people don't put value on hard work anymore; they don't put value on taking time to do something and spending years and years on trying to achieve something so that when it's done they can go back and listen and be like, "Wow, I did this," because everything is so quick—it's just double click and you're on. People are so impatient they don't have the attention span to nurture something or the time and energy.

What Does It Mean to Be a Musician? To me it's all about fulfilling that need or passion to keep growing and keep getting better. It doesn't matter if I'm just in Hawaii and I'm practicing, as long as I feel like I'm getting better. But the problem is that when you're standing in one place, it's hard to grow as a musician. You have to travel and you have to hear other musicians and experience other things in life. It's about studying people, different cultures, different types of food, checking out different styles of architecture in places, all of those things. Like falling in love, having your heart stomped on, all of those things make you a better artist.

The ride should never peak, that's what I believe. The highest point should be when you die and you should always have that; for me I just want to keep this passion and desire to understand myself. To keep understanding myself more and more every single day.

This is all I want to do. Even if I get married it's going to be a part of this. I think that's the great thing about the arts; it's not about touring or traveling, it's about self-discovery. The more I understand myself the more I can be comfortable with myself and be more composed at every second of my life; just be in the moment. That is what will make me the best artist that I can be. You keep finding new things about yourself and I'm sure as you face death you discover something completely different too. So up until the point that you die you always will be learning.

When you're performing you want to share your life experiences and what you've seen. With music you can do that in the purest form, and without words (because words have certain feelings attached to them) you're just communicating human emotion. To me that's the greatest fulfillment because everybody just wants to express themselves and tell others how they're feeling. That's what it's all about.

I do spend a great deal of time in Japan. It would be nice to converse or make jokes with people onstage. But I've always felt that sense of fulfillment just performing in front of a Japanese audience, because I believe music is a universal language.

The Fortune Cookies

Joann Lee

Joann Lee was a member of the Fortune Cookies, a girl singing group in Chinatown, New York, during the 1960s.

I was about fourteen years old; we were going to junior high school at the time. There were four of us—me, my sister Sue Jean, and another set of sisters, Joanne and Rose. We all got together and started this group called the Fortune Cookies. This was in the early sixties, when girl groups like the Shirelles, the Ronettes, and the Supremes were hot.

We had a music teacher, Mr. Barr, who wrote songs for us, and my sister's English teacher, Mr. Hoffman, became our manager. It was the stuff teenage dreams were made of. We wanted to sing; rock and roll was what we listened to, and in Chinatown we didn't see ourselves as different—we thought we could make it, just like any other girl group out there. Those were the days when even guys hung out in hallways and sang hits, like Dion and the Belmonts, doo-wop kind of stuff.

We would practice after school. Mr. Barr wrote these two songs for us, and we were thinking, maybe a record contract, maybe our own 45. (In those days, it was 45 rpm records—everyone took 45s to parties and played them.)

Recording Contract: One day Mr. Barr said we would be cutting the record in Midtown, in a music studio, under the SMASH label. It was in the Times Square area, and we got there at three in the afternoon. There were all these musicians when we showed up—violinists, sax players, drummers—a seven- or nine-piece band. It was like stepping into another world. I hadn't ever been in a recording studio before. Yes, I had ridden the subway all over the city, but this was the first time I was more than an observer outside of Chinatown. There were these middle-aged men in jackets and ties with their instruments, and they were there to play music so we could sing—all four of us, ages fourteen to sixteen, from Chinatown.

The session went on and on; we just kept singing the same thing over and over again. My sister Sue Jean and the other Joanne sang the lead. Rose and I sang background. But it was nonstop, and we didn't have a clue as to why they wanted us to do it over and over again. By the time we left the recording studio, it was 3 A.M. That was it.

The next step: we had to get our parents to sign the recording contract. But my dad, an educated person from China, felt he needed to get a lawyer to represent us. Things didn't go well in the contract talks. At that time, I believe they were going to give us 3 percent of any profits from the record, which I understand was the industry standard. But my father felt that would be an injustice, so he just wouldn't sign the contract until the terms were changed. This led, I think, to very hard feelings with the record company, and they basically didn't end up promoting the record after that. It was released and played a few times on the rock stations in New York City, but that was it.

My sister and I think back about what if Dad hadn't made such an issue over the contract; maybe we would have been as hot as the Shirelles or the Supremes. But that's the sort of stuff we can only think wistfully about today.

So we continued to sing and practice after school, and even got together with a group of guys—two guitar players and a drummer—and we started playing parties, like Sweet Sixteens, in Chinatown. In those days, there were dances in Chinatown almost every weekend,

The Fortune Cookies, 1965 (top: Joanne Lau; bottom, left to right: Rose Lau, Sue Jean Lee, and Joann Lee)

on Fridays and Saturdays. Looking back, we were so young then, the world just seemed to be full of excitement, promise. The guys were called the Dynasty, and they played all sorts of rock songs at parties—from fast stuff like "Wipeout" to slow songs like "Sleep Walk." We sang songs like "Soldier Boy," "Johnny Angel," "Leader of the Pack"—the top hits of the sixties.

This was around the time of the Beatles, so we wore outfits, like ties and suspenders and short skirts. We didn't have much money, so we had to figure out how to look cool and together without spending much.

We would play at these parties sometimes for free, sometimes for $200 or $300 a night for the whole group. It was a blast. We didn't think about what it meant, we didn't think about the future—we were just kids, having a great time, and no one else in Chinatown was doing it. Our parents were okay with it, they didn't have much time to spend with us, essentially. Mom worked in a sewing factory and Dad worked in a restaurant pretty much all day.

I still have the songs, converted from the 45 record to an MP3 file that I share with my son, nieces, and nephews—the next generation, because they get such a charge from hearing that we did this.

The first song, which was to have been the designated hit side on the 45, was called "It Should Have Been Me." The other side is "Girl in Love." Both are in the vintage of the sixties: girl is desperate and in love kind of stuff. Now I listen to it and I giggle that we were ever that young, that we were part of that time in rock and roll in American culture. They used to play our record at all the dances, and kids in Chinatown, many knew the song, knew we had cut a record.

All in all, we started out doing something because it was fun, and gradually it evolved into this wonderful moment in our teenage years.

We stayed together as a group, playing parties, pretty much for about three years. By then, one of the sisters, Rose, left, and my sister, Sue Jean, went off to college, and we stopped performing together.

I guess looking back at it today, the best part of that was just doing it—singing the songs of the sixties because it was *our* music, it was just rock-and-roll, the stuff that made us happy, that brought us closer to being teenagers in a time when girl groups were hot. We were even featured in a few teen magazines. No one told us that it might be an impossible dream to pursue, or that, being Chinese, we might be viewed differently. The thing is, we sounded pretty much white; we sang music written by a Jewish music teacher and we sang without accents. How much more American could the experience be?

GROWING UP

From Laos to Iowa

Steve Thao

Steve Thao is a Hmong American living in California and working in the area of media. He and his family settled in Pella, Iowa, in 1976.

Pella, Iowa, is a town settled over a hundred years ago by Dutch immigrants who were trying to leave persecution, so it's known as a city of refuge. There was a documentary done about the town and our family as the second wave of immigrants taking refuge there.

I was four or five. I came with my younger brother and sister, and my parents. Two years after that my youngest brother was born in America. Shortly after we arrived we sponsored other families. My dad's brothers and sisters came to live with us. It was a small town, about seven thousand back then. We were sponsored by a Christian Reformed Church in town. I think there were three or four Christian Reformed Churches and each church sponsored a family. It formed my core values as a child going to church to understand about the Judeo-Christian tradition.

But a lot of Hmong are still traditional and practice the old country's religion: atomism. The Hmong traditional religion has a shaman who heals by way of talking to the spirits, and that has been documented in mainstream media and Hollywood, just recently on *Grey's Anatomy*.

Growing Up in Iowa: You're a kid growing up, reading fairy tales, Hans Christian Anderson fairy tales, and you think you're like everyone else, but then you grow up and understand you're different.

I didn't know any better. I loved it, I loved the small town. We lived in a small town in a time where you didn't lock your doors and you could walk around and didn't have to think about child molesters and being kidnapped or things like that. I think I had a pretty decent childhood in that aspect.

Originally we were in Laos, and after the fall of Laos[1] all of the Hmong people who sided with Americans had to escape to refugee camps in Thailand. Then we would go to a country that would accept these people as political refugees. When my parents got here, my father worked as a janitor for a couple of years and then we moved down to the capital of Iowa, Des Moines, which is forty-two miles away. I was in third grade by then. He worked in social services, helping refugees, Southeast Asians specifically, find work and get acclimated to American life.

In Laos he worked with the military, something like an air traffic controller or radio dispatcher, so he had to learn English. So coming to America he knew some English already. My stepmother did not know English. I guess she learned through living and talking with our sponsors before we came.

In Pella there were probably four or five other families, relatives that we helped sponsor and helped other people sponsor. I think it grew to maybe six or seven at the peak. The town was great. It had a tradition—it was called a city of refuge. I don't really have any recollection of any bad memories of any people saying this or that, so I think our experience was very positive. It was a very conservative town and I think they accepted us, or most of the people knew that they were going to have Southeast Asian refugees.

There were more Hmongs in Des Moines.[2] It's the largest city in Iowa; it's much more diverse. There are African Americans, Hispanics, Latinos; it was a very big change for me, just because for the first couple of years Pella was a very homogenous area. I think probably the population in Des Moines was two hundred Hmong families, so it was huge.

This was the early eighties; during that time people were not as

used to seeing Asians everywhere as we are now. It was a big culture shock for me. In Pella everyone knew everyone and nearly
everyone went to church together. In Des Moines, where the
classes were so mixed, I did feel weird, even as a kid. As a third and
fourth grader, I got taunted with names and things like that.

I see myself as Hmong American, not just Hmong, because politically we're Americans. I grew up in a town where I learned to
have the American dream.

The American Dream? It changes, as I'm an adult now. You
grow up and you don't feel that you're different. But as you go
through experiences and life, you see how people react to you.
Also, it's the institutional restrictions on you. You feel that it's
based on who you are and how you look.

I look at the American dream as a young kid—you would talk
about careers and you would dream about becoming a president of
a company and you would think that's very attainable. But I think
it's very hard for Asian American men or persons to be able to do
that. That general American dream is not very realistic for a lot of
Asians. What they do, I think, is find their own American dream
and success within their communities.

I've bumped up against the ceiling many times. I wrote a
screenplay about it. Politics plays in everything. In the military,
in corporate, any job you have. I was in the ROTC in college—
Gonzaga University in Spokane, Washington. The cadets who were
welcomed and fraternized well within the ranks of lieutenant colonels and captains were white males, and those who were able to become friends with them were young white males, who acted like
them and talked like them. So it wasn't really based on scores or
anything else. I had a friend who was Vietnamese and we scored
very well on our physical tests and on our other tests, but we were
never given positions of power or leadership. So I think we came to
understand that this was going to be our life if we continued a career in the military. That's one of the biggest times when I encountered how the world was going to be.

After College: After college I moved to Fresno, California.[3] Fresno was probably the so-called capital of the Hmong community in the eighties. The leaders were here and the population was huge, upwards of thirty thousand back then. It's still huge. My family moved here to do business because my father encountered a glass ceiling and he realized if he was going to have any success it was going to be within his own community. He started a small business catering to the Hmong American community, so I came and helped him for a couple of years.

We were the first Hmong company to do documentaries and movies. He was right at the crest of the video craze that was sweeping America. The technology was making it easier for people to have their own cameras. So we started a video company and began making the documentaries, going back to Laos and taking videos of people in Laos, China, Burma, and Thailand and showing how they lived back then and showing some of the places we were visiting.

Right after that I went to Minnesota and worked as a television producer. I did community TV and produced a Hmong television show that was shown in Minnesota and also nationwide on the International channel. We did radio and I published a Hmong newspaper up there and the TV show. I just came to Fresno last year to run the radio station; I'm a general manager there. It's 1210 AM in Fresno. I speak Hmong better now through working with the community the last ten years. But in high school and college my Hmong was probably very elementary. It probably still is, but I've probably expanded my vocabulary about four- or fivefold.

As a Hmong American, I feel very fortunate to be a part of this community. Even though within every community you have problems—you have political problems where people are fighting— I think in my college years I found a sense of love for the community. That's my thing about being a Hmong American and that's why I have chosen to work with the Hmong community and in media throughout all these years after college.

Harlan, Kentucky

Albert Lee

Albert Lee is a journalist who lives in New York City. His parents are from Korea.

My father is from a city in Korea, Tageu, and my mother is from Seoul. They immigrated to the United States around 1970. I am the youngest of three children, born in Kentucky, where my parents live today.

My father was a doctor in the Korean military, so when he came to this country there was this deal whereby if you have certain skills and you go to underserved areas like urban inner cities or rural areas where they need doctors, then they will sort of put you on a fast track toward getting a green card. So that was sort of the deal that my dad did. He's still there today because in Kentucky there are few doctors and they're desperately needed in poor areas and really in rural Appalachia where I grew up.

"Asian American"—I never heard that term growing up in Harlan, Kentucky. I didn't know what that was. I mean the word was only necessary in the sense of designating a group. And it was only me and my family. We were the only nonwhite people around. It's like how the Eskimos have forty words for snow—well, because there's so much snow. Is the word Asian really going to be necessary when there aren't any Asians around? "Oriental" was the term of art. I loved growing up there, but of course there was a lot of racism.

Growing up, I had a great deal of self-loathing. I wished I was white—I kind of felt like I was born the wrong way because I didn't know. I had no conception of trying to think of the right way to say this. To me being white was "normal." In my childhood logic that's the way it worked. So I would look in the mirror and say "I wish I never had these slanty eyes." Of course I thought about that. Later I grew up and thought how stupid it was. But that was very real and very palpable.

It got really hard for me as I got older. It got so bad for me that I think my mother had her sixth sense and suggested the idea of boarding school. I hated the idea of going away because Kentucky was the only home I knew. But I thought, Mom has this idea and I'll just let her send out for catalogs and do what she needs to do and get this idea out of her head. Getting sent away for school was something that happened when you were being punished. It was a very foreign idea, but the more I thought about it the more I thought, I do have to get out of here. The worst was when this kid pulled a knife on me in the locker room in seventh grade. That's when I really knew it escalated. I mean kids—they're just so brutal. He always called me names—chink and whatever—tons of names. So he just had it in for me. He wanted my lunch money, which was so cliché. But it's actually what happened.

As for dating, I was only in Kentucky until the seventh grade, so I wasn't really dating anyone, obviously. And socially I lived on a side of a mountain and I played with the other kids in the area and I did typical things that kids in the area did. We went camping and hiking and hunting and we shot BB guns and caught frogs and played, pretended like we were pro wrestlers jumping on trampolines. You know, stuff like that.

So I did not grow up around other Koreans or Asians. In particular, Koreans are centered around Christian churches. Honestly, I've met only one other Korean American in my entire life who wasn't Christian—which is kind of shocking to me when you think about Korea, because Christianity is a minority religion there. Both my parents are Buddhist, so I grew up without any of that. They were more of the assimilationist string. I think there's that certain strain in immigrants. When I inquired, my parents showed me things about Korean history and the language. But I do not speak Korean. I went to Exeter, in New Hampshire, for boarding school. Until then, the farthest I had ever gone from Kentucky was Disney World.

After I left Kentucky, I was shocked to see other Asians. I saw a Chinese restaurant—it was bizarre. I remember it very distinctly and thought it was so strange. I have never seen so many minorities in my life. Asians, blacks, Hispanics; it was just shocking to me, completely shocking to me. I grew up in Kentucky in the rural mountains, a very backwater part of the country—one of the poorest areas. Whenever you see those commercials on TV with some Christian charity guy saying poverty is in America too, and they have kids who are barefooted with no clothes on and they're hungry and dirty—that's my hometown. That's exactly my hometown. I think the poverty rate in my hometown is literally 30 percent. And double-digit unemployment. I mean it's a coal-mining town—it's very poor. So that's sort of where I came from.

Here I was going to a prep school environment with some kids coming from similar backgrounds as mine (and very fantastic financial aid programs) and kids also coming from more privileged backgrounds, and from different areas—New York, California, and foreign countries. From there I went to Princeton University, which is where my middle sister went, which is how I ended up in New York, because it was so close.

In high school and college I tried to go to these Asian societies or the Korean American Princeton student group. But I never really felt like I fit because many of those groups were very cliquey and only Asians. I mean, you'd go to the cafeteria and it was the table of Asians, and my friends were the people I lived in the residence hall with in college. And also, more to the point, oftentimes I found these groups were strongly overlapped with the Christian and

Evangelical student groups. It was literally like the memberships overlapped completely. So oftentimes you would go and people would evangelize. It happened to me a lot and I was not interested at all.

My parents are Buddhist. My father is typical Asian—he's a man of few words, so I haven't the faintest idea what he believes in. He never really speaks about it; he's not a really religious or spiritual person. My mother is still Buddhist. Born-again Buddhist, actually.

I used to speak Korean when I was a little kid but I just lost it because I never practiced it or had an occasion to speak it. Both my parents speak English fine and I speak with them. They still speak Korean with each other from time to time. They also speak English to each other.

Look at it this way: my parents have lived in America longer than they lived in Korea by now. So this is their home. They've talked about going back, and oftentimes when we were younger we would say, Don't you want to go back to Korea to visit? And they don't really. They say when they go back there they just don't fit in. They feel like even the language is different to them, and it is. It's a democracy now and it's so modernized. They don't recognize the country anymore and they've lived in Kentucky and America so long that they feel most at home here.

My parents often visit my sister in New York. She is an accountant, and my other sister is doctor. I think they're happy. I don't think they see it as a metaphor for the American success story, the American dream. I mean, certainly they came to this country to pursue that, but my parents aren't very big into self-mythologizing. My whole family's that way. We very much live in the present. And I don't think we would ascribe larger meanings to things like that.

Growing Up in Los Angeles

Daniel Jung

Daniel Jung, a college student at the time of this interview, was born in Salinas, California, and attended high school in the San Fernando Valley. Both his parents are from South Korea; they immigrated to the United States in 1982.

Los Angeles Riots: The riots happened in 1992. My parents didn't own a liquor store at the time, so I was never really affected by them. I remember there's a Korean plaza maybe a few miles down the road and they had shops there. I was really young but I remember going to this meeting with my dad and I know a lot of the Koreans took up their own arms and had guns and stuff. I remember sitting in the room and they're asking each guy, Do you have a gun, do you have a gun, do you have a gun? But since we live in the Valley, that complex never really got threatened by the rioters. I know a lot of Koreans dislike African Americans because of the riots. Some Koreans have the image of, Oh, African Americans are going to try to rob or steal from you, so they're always kind of afraid of them, like maybe my parents are. For me, it's not like that.

I remember when I was in eighth grade this guy came in and tried to rob my parents' store and he actually shot my dad in the face. I remember he was hospitalized for a while and my mom just kind of looked after the store. Because of that incident, my parents really dislike African Americans, especially my dad. He is fully recovered, but he's always really careful.

It was 1997, September 15. After that, my dad saw a counselor—a psychiatrist. I'm not sure that even helped him out or not. But I see my parents as being really strong people; my dad went to work and he never really talks about what happened. My mom went to work the next day and she just opened up the business. I know it's really hard; my parents work seven days a week. But I know they want to do it for me and my sister—pay for our education and stuff.

Their success story is my parents' owning their own business. My dad started owning a liquor store, because his friend did it and it's a pretty good business in L.A. So he kind of just followed in those footsteps. The store is actually a little south of where I live, west of L.A. I think of that area as a really nice area, Santa Monica. It's on Fifteenth Street, near the beach. My parents have never had any problems there except for that one incident. Hopefully they'll retire soon.

I definitely don't want to run the liquor store. I don't think my father would want me to do that. It's hard, opening up 365 days a year, working long hours. For them, if I came home and I just took over that business, my parents would see me as a disappointment because they sacrificed their life for me and my sister to have a better one, so for them to sacrifice their life and for me to just do that wouldn't be right.

I'm an international relations major, studying international business and economics in East Asia. Hopefully I'll find a job somewhere in the corporate world in accounting or investing. Since I have the education and background I think it would definitely be easier for me than my parents.

Growing Up in L.A.: Childhood was pretty good. We pretty much lived in suburbia, so I had a lot of friends in my neighborhood. During the summer we'd hang out, ride our bikes, play basketball, go swimming. So, it was a pretty good childhood experience. Front lawn, big backyard. It was pretty good. There was a Korean family that lived across from our house, but they ended up moving. So we were maybe the only other Asians on the block. There was another family down the street that we saw here and there, but we never really had any contact with them. And pretty much Caucasian or Latino families.

There are so many Koreans in L.A. Even in my neighborhood there are two or three huge Korean supermarkets and there are so many Korean churches around that area. I don't really think of myself as the only Korean or Asian American. I remember going to elementary school and being the only Korean or Asian in my class. That was kind of weird. I remember going to birthday parties and everyone was different. It was weird going over to their house and then coming back to my house, because I knew my mom wouldn't let us eat junk food, so there was no junk food in the house, like no soda. If my friends came over it was, Well, do you want water, do you want juice, or do you want some fruit? So that was kind of weird.

At my friends' places, they'd have pantries just stuffed with junk food like fruit snacks or chips or cookies and all that stuff. But when my mom went to the supermarket, it was only one or two things and that's pretty much it. We would have to say, We want this or we want that, instead of our mom just picking it out for us.

I have one sister. My dad's side of the family lives in Korea, except for one aunt who lives in Anaheim, which is south of L.A. My mom's family—pretty much all of them—live in Southern California. I speak Korean at home. That's how I communicate with my mom and dad. When I talk to my mom, I don't really understand some of the stuff she says. There are times when she doesn't understand me, and it gets kind of frustrating because you have to keep explaining yourself. I know there are numerous times we have argued because of language issues.

What is their idea of success? I guess my mom just wants me to graduate college, have a good job and good family, and be able to take care of them since I'm the oldest son. So I guess that's her success story for me. Also not getting into trouble in school or getting arrested, which I never did. For her to raise good kids, like me and my sister, that's good. When we went to Korea two years ago, my aunts and uncles, whom we met for the first time, they were always like, "Oh, your kids are so well-mannered," and stuff like that. I guess when you hear that and they tell it to my dad, it's nice and it shows my parents raised me right.

Education: My parents stress education a lot. We went to Korean school on Saturdays, and I did tutoring when I was little— math, English, science. If I wanted to go out and buy a book, my mom was like, Okay buy the book. If I wanted a video game, then my mom would say, Why are you buying a video game? I guess cost wasn't really an issue, especially when it was toward my education. I remember in sophomore year I barely had a 2.0 because I was on the basketball team and was focusing everything on basketball, so my mom took me off the basketball team and my grades just went up.

Academically they've always been harder on my sister than me. I don't know why; I never really asked them that. But when I got my report cards and my grades weren't as good as hers, my mom never got down on me. She would just say "Try harder next time," or she would take me to tutoring schools. I remember doing a lot of that for my SAT prepping. It was stressful. My mom would send me there, but I would never complain; my sister always complained. She hated going to SAT prep schools, taking prep classes. I just did it.

My mom, she always wants me to go to grad school: Oh yeah, when you get your MBA you get this much more money—she's always telling me that. I tell her I'm graduating, I'm kind of sick of school right now, I want to get a job, just live a little bit, and if grad school comes up I'll go. I guess just looking at the success stories of Japan, Singapore, or Korea, there's more respect if I get a job, and if people over there are doing it, I can do it too. Going to school you learn about the Asian economies but I never correlated it to my life or what it would do for me.

Parents: My dad's really traditional with the whole respect thing. Because of it, I don't really have a close relationship with him. I guess he went through a lot of that with his dad, and he has this mentality that he knows more than me and my sister, which is not really the case anymore, because my sister and I are more educated since we live here. So he has to demand respect from me and my sister. If we're watching TV he'll say, "Dan and Laura, come outside, I need to talk to you," and he'll lecture us. I'll fall asleep and he'll keep on lecturing—things like, What are you doing with your life? And its funny, too, because he gave me a lecture about making friends and how you can't trust them, and I was like, What are you talking about? You can't even argue back with him. You just have to sit there and listen to it and just hope Mom comes in and says, Listen it's late, let the kids go to sleep. I know my mom is more relaxed, so my sister and I could always talk to her about anything. My dad doesn't know anything about my sister and me; he has to find out through my mom.

I do think it's hard keeping a balance though, between the Korean culture and the American culture. Growing up, even talking back to your elders or disrespecting them or telling your dad or parents what you think was forbidden—there are so many times I wanted to tell my dad, "No, you're wrong," but I just kept my mouth shut. Do I think he understands my culture? I think he thinks he does, but he doesn't. I don't know if you've heard that a lot of Korean sons have difficult relationships with their fathers, but they do. My dad has always been so hard on me—even when he would come to basketball games and I would do really well, I always thought it was a competition between him and me for pride or whatever it is. I don't think he's ever given me a compliment in my life. Even this past winter break, we went to go play golf together and I killed him on the course and he'd always say, "Oh, next week I'll beat you." It's always a competition between me and him. We'll go play golf and I'll see it as fun and I'm sure he does too, but I'm sure he doesn't want to lose to his son.

When I was growing up, my mom told me one time she was real angry with me and she said, "You're going to be just like your dad when you grow up." I was so angry at her for saying that. When people compare you to your dad—yeah, he's a really strong person, but his attitude and how he treats others—I just don't see myself being like him; I'm just the complete opposite of him. I guess when it comes to owning your own business and stuff my parents are really successful, but maybe socially or culturally he's not that successful.

Before my parents owned the liquor store we would always sit down and eat as a family. But after that, since they had to work, it was usually just me and my sister, me by myself, or me with my friends. But on Saturdays and Sundays, when my mom had time in the mornings, she'd always cook for me and we'd sit down and eat together for breakfast or brunch and that was always nice. Often they worked late hours and stuff so they usually just gave me money to go out and buy something to eat. For dinner we probably just never really ate and sat down as a family much.

Korean Identity: I'm proud to be Korean and to be who I am. I always think of myself as an American, then Korean American. I know that when we went to Korea our relatives would always tell us, You're Korean first, then you're American, and remember your last name. I think I'm pretty well assimilated into the American culture, so I don't really think about things like that.

Do I ever think about World War II and the internment of Japanese in this country? I don't think I have, because World War II was in the 1940s, before the civil rights movement, and I guess nowadays people are more educated and more liberal. I guess if World War III happened in Korea I don't think I'd be in an internment camp, so I don't really think about that.

Going to college, you just want to meet friends and people. I know a lot of the Asians and Koreans here at Boston University like to hang out with their own cliques, so once you hang out with one of them you hang out with all of them. You just get comfortable with them. There are so many more Caucasian kids here but I can't say I'm really good friends with any of them. When I go home, then I can say, I'm really good friends with Mike or Ryan or

Brandon—non-Asians. I knew I had more of a mixture of friends
back home, but I never really thought of why. When I see someone, I see if they're going to be my friend, not if they're, Oh, you're
Chinese, or you're Korean—definitely not that. Just be friends
with whomever you can be friends with and be happy you're
friends with that person. For me, personally. I don't really care who
my friends are.

Stereotypes of Asians today? Probably study hard, good in
math, going to be doctors. I don't think the stereotypes have really
changed all that much from when I was in high school and even after college. I really don't think it's that valid. There are the Asians
that study well and work hard, but with my friends I don't think it's
really valid at all.

I don't really pass as being Asian; people think that I'm Hawaiian or Samoan or from the Philippines, and some are like, Are you
Latino? Plus I'm dark too. Coming from L.A., where it's kind of hot
and you're outside, I tend to tan really easily.

Do I think being an Asian male today is positive, negative, or
neutral? I never really thought about that. I think I did when I was
younger, but that was only because I went to a private Christian
school and I was always surrounded by white people. So in that
sense I thought about it more. Even in high school most of my
friends were Asian and in college most are Asian. So it's hard to
think, Oh, I'm Asian—because I'm always around Asians.

In junior year of high school we had a race and gender unit, and
they asked a lot of similar questions and I remember the answer
five years ago was that whites in society always have a head start—
like if it's a fifty-meter race, they always have a fifteen-meter head
start because of their race. I guess I thought that when I was in high
school. Only because we're first generation my parents didn't really
have that much information about school or how college worked,
so I always thought some of the other parents who went to college
here or could speak English knew what to do when applying to colleges or getting a job. I think now graduating with a college degree

I can see myself on the same playing field as a white guy or another guy. So I don't see race as hindering me in any way.

Have I ever experienced racism in Los Angeles? Yeah, when I went to elementary school I experienced a lot of it because I was the only Asian kid and everyone else was different than me, so I got the typical racist, Asian racist, jokes. The white kids would pull their eyes back and if a kid had an Asian accent they would try to imitate that as best as they could. It was such a long time ago.

What changed? In high school I had more of a mix of friends. I had Caucasian friends and I was on the basketball team, so I had African American friends. The Jewish kids and the Asian kids were all pretty open, so we made jokes. I guess when you hang out with a group of Asians and there are more than two or three of you, in that sense it's easier to take in. But when you're that one kid, and everyone's picking on you, its kind of harder to accept.

What do I think about the images of Asian males on TV and movies? You don't see them on TV at all. Even in high school we were talking about this. They always play the bad guy, they always know martial arts. I always see that on the TV or in the movies today. I guess I'm kind of indifferent toward it. I've seen it so much I kind of don't think about it anymore. Whenever you watch a kung fu movie that's what you see. In the entertainment industry you don't really see a whole lot of Asian superstars really. I guess that's just how you're raised by parents. When you say, "Hey, I want to be an actor," your parents aren't going let you be an actor. They're going to tell you to go to school, get good grades, and go into business or be a lawyer or a doctor. The parents kind of steer you away from that industry or field.

Dating: Right now I'm dating a girl who's half Chinese, a quarter Indian, and a quarter Ecuadoran. I know my parents always wanted me to marry a Korean because I'm the guy and they want me to carry on the family's last name. My mom always tells me, Oh, you're going to marry a Korean. My sister doesn't really like

Korean guys all that much. My mom kind of knows that too, and she doesn't really say much.

You can't help who you like or who you love. If I do end up marrying a Korean girl and my mom is happy, then it just worked out. But she's always saying, You can't marry a black girl or a Mexican girl. And my mom doesn't know that I'm dating this girl right now. In the past I've dated mostly Koreans, Asians, not Caucasians. I'm not sure why. For me personally, when hanging out with Asians you just feel more comfortable around them, and there's always a stereotype that the Caucasian girls don't like Asian guys. It's weird because you see a really good-looking Caucasian girl and think, "Wow, she's really hot," but I wouldn't go up and ask her out on a date, because she probably wouldn't be interested in an Asian guy, I think. I don't know.

I don't really see myself marrying only a Korean girl; my parents do. I find myself more comfortable around them than other races, but if I like a Caucasian girl and I ask her to marry me, I know my parents won't approve but you can't help who you like or love.

Portland, Oregon

Jeff Andrada

Jeff Andrada was born in Vancouver, British Columbia, and raised in Portland, Oregon. His parents came to the United States from the Philippines in 1966. He works in the insurance industry in Boston.

As my parents were driving down from Vancouver, they saw this nice little quiet city, Portland, that they liked, plus my dad had one or two friends that lived there. I spent my life in Portland, went to college in Corvallis, which is about an hour and a half from Portland, graduated in 1994, got my first job in Portland.

Growing Up in Portland: It was good; I had a great upbringing. Great parents. But as far as other Filipinos or minorities, they weren't around. Most of my friends were Caucasian, white. The only real Filipinos I knew were my cousins. They immigrated, stayed with my parents, who sponsored them, and most of my aunts and uncles. Most of my Filipino friends were my cousins. I didn't feel like a minority growing up. I didn't really feel that I was any different in elementary school, grade school, high school.

My parents were part of the Filipino American Association, so they would have Christmas events or just events throughout the year, big gatherings, and they would put on Filipino cultural events, different dances, that sort of thing. That happened maybe two or three times a year at a cultural center.

After church and on birthdays, we would have big gatherings with my cousins and they would come over. It was like a potluck. All the aunts would make stuff and we would all eat and just bring various items and that was pretty much the party, eating and socializing.

What did I like to eat? My parents really like fried fish, fish stew, fish heads, the standard chicken adobo, and beef intestines cooked in cow's blood. Once it's cooked, it looks black, like chocolate.

On Sunday after church my mom would make spam, eggs, rice, and this Filipino fish called tuyo. But you would have to cook it outside because it stunk up the house.

Education: It's very important. My grandparents put every child through college in the Philippines, both sides, with an exception of one or two. You had to go to college. All my aunts and uncles are either nurses or engineers. They had no choice. My grandfather worked overseas, everywhere—Iran, India—and was away from his family, and my grandmother raised the kids so they could have money to put my aunts and uncles through school.

My grandfather worked for an electrical company; he wasn't a maintenance man, he climbed the towers and did certain things for the electrical company, I think based out of Vietnam.

Both my parents came here in their twenties. My mom was a registered nurse; she did that for thirty-five years. My dad is a civil engineer; he designs power substations. Their expectation of me is that I go to college, get a degree and a job.

What does it mean to be a Filipino American? I think of that question more in terms of my parents, growing up and learning from them, the family working together like they did. They came from the Philippines without knowing anyone and they worked hard. So I think they just instilled that in me. It's not necessarily too much of the Filipino culture versus someone living there, but more so the values of working hard and the family and loving each other. I guess from that standpoint that's what stands out as the Filipino American. Just hard work, coming to the States, not having much, and putting my brother and I through school. The one thing I wish, and my cousins too, was to have learned the language.

I could understand it growing up but they didn't really enforce it, or teach me or my cousins the language. But my relationship with my parents is very strong.

Work: I am a manager at an insurance company now, in personal market claims. Do I feel that as a Filipino American there's a level playing field in the corporate world? Yeah. I think it's level. The company's very diversified. They have a diversity network, programs, a program for minorities in colleges. I'm mentoring a student this summer. I really haven't come across any situations where I didn't see it level. I don't have a sense of any glass ceilings. I think if you work hard and you perform, and it's evident to the others, then the sky's the limit.

Do I feel things are easier for me, speaking English and being educated? I think times have changed, kind of evolved to where it's just accepted. You've got all these laws now as far as equal opportunity, employment and diversity networks, making sure you have a certain amount of minorities hired. Even with schools you have a certain amount of minorities and I think it's changed in that regard because of laws and procedures. With companies it's easier because of these changes.

Identity: I see myself as an Asian American. But when I meet certain Asian Americans—like some Chinese friends who speak the language—I compare myself with them, and they're a higher degree of Asian American than I am in regards to the Asian part. But I consider myself an Asian American to the degree I said.

Was it hard being a nonwhite growing up? No, not at all. I'm not aware of any racism. I mean you can never really know indirectly when somebody is thinking something. Me, I don't think about that. I'm Asian American, I'm American. When people ask me where I'm from I say, Portland, Oregon. That's it.

We were raised Catholic. My brother went to Catholic school growing up. My mom, she's a devout Catholic, goes to church every Sunday and says the rosary everyday. It was a strong part of my life growing up. Every Sunday, midnight mass. I was involved

Jeff Andrada

in some Catholic church groups. But I'm not as devout as my parents are.

They prefer me to date Asian, Filipino. Even to this day they would prefer me to date an Asian. But, they also know if I'm dating a Caucasian and I'm happy, they would be okay with that. My brother dated and married a Caucasian. I don't have any preference: Caucasian, Indian, as long as I'm happy and have feelings for the girl.

But growing up it was hard. First off, my parents did not want me to date in elementary school, or junior high school. Even my sophomore year of high school they wanted me to focus on school and graduating and going to college. So they didn't want me to date. I don't think I had a girlfriend in high school.

Do I think people look at me ethnically when I invite them out on a date? No, I don't think so. I'm currently dating a Caucasian girl and we actually had this discussion a couple of weeks ago. I don't think it really crossed her mind—her thinking, What are my parents or friends going to think—we just got along.

The Philippines: The United States is my home. But my parents are eventually going to move back to the Philippines. For them the goal next year is to live six months in the Philippines and then six months in Oregon.

I was there two or three years ago. It made me appreciate my parents and the United States more—just in general how people, kids, have it lucky here compared to the kids there. It's a Third World country and I remember very distinctly walking out of the airport and getting bombarded by a combination of homeless folks and poverty—people running around with no shoes, especially in Manila; it's crowded, pollution, a lot of poverty, and kids running around. My grandparents live about six hours north of Manila in another province. And same thing, crowded. I have five or six cousins and they're my age, they're unemployed, most don't have jobs; it's hard to get a job. They drink everyday and have nothing to do. [They] go out on the town and just laze around during the day and it's pretty much like that all over in that neighborhood. I liked it because that's where I'm from, but it was hard seeing that environment, that poverty; it was very hard. It made me really appreciate living here.

Growing Up in Hawaii

Jake Shimabukuro

Jake Shimabukuro is a twenty-nine-year-old musician, born and raised in Hawaii.

I never really thought about what it meant to be Hawaiian, or Japanese, growing up. I just kind of looked at everyone as a person and that's about it.

Growing up in Hawaii was great. I love the beach. There's a strong sense of community and family and helping each other and working together, loving your neighbors and treating everyone as if they are a good family friend. You call everyone Auntie and Uncle whether you're related or not. I think that is a great way to grow up. You don't get jaded as much and it expands the capacity to love in your heart, to be open to other people.

A lot of people who don't grow up in that type of environment feel like they always have to look out for themselves because no one is going to look out for you. With some young people the perspective is, you do it on your own, you have to work hard for what you get. When I was growing up there were a lot of people who helped me get where I am today, so I'm going to help this younger generation.

On the mainland it is a little bit harder compared to growing up in Hawaii. I come to New York and people don't know if I'm Japanese, Chinese, or Korean. In Hawaii you would never get that because people know. They're around enough Asian people to know that person is Vietnamese, that person is Korean—by looks, because there are little subtleties that when you're around them enough you pick up. Even accents, like a Chinese accent if you're growing up in Hawaii.

But growing up somewhere like Nashville, when an Asian person walks through Nashville, they won't know. I've done some shows in Idaho and they don't know. I mean, I don't feel weird or anything, but it's just funny when you realize how lucky you are growing up in Hawaii because I'm happy with my outlook. There are times when you open up a little bit too much to people and you can get conned or get ripped off. But I'd rather live life that way than the other way—closed up and trying to protect myself.

My mom is fourth generation and my dad is second generation, from Japan. That makes me fifth generation on my mom's side. I have a younger brother who is five years younger, and my mom and dad got divorced when I was in sixth grade. My brother and I lived with my mom. We never traced back to how my mother's side came to this country. I know they're from Hiroshima, but that's about it.

My dad's from Okinawa but we don't know exactly where. My grandfather was actually adopted by a family in Hawaii. So we don't know anything about my great grandfather—we don't even know what his name was. My grandfather fought in the Korean War.

Neither of my parents speak Japanese. My grandma speaks just a little, real slight, but on my dad's side no one spoke Japanese. As far as Japanese holidays or traditions, we don't really observe any. In Hawaii, everyone is pretty well educated about other cultures, especially Asian cultures; we celebrate Chinese New Year and all that kind of stuff. So it wasn't a big shock when I went to Japan for the first time because being in Hawaii you grew up with all that stuff.

In our family, growing up, we never talked too much. It was always like that with my mom, and she was like this with my grandmother too—where the parent and child don't really communicate. You do what you have to do and you get scolded if you do the wrong thing. But we never talk about emotions or feelings or say, "good job," or "I'm so proud of you." That never existed. It's always, Did you finish your homework? Finish your homework. Eat your dinner. Or, Don't forget to call so and so. You never communicate on a level like you would with a best friend. We're a very close family but it's almost like we wouldn't sit together at dinner. I might be at the couch eating, my brother might be in his room eating, and my mom might eat a little bit later. So it wasn't like you saw it on TV, where the whole family sits together.

I use chopsticks when they are available. I prefer them. But not all places have that. Even things like taking off your shoes before you enter the house, and bowing, I'm always bowing. It's just something I can't get rid of.

Asian American as Identity: I don't know how people see me. I think everyone should feel proud about who they are, because it's about celebrating life, celebrating everything.

There was a time when I was going through a crisis when the Japanese vessel got hit by an American submarine. It sank and killed nine Japanese and it was in American waters.[4] When that happened I had actually written a song for the families of the missing victims. During that whole situation I was getting interviewed by all these different media people—by American and Japanese media—and they were asking me if I wrote this as a Japanese person, as an American person, or from Hawaii? Almost every interview they asked me that. My response was that when I wrote the song, one of the students that was missing was the same age as my younger brother, and I thought, Wow, that could've been my brother. No one wanted to take the blame, but the whole thing was that nine missing human beings were out there in the ocean, so let's find them. That was kind of my whole take on it. I never felt like I had to speak as a Japanese person or an American person.

Did I Ever Learn About Internment? The camps and all

that? Oh yeah. I've talked to a lot of the vets that were in the 442nd,[5] and I've had ongoing discussions with them as I used to be a member of their educational foundation. The whole goal is to preserve the stories of these Japanese American veterans firsthand through interviews on video so we can take those stories directly from the horse's mouth and educate kids. It's different when you read it in a text rather than hear it from one of the veterans actually speaking to you on video.

I first discovered that group when they asked me to do the entertainment at a fund-raiser. Though I've always known their stories, to actually meet the vets and to hear their stories in person was so powerful that I felt I was back in elementary school. Among my peers we were never caught in a situation like the 100th battalion;[6] we never had to go through those unfortunate times.

Do I think Japanese will ever be confined again? It's sad to think that, but really, anything can happen. Who knows, there may be another shift in power. I don't think it's so much a matter of what Japanese Americans can do to prevent it because at the time, they didn't do anything wrong. I look at everything as there's good and evil in this world. There's going to be a constant struggle to balance that. Whether people take it in the form of racism, whatever it is, there's always going to be that struggle. And I think we just have to constantly educate ourselves.

Language: I have a pretty large Japanese vocabulary—I just can't have a conversation. If I was to meet someone on the street, I wouldn't be able to talk to him. I can ask stuff like, Hi, what's your name? How old are you? Where's the bathroom? That kind of stuff. But I can't convey emotion. Even with English I have a hard time with that. I want to tell you how I'm feeling but I don't know how to describe it or say it and those are the things that frustrate me. With music I feel like I can do that.

I wish I could speak Japanese, if that's what you're asking. But I also wish I could speak other languages as well. That would be awesome.

Between Continents

David Tang

David Tang, a Chinese American, was attending college at the time of this interview.

When people ask me where I'm from, I just say Hong Kong, even though I'm not a Hong Kong citizen, I'm an American citizen.

My nuclear family is in Hong Kong. That's where my mom, dad, and my brother are. I guess I call it home, but I kind of don't. That's one thing that I've never fully reconciled.

I was born in New York. My parents both grew up in Hong Kong, but they went to New York for college, City College of New York, CCNY. That's where they met. After my dad graduated he went to business school, to Carnegie Mellon. He ended up getting a job at Citibank and he's been bouncing around—to Saudi Arabia, then we lived in Athens for awhile, then went to Hong Kong and Singapore. He's retired now; I believe he was a treasurer of the Southeast Asia region for Citibank.

In high school, my parents sent me to boarding school in Connecticut to give me a more stable environment. It was Choate Rosemary Hall, a predominantly white school in New England. When you're growing up, especially between high school and middle school, it's this big leap in terms of social development. That kind of messed me up because I didn't know what to fully be a part of. Did I want to fully immerse myself in Choate? I didn't want to fully immerse myself when I went home for break to Hong Kong, because there wasn't that much stuff to do.

When I came to the United States for school I wasn't fully international because of my background and then I wasn't fully American. So it's like the whole black sheep thing.

My parents didn't understand why it was so weird for me. Whenever I went back home to Asia all my friends were back in the United States, so I was just sitting around. My brother was there, but it's just not the same hanging out with your brother or parents when you're used to hanging out with your friends. I just tried to get by when I went back for break, because there was nothing much there. I mean I could walk around and shop or go to the zoo or something.

Education and Expectations: I'm about to graduate from college and find a job; I can't rely on my parents for forever. After I graduate I want to be financially independent.

How do I see the world? I know I'll never be a pro athlete or something like that. I have a pretty open view; I don't see myself getting pigeonholed. I originally thought because I was a bio major I was going to have to work in a lab or cure cancer or save a panda or something. I mean that'd be nice, but I don't know if I personally want to do that. I might end up in business like my dad, even though I'm a bio major. That's what happened with my brother; originally he was a bio major, and now he's working for Citibank in Hong Kong.

Education's really important to my parents. They always had big dreams of me and my brother going to Harvard, Yale, Princeton— those big Ivy schools. We both went to prep school but my brother ended up going to Chicago and I ended up going to Boston University. I think they wanted me to be a straight-A student and go to Harvard, get a 1600 on the SAT, pretty much the stereotypical Asian kid from my parents' generation. I wasn't perfect, pretty far from it.

For some kids the expectation may be unreasonable. But I can understand why my parents felt that. My dad was the oldest son and he had a big family. He came to the United States, was waiting tables everyday just to get through college, and would send money home. Later, he sent money to bring his brothers and sisters to the United States. He was the first one to come over. I guess he needed good grades to get where he is now. So I understand perfectly why they want their kids to get straight A's.

I think for most of my parents' generation, those who came here, that's pretty much all they did, just get by. My brother and I and most of my generation are extremely lucky to not have to go through that.

There was a whole lot more adversity in my dad's life than in ours. In some sense I feel guilty because I never really had to work as hard as he did just to get where I am now. It's fortunate that we ended up in this situation, but in some sense it's unfortunate that we haven't really faced real adversity.

My priorities? That's one thing that irks my parents. I don't look into the future that much. I don't know if it's just my way of dealing with things, but that's the way I live my life. I live in the moment.

On Racism: I've been hated on before. This white guy, during my first year in high school, he just came up to me and said, "Hey, you're a dirty chink." And he called my other friend from Hong Kong that, and my friend didn't know what a chink was. There's still a lot of bigotry in this country. I think it'll always be there. There are bound to be differences and there are going to be people who accept them and people who hate on them.

I think my generation is a lot more desensitized to it because we didn't live through total outright racism. You read about outright segregation with whites and blacks and stuff, but that's like a degree of separation because we didn't live through it. There's only so much you can get by reading about something. Living through something is totally different. I guess my generation has a bit of a rosier view on racism than past generations simply because we didn't experience

David Tang

what happened. It's one thing to talk about it, but it's another to live through it.

Stereotypes of Asians: Good at math? I kind of laugh at it because I'm terrible in math. I almost failed AP Calculus in high school. I can understand about the math thing though—it's pretty much memorization. I went to an after-school program, and they drill you and time you. Did it for a few years, hated it. Pretty much you go there and they just give you a book full of equations and stuff and you keep going through the book page after page.

Math is the one thing you can excel at that doesn't require much English comprehension. Everyone deals with the same numbers, so if you're not good in language, you might as well succeed in math.

Identity: Ethnically I know I'm Chinese, my parents originated from China. It's just that the mental aspect of it is fragmented. I wouldn't say I didn't have a stable environment, because my family was there and there was always food on the table. It's just the way things worked out—I was kind of displaced from two different cultures, the whole black sheep thing. This guy sticks out because he doesn't know where he's from, or where he calls home, which is why I'm surprised I turned out decently, okay. Because identity is a big thing—not just racial identity, but identity in general. I've been fighting with my identity for a very long time.

I don't think of myself as Asian, or Asian American; I think of myself as David. That guy David. That's what he does, this is how he's wired. It's just like being Asian is a detail but that's it—it's not the entire thing, it's a descriptor. But one descriptor is not going to describe the whole person. That's one thing I've come to learn—knowing someone and understanding someone are two different things.

I think we all want to be good kids, for the most part. I think that's pretty much universal, but obviously I'm a poor example of it because I've done certain things to mess things up and I won't deny that. I respect my parents, I still love my parents, and I'm grateful for them. Obviously the connections I've made outside my family are stronger than in my family.

EDUCATION, EXPECTATIONS, WORK

Cultural Anchors

Laura Jung

Laura Jung, a Korean American, was born and raised in California and is the sister of Daniel Jung.

The strongest part of my culture is what my parents taught me—that a person should be honest, be proud of who you are, and strive for success. Make my dreams come true, find the job I want, make money, support myself, and have a family. I think that's what's expected. I'm proud of people like my parents who work hard and don't care about the superficial things.

I speak fluent Korean, and I have a good relationship with my mom, and I think our relationship got better when I went to college. But my relationship with my dad has been the same since I was a child. I don't really know him. I think it has a lot to do with culture and how he was raised and how Korean men are supposed to be. They're supposed to be unemotional and stoic and they aren't supposed to communicate their thoughts and feelings, and my dad never communicated with me. It was either do this or do that. So basically that was it; there was never any communication where he asked me my opinions or anything like that. We never have conversations. I guess my expectations are a little different because I was raised in the American culture. I see my friends and they have really good relationships with their fathers and they do things with their fathers, so it is different.

I definitely think my mom is my hero. She works so hard. I feel like nothing ever gets her down. She doesn't really speak the language yet, she's successful at her business. They own a business together. It's a market. Market/liquor store. I just feel like she's really optimistic all the time, but she does house chores and runs the business. I feel that she cares about other people and is willing to listen to them; that's why she's my hero.

Education and Expectations: My parents view education as very important. I think because my parents never had that opportunity they pushed us to achieve as much as we can. They have this idea that without education we won't be able to succeed and do what we want here. Sometimes I feel I have a responsibility to them because they've done all of this for me to get here, so I can't really let them down, so there is some sort of pressure.

I'm at the Harvard Graduate School of Education in the risk and prevention program. Eventually I want to go into counseling psychology. I want to work with Asian American and immigrant adolescents, because I think there's such a stigma against mental health assistance and I think Asian adolescents do need it. They encounter so much stuff academically and just the pressure to succeed—they have all these stresses. I was reading up on Asian American immigrant mental health statistics and the suicide rate is ranked number five or something for suicide rates and I was really astonished by that because you don't see a lot of Asians complaining that "I'm so stressed I can't handle it." I think a lot of people internalize a lot of these things. Another problem is fitting in. Especially for the immigrants, assimilation and acculturation are very hard.

Being of the second generation, there is sometimes the stress—hardship—of immigrant parents. It stems from kids who have to take over that parental role like helping their parents with English, paying the bills. I think we have that duty toward our parents because they gave up so much to come here for us. So we can't leave them.

I'm going to live my own life. You say that, but it's not really like that. I feel they sort of have that pull on me. The unsaid expectations are to help them out financially, and to take care of them. I think finance has a lot to do with it. Asians look at that a lot because it's also how they measure success—by how much you make in the year.

Being the oldest, I think that also plays another role in Asian families; there's a lot more responsibility placed on the oldest child. Growing up, my parents put a lot more pressure on me academically than my brother. I got straight A's. Up until mid–high school and after that it became difficult. I was more upset with myself because I thought I was letting them down. They said, "It's okay, you still have good grades," but I felt that pressure. It was almost a silent pressure. I knew they had wanted that for me but I couldn't do it, so it was kind of a letdown for me.

I think I put that pressure to succeed on myself now. In high school it was, I need to get good grades so I can get into college. If I don't get into college then I'm going to be a failure and I'm not going to get a job. Now I think if I don't get good grades I'm not going to get into a good Ph.D. program. It just continues. It's like the grades sort of measure what my success will be in my future. In general I think Asians feel the need to succeed.

I was in journalism in high school and I really liked writing, working for the newspaper. I wanted to be an anchorwoman on television, do reporting and be on the scene. It just sounded really exciting, traveling to a lot of different places and reporting from there. I went to NYU as a communications major, figured I would get hooked up with an internship and start my way up.

In college I changed my mind. I interned at a PR firm that dealt with a lot of people in the entertainment industry and I just didn't want to be in that kind of environment where everyone was there and selfish for their own reasons. I wanted to be in a place where people cared about other people and were willing to help others. I wanted to get more involved with community service and volunteerism and that's how I ended up with my current major.

Speaking Up: Outside of the Korean culture, I think there are stereotypes too—like being an Asian woman—that we're supposed to be passive and submissive and very quiet. Sometimes I fit that role but sometimes I don't. Because I'm an Asian woman, people think I'm that way all the time, but I have a lot of personality and characteristics that are part of me. In films they're portrayed as this fiery, exotic, sexy woman or this demure, quiet type. But that's not how all Asian women are. And I feel pressure to break that idea that people have even though I don't know why I do.

Sometimes I think it's hard for me talk about it because I was kind of taught that we don't speak up. That's what my father ingrained into me. We're taught to not really have a voice. I'm just supposed to follow what he says; I'm not supposed to have an opinion. I think it's something I've struggled with, especially in class, because there's a lot of participation and discussion.

I think that's why it's hard for someone who's growing up in this culture. We were taught not to speak up at home because our parents were always right. So when you go to school it's the total opposite; you're confused, you don't know what to do. It's two separate values being thrown at you, so I think children get confused.

I don't know if I ever got over that; it's still in the back of my mind and it's something I still struggle with because it's part of my identity. Even now I have a lot of difficulty participating in class. It's definitely hard. I have opinions, not that they're not worthy to be shared. I think it's the way I'm trained. I actually had this conversation with a student who was a minority—she wasn't Asian, she was Hispanic—and she said, "Like in my culture, I'm taught not to speak up. My parents are right and my dad is a chauvinistic guy." And I was like, Maybe that's the way we are. Yeah, because she has opinions but has a lot of trouble participating in class too.

Dating: If I dated a Caucasian guy that would be okay. But if I brought home a black guy or a Hispanic guy, my parents would kill me. I think a Korean guy would be the ideal because my parents would want to communicate with him and there wouldn't be the language barrier, but I think other Asians are fine too. I think they just want me to get married. In terms of whom I'm attracted to, I'm definitely attracted to Caucasians and Asians.

Growing Up: We didn't really grow up in the city; we were sort of outside Los Angeles in the suburbs in the San Fernando Valley. My parents moved to L.A. as we had family there. I guess in our neighborhood there weren't many Asians around. It was a pretty white neighborhood. I think my brother and I grew up with a lot of diversity. There were a lot of Hispanics next door so we got to learn about other people and experience other cultures.

I think when I got into middle school is when I started thinking about the whole Asian thing, wondering about my culture and things like that. In elementary school I never questioned that I was different than my peers; they were just my friends.

Along with the whole adolescent awkward stage there was also the fact that I didn't really fit in with the Asians. So I kind of hung out with the mixed group. I guess I had my biases against them. They seemed superficial—what kind of car does your mom drive, and the latest Calvin Klein shirt—and I wasn't really into that. I just didn't really feel comfortable around them.

I started noticing that the Koreans hung out with each other, the Chinese hung out with each other, the Vietnamese hung out with each other. It was like there was even segregation among the Asians; it wasn't like a bunch of Asians hanging out. I think even among Asian groups there are biases among other Asians and stereotypes as well and I think those come into play.

I consider myself Korean American. I guess I think that to generalize as an Asian American is sort of wrong, but to specify and say Chinese American or Korean American, that's perfectly fine. I had a lot of trouble making friends in Korean school. I was always the girl in the corner reading my book. Everybody else had friends because I think they also went to church and I think for Koreans that's where all their social activities take place on Sunday—they have church and church groups and meetings, and my family never got involved, so I didn't know them in that way.

On Being Asian: Is it an advantage or disadvantage? It depends. I think Asians are coming up in my field, but there aren't many Asian Americans or Asians in general in psychology and there aren't many researchers that are Asian doing Asian research. So I think I have an advantage that way.

I guess in education people see the Asians at the top, so it doesn't really apply there but I guess it does in the corporate world.

I think if I went into the corporate world it might be a disadvantage, because my parents talked about it. When I was younger my parents used this example of my aunt when she went to a hospital to become a nurse. She was up against this Caucasian woman and the Caucasian woman got the job. They're always talking about how it's harder for us because we're a minority so we have to work extra hard. I think because they said it when I was younger it was sort of engraved in my head. I don't know if I necessarily feel it when I'm in job interviews, but it does come up sometimes.

I don't really think I've had a negative experience as a Korean. I guess that it was in high school that people realized I didn't really hang out with Asians and that was when I actually encountered racism from Koreans themselves; they called me Twinkie and things like that because I didn't hang out with them.

About cultural expectations: among Koreans, if you don't love everything about our culture you're not Korean. I'll give you an example. I was talking to a lady who was very involved with the Korean culture group, and they watch Korean videos and listen to Korean music and know everything about Korean pop culture. I said, "I don't listen to Korean music but I watch dramas every once in a while," and she was like, "Wow, you're so not Korean." I speak the language, I eat the food, I am part of that culture, but I'm not necessarily into everything, and she assumes that is being not Korean.

North Korea: I feel bad for the North Koreans. I sort of see it as a different culture; they're not really part of my culture so I don't really see it as affecting me. It's scary to think about what they're doing, but I don't really relate it back to me. When people ask, "Oh, are your parents from North Korea," it angers me. I don't know why, we're all from Korea. But there's that North Korea, South Korea divide. No Caucasians. And people come in asking, Oh, did you hear about what happened in North Korea? Are you from North Korea? And I'm like, Wow, you should really educate yourself. North Koreans can't get out of their country and come to America. I don't know why there's that anger when people ask if I'm from North Korea. They're sort of seeing us as the enemy, like we're somehow involved.

I don't worry that what happened to the Japanese during World War II might happen to Koreans. I feel like America has progressed, hopefully. And they wouldn't characterize all Koreans to be enemies like they did during that time with the Japanese, and put them into camps.

If I see an Asian in a film, and they're portrayed realistically, I'm like "Wow, that's cool they're including an Asian," but if they're portrayed in a stereotypical way, it angers me. Even in regular TV shows you see it; they portray Asians as the model minority—they're always doing well in school, especially in math and science, the nerd, or it's the other extreme.

Of Work and Family

Agnes Braga

Agnes Braga, born and raised in Manila, talks about self-perceptions and expectations as a Filipina.

I came from the Philippines at age twenty-three. This was in 1977. I had already finished college with a bachelor's degree in science—a business administration degree. My hopes were to earn a living. At that time in the Philippines, and probably in most of Asia, if you're a woman, you're what? A second-class citizen. Or maybe not that bad, but it's difficult for you to get your foot in the door.

I was itching to get out of the Philippines even when I was in high school. It's funny; the feeling was that I didn't belong there. I saw my friends, my schoolmates, their idea of being a woman—it's almost like a low self-esteem thing. Like, I'm a woman, I can only go this far, I can't be up there. I'm not going to have the opportunity. So a lot of my high school friends were like, Oh, I'm going to marry someone rich so I can go higher up in the food chain. That's how a lot of them thought. It was disgusting. That wasn't my idea of a life at all. I can't think this way, I can't function this way. I can be better off on my own terms—my own sweat, my own blood—and not because of someone else, a husband or a family that can put me higher up in the food chain.

The types of careers that were geared toward women were teaching or accounting. I couldn't do that. I thought of maybe becoming a doctor. But that was too long, eight long years. So my second option was to be a chemical engineer. But at that time, for engineering courses and being female, I would probably just end up teaching instead of working in an office or out in the field. As my mom pointed out to me, I don't have the temperament for that. Her exact words were, "I could just see you driving a pencil in your eyes because you couldn't get the solution to the problem or something like that." Then she said, "Why don't you just be an accountant like your sister? You'd really like it." I didn't make good grades, but I passed and then I took the CPA board and passed it the first time.

When I came to the States I was hoping I'd get into something worthwhile. I ended up in an insurance company—customer service. Then I became a liaison between the client side and the data processing side, so I got interested in that. Then I took some technical classes in data processing and so now I'm a programmer.

Eventually I settled in Los Angeles. As far as working, that's what I thought it would be—that I would be self-sufficient. But I had this idea that I would be on my own and have an apartment with just me. But then again it didn't quite turn out that way, because Mom and Dad joined me.

I'm not married—maybe it was the influence of my friend at the time, and the picture she painted for me: when you get to the States and you're earning a living, you can make it on your own and you really don't have to have family with you and things like that. In the Philippines it's always an extended family household. So I thought it would be totally different than that, maybe a 180-degree turn.

As I made my observations with family and friends today, it's not what she painted for me. It's about the same as living back in Manila, except that every member of the household is earning a living, or those who are of age are working; it's easy to find a job, not like the Philippines. That's the only difference.

At the time the opportunity of marriage presented itself, I wanted a career and the guy I was dating, he would want me to just stay home. I didn't know why he had that idea. I think he thought that being Asian, you should just be submissive and you should just stay home. He wasn't Filipino, he's American. But I wasn't quite the typical Filipino—I was more atypical than anything.

Expectations: I've worked with a lot of British and American programmers. Most of them are male, and it's like their expectation of Asian women is being submissive—that it's easier to get along with an Asian than a Caucasian woman—in the workplace and even at home. The ideas of these guys—there were a couple of them in the workplace—were, You're Asian, you're used to the home life, you're used to serving your man. You can just prepare the meals and do everything, it should be easier to get along with you. These are male co-workers, Americans.

My response is, You're looking at Asian women to be in servitude. You don't need a wife if that's what you're saying; I think you need a maid, you want a maid. And they say, No, it's just that with American women they're more opinionated. At a provocation they will tell you what is in their head; they will vocalize. Whereas with Asian women, they said, they would tend to keep quiet, keep it to themselves—a different approach, and then later, when the man is calmed down, they would talk about it. But still the man's word is the world.

I felt that way at work. At the time that I started programming, which was in 1983, there weren't too many women programmers; it was mostly males. Today, it's different; there are many more women. Back then, they gave me whatever they wanted to give me as far as work went, and I just went straight up to the boss and said I think I deserve more. I [said I] came from the client side and know what's happening on the other side, so you can't give me the runaround.

In the beginning I encountered that a lot. Eventually, when I built up my skills and confidence in my work, it diminished. As long as I'm vocal and I tell them my opinion, and I can do my work right—sometimes in a shorter amount of time—then they realize your potential and they back off. It's always like you have to prove yourself first. But when it came to another male programmer, it wasn't like that at all. It was more of a buddy system and a boy's club.

As for dating, in the early eighties the expectations of the Filipino woman or Asian woman was, Well, we are obedient and you just stay quiet like a wallflower. Now it's not that way anymore. You're not just a wallflower, not just somebody who would sit in one corner of the room and stay quiet the whole time.

For Filipino men the expectation for a traditional Filipino woman would be that you would always recognize the man as the head of the household. Even now I still feel that. Let's say in a husband and wife situation, both are working and that's fine, but when it comes to making decisions the woman would still defer to the man for the most part. My dating preference would be a non-Filipino, because Filipino men, they're not comfortable with you voicing an opinion. Maybe it's just me, but I think they just want you to be more quiet than more talkative.

Do I See Myself as an American? No, not quite. My mom's with me right now and she's eighty-eight years old and in her condition she needs to stay with a family member, and I guess I'm it. Would I have an American counterpart who would take in her mother and live with her? I think it's far and few. In the American family, the parents would be either in their own place or maybe in an assisted-living facility. In the Filipino family, they know that the parents will be with one of the children, most likely, rather than in an assisted-living or nursing home. I don't see very many American families where the parents are with one of their children under the same roof.

Basically I see myself as a career woman. When I was thirteen I decided I didn't want any kids. At that time I knew that most likely I wouldn't be married, or if I would be, there would still not be any children. So my life basically worked out the way I wanted.

An Editor of Entertainment News

Albert Lee

Albert Lee is a senior editor at Us Weekly.

I don't think of my ethnic identity, ever, in the course of my work. It doesn't inform what I do. It's not going to change how I cover the Oscars, or who we think are the best-dressed at the Golden Globes. It doesn't directly inform my job. If I were, let's say, an education reporter, I'm sure it would, because there are huge issues about affirmative action, particularly in California, about the percentage of Asian Americans that make up the student body at the state universities, that becomes a huge issue. But covering celebrities—first of all you don't really have a whole lot of Asian celebrities, and we're really driven by just who happens to be big movie stars and big TV stars. We cover Sondra Oh a lot. But it's not because she's Asian. It's because she happens to be on one of the biggest shows on television now, which is *Grey's Anatomy*.

Getting Started: When I first started I always imagined myself working at one of those very serious literary journals like the *New York Review of Books* or *Commentary*. But like any recent graduate I took whatever job was available. I don't think a lot of people have the luxury of necessarily deciding what they do. So my first job out of college was for a magazine called *Hamptons Country*. It was a magazine that covered the Hamptons in New York. We basically covered socialites' parties and new restaurants in the

Hamptons, blue-blood families and that sort of thing. I mean this was a very stupid way of going out and finding a job, but I literally opened up the Yellow Pages and turned to periodical magazines and started calling people and asking if they were hiring. And that's how I got the job.

I don't have formal training in journalism. I went to Princeton University, which is a liberal arts school, and I majored in religion. They didn't offer journalism classes and I certainly didn't have any intention of going to journalism school. During the summers I would intern at places like the *Village Voice*. I interned at a company called Metro Beat and it's now been acquired by Citysearch.com. I freelanced for some dance publications. I used to write for *Dance* magazine.

If I could have made a living writing for dance magazines and arts magazines I'm sure I would still be doing it today. But the truth was when I wrote for those dance magazines I got paid very little. You'd get paid like $100 for a thousand-word article. That's like ten cents a word, and then you write for an entertainment magazine and you get two dollars a word. Well, obviously, you're going to take those jobs more frequently because it pays the rent. You're struggling to live in NYC where rent is out of control and that sort of thing.

So I think that I started out and kind of had aspirations of working in more serious areas of journalism, but frankly I followed where the money and jobs are—which is in the celebrity sector, the entertainment sector. That's one area of the magazine industry that isn't going into the toilet right now.

I've worked at *Us Weekly* for about four years now, but before that I was freelancing for probably like two or three years doing articles about the entertainment sector. I would say that, in terms of doing hardcore celebrity news and nothing else, it happened when I joined *Us Weekly*. These types of magazines didn't really exist—certainly in the volume that they exist now—when I started doing it.

My primary responsibility is to edit the front section of the magazine, which used to be called Faces and Places and is now called Hot Picks. It's basically the first fifteen or so pages of the magazine, of pictures and captions, which include US Weekly's signature feature stars. Any time we do any kind of big awards coverage I oversee all of that. I oversee the Oscars, I oversee the Golden Globes, MTV Awards, Grammys, Emmys—basically any big awards show I'm editing. I'm the one who works directly with the photo editors, the designers, and the writers to put the layouts together.

How is my job different from a regular journalism reporter's job? I don't really think it is. I've worked at *Hamptons* magazine. I worked for Tina Brown's *Talk* magazine, which is more like a general interest publication. It's basically the same thing. Like any journalistic story, you look for compelling stories and interesting news events and you identify characters and conflict in a story and you piece that out into a narrative that you tell your reader in a way that's visually interesting and fun for the reader to look at.

There are numerous Asians writing in the entertainment industry. The editor-in-chief of this magazine is an Asian American, and before this she worked at *People* magazine. For a long time the number two editor at *People* magazine was an Asian American. So I think there are plenty of Asians in the industry in that sense, even though we're not like the majority.

As for my parents, they were very nonjudgmental—I mean they make jokes like, Hmm . . . *Us Weekly*? Maybe you can go work for *Time* magazine. Or *Newsweek*. Something more serious. But you know, *Newsweek* just put Paris and Britney on the news cover. That shows you where the market is heading, where the industry is heading, and what people are interested in reading about. But no one ever had the gall or lack of tact to be saying to me, You're an Asian—I expect you to be reporting about science or something like that.

Right now my work is mostly managerial. I used to be a reporter and I would go to movie premieres and I would interview Nicole Kidman and ask her embarrassing questions about her sexual life and that sort of thing. I mean, reporting and going to movie premieres and parties and nightclubs—that's a young person's game. So we have other reporters who go out and do that.

Entertainment news, I think, is very similar to what makes an interesting business story. It's what readers are responding to. It's about news value. It's a very subjective judgment. That's why editors-in-chief are fired and hired every year, every month. It's a constant merry-go-round with different editors because in some sense it's a subjective opinion. On one level *Us Weekly* does focus groups. Also, on a certain level, you go with your gut. It's a story like Britney Spears shaving off her hair and going into rehab—you know there's a concern for her children. On a certain level that kind of writes itself. It has all the hallmarks of an interesting celebrity story.

Will there ever be an Asian American superstar at the level of Nicole Kidman? I think so. I think Shonda Rhimes, the creator of *Grey's Anatomy*, made a huge step. It's amazing how one person can affect Hollywood in that sort of way. There are oftentimes perceptions that Hollywood is behind and hasn't really caught up. There is a huge sector of activism going on in that area. I think all it takes is one person like Shonda Rhimes. She decides to cast minorities in lead roles. So you have James Pickens Jr. playing the chief of surgery, and Sondra Oh as one of the interns, and Sara Ramirez. This has been going on for awhile. Latin representations certainly in television are exploding, like America Ferrara, the star of *Ugly Betty*, which is one of the biggest shows in our demographic and a huge ratings bonanza for ABC.

It's interesting now to see who becomes a big star, since celebrity has become divorced—increasingly divorced—from actual talent. You look at someone like Nicole Richie, Lionel Richie's daughter, who became famous for basically becoming skinny, too skinny, and that's kind of a very odd thing to become famous for.

Race always plays a factor in how readers of a magazine or viewers of television see celebrity and how that informs their interest; whether there is a TV show or a magazine story, of course that's going to affect an editor's decision.

VIEWS FROM WITHIN

Chinatown, New York

Corky Lee

Corky Lee, born and raised in New York City, is a photographer and community activist.

Chinatown is a part of my soul as well as a physical part of my being. I'm born Chinese American and I'm probably more American than I am Chinese.[1] I think that being in this country you get the best of both worlds. You have some individual freedoms that I would probably not have if I was in China. But in order for this to be a really free democratic country you have to struggle constantly with forces that want to take some of those liberties away. That's why people call me not a fighter, but at least an activist, and I will probably continue to do that.

Photographically I tell people, Yeah, I practice photographic justice. Because I can probably speak louder with a camera than with any words I write.

The perception among Americans out there is that Chinatown is a very inexpensive, good place to eat. But there's more. There's art, there's culture, there are politics, there are issues with parking outside. If you take a look at every other car that's parked out there, it has a police vehicle license allowing them to park. That means people like you and me who want to drive and park in Chinatown to shop, to eat, to worship, will have a harder time during the week. There's a big, major issue about parking in Chinatown that's been festering since 9/11. The general public doesn't know about that.

Changes in Chinatown: Before 1965, this was predominately a Toi Shan community where pretty much people knew each other. After 1965 a lot of immigrants came in principally from Hong Kong and eventually China.

Chinatown went from mostly Toishanese- to Cantonese-speaking people, probably about the early eighties. Normalization with China took place in 1979. Today a lot of the elementary school children are actually speaking Mandarin because a lot more people from the mainland came over.

On the other hand you have the emergence of snakeheads—these guys who smuggle people in for $40,000 to $60,000 a head. You also have a Fukinese community coming up along East Broadway because that was sort of the fringe of Chinatown. The Fukinese actually put up a statue of Commissioner Lin, who was responsible for burning all the opium in the opium wars. Toishanese and Cantonese put up a statue of Confucius, so they, the Fukinese, took pride in putting up a statue of Commissioner Lin.

There are places along Division Street where almost on a daily basis restaurant vans would pick up Chinese workers and drive them out to Connecticut, maybe New Jersey. For longer distances, there are these competing bus services that are very cheap. People take the buses to restaurant jobs outside of New York, to Washington, D.C., or Boston, for like $30 round-trip.

They go to find work. They would probably live near a restaurant six days a week and come back one day a week. These immigrants would look at the area code and they would know how long the bus ride would be to get out there. They may not know exactly where it is, but they are sent by Chinese employment agencies. A lot of employment in restaurants outside of New York actually germinates here. So New York is probably a real hub. And then satellite hubs would be Boston and Washington, D.C. After they have a job there, if there's an employment agency in Washington, D.C., they may find another job elsewhere, or they may come back here on their day off. They'll say, Well, I don't really like the way I'm being treated in this restaurant in Rockville, Maryland, or something, and they'll come back here and look for another job and they'll go elsewhere. There's actually a lot of mobility and competition among these bus services.

There have been at least one or two homicides and some violent attacks among competing operators. Right after Chinese New Year, there was a shooting and it was close to one of the departure points for one of the buses, like a block away.

Gradually the news about these buses has filtered out among a lot of college students. You can actually go online now and order tickets. So that's a pretty thriving business. There are probably at least six departures daily but the times that they leave are much more convenient to restaurant workers who get out after 12 or 1 A.M.

The Future of Chinatown: After 9/11 the tour buses don't come into Chinatown anymore because they can't park here. They have been gone for more than four and a half years. If you had the tour buses, people would know about Chinatown and may come back down after the tour. All they would have to do is get in a cab. Every cab driver in New York knows where Chinatown is. They'll come eat here or do some more shopping. I think tour buses would be a step in the right direction. When I was younger, there was a protest against the tour buses. They really didn't contribute too much. But I realize now that they actually did. I think at this point you need every nickel and dime to keep this community going. You have landlords hanging out "For Rent" signs here. Before, you would never see a "For Rent" sign in Chinatown. But now people can't afford the rent. And the apartments, little dinky apartments, are probably going for like $1,500. You have non-Chinese moving into Chinatown because they like the neighborhood, because it's safe, it's pretty cheap to eat, and you just have to pay a lot of rent to stay here.

So I think you have to kind of continue to nurture it—be they Chinese immigrants or people who want to move back into Chinatown and want to make this a community.

Right now there are a lot of condos coming up, so its going to change the character of Chinatown if that continues to happen. What's very viable is Confucius Plaza. It's six hundred units of affordable housing, middle-income and so forth. No other Chinatown in the history of this country has that big of a presence. San Francisco has a smaller community housing project. So I would think more affordable housing would be one way to keep the community base here.

Look at L.A.'s Chinatown; no one lives in L.A.'s Chinatown anymore. After six or seven o'clock, after the restaurants close, you have all of these derelicts that come into Chinatown. Same thing with Little Tokyo. Nobody lives in Little Tokyo!

If you don't have affordable housing I think the market is going to shrink. You have tenement buildings; a lot of them are really old. Ninety- to a hundred-plus years old. So you have to build new housing and start new businesses.

Elected Representation: Get someone elected so there is representation. There's taxation without representation in Chinatown that's been going on for far too long.

There's John Liu, who was elected to the city council from Flushing, but no one from Chinatown, Manhattan.

I think political representation has to be pretty primary. You can do a lot of other things, but once you get political representation, there will be a coming of age. In the last city council election, they tried to get one of the two Chinese candidates to give up and then run with the other, because when the numbers finally came out, if the two of them got together they would have enough to override the guy who won. The numbers were there. I think at least for the first elected city council member from Chinatown you have to think outside the box.

Oftentimes when they do go and vote, there are a lot of obstacles for immigrants. One is bilingual balloting. I actually testified a number of years ago (this is before 9/11) that you can't convert the candidates' names, even if they're Chinese, into Chinese names on the ballots. They couldn't do it. You can do it in English and you can do it in Spanish, but there's no room for Chinese.

Federal law mandates that if 10 percent of the community is of a particular ethnicity or nationality, you have to offer the voting population that option. Their names should be in that foreign language, be it Russian, Polish, or in this case, Chinese. So they said the only way they could do it would be to have these paper ballots. But paper ballots can get burned and they're actually pretty big sheets. They're seventeen by twenty-two inches.

My feeling is that if they spent some time and effort to put the characters in Chinese, they could do it. When you're able to vote and can't vote, it is discouraging. A lot of Chinese people were turned away in the past. I think once you get that done, you have a much better chance of getting a Chinese individual elected.

I think racism has taken a different form from twenty to thirty years ago. It's probably a lot more subtle. I think it comes in the form of comments, be they on major media or in political cartoons, things of that nature. There's a commercial on TV for a car. There's an Asian guy, an Eskimo who has a dog sled, and the white guy's driving the expensive car. The Eskimo has buck teeth, and I'm like, come on, that's politically incorrect.

I consider this idea of America being a melting pot a misnomer; it's more of a salad bowl. It's probably not a total meltdown of cultural and traditional ethnic value but an appreciation of diversity and acceptance.

Through Photography: As an Asian Pacific American, what I have done, particularly about 9/11, is try to get the news out about what was going on in Chinatown beyond the ethnic press. I would send my stuff primarily to a community paper called *Downtown Express*, which also owns the Village weekly newspapers. *Downtown Express* addresses everything south of Canal Street, going down as far as Battery Park. I'm probably the only consistent Chinese American or Asian American contributor, photographically. If I know about a story, I would make the pitch then I would try to get the photograph into the publication. Eventually the *Downtown Express* started to do more stories because I was submitting them. I was only paid per story. When the articles started to appear, a lot of the other organizations started to send in their press releases.

There are also many other journalists who have come through wanting to know about stories and have heard about me in one form or another from the AAJA (Asian American Journalists Association). Taking them around, I've heard of other stories that I didn't know about. So I feel it's my responsibility to do that.

It's the continuation of what I started three, four decades ago. At the time I started I knew there wasn't anyone that was photographing. And I didn't really think of documenting things. I wanted to get into the papers and I figured if I could get into the papers it was a form of documentation—showing that Chinatown or other Asian Pacific Americans are part and parcel of the larger landscape. There was a void.

I felt like Don Quixote, taking on a campaign, even if it's just one person. Eventually I figured one person can make a difference, after spending time at NYU as an artist-in-residence. There are some students who have heard me speak and seen my photographs. They come looking for me to ask for advice or support.

Maybe in a strange sense I'm very provincial. In another sense, if I take photographs and persevere in what I do, I can send that message out to other people: listen, you should take another look at what you perceive to be Chinatown.

Of Japanese Towns and Cultural Communities

Dale Minami

There are only three recognizable Japanese towns left in the United States and they're all in California: Los Angeles, San Jose, and San Francisco.² Excluding Hawaii, the internment and the incarceration of Japanese Americans had major psychological effects on my parents' generation as it flowed down through lineage. We were taught to be 100 percent American, to really succeed, to try hard, and as a result I think we were taught a sort of assimilative model to follow. As a result, you find the out-marriage [marrying other than Japanese] among Japanese American women, for example, is over 50 percent. For men it's lower, but there is a high out-marriage rate because we, and I should say not they, were taught to be as white as possible. To that extent I think there is also shame about being Japanese American. It was not something to be proud about until we learned the lessons of African Americans and Hispanic Americans who fought the civil rights struggles and kind of blazed the path for Asian Americans to walk upon in their journey not only to equality, but to self-pride, self-worth, self-dignity. So I think of Japanese Americans as the most Americanized of groups, even though they weren't the first Asian American group to immigrate here. I think the Chinese were, en masse, but because of the Exclusion Acts, the Chinese couldn't build stable families.

The Japanese could build stable families—that's why we still count in generations. But the camps, I think, had a major influence on essentially dispersing the entire community—in terms of creating a psychological vent to not just stay with your own kind. Being in a Japanese American community was not thought of as the optimal safety net for you in case this thing happened again. It made you feel that if you were associated with Japanese Americans too much, the same thing could happen again as did during the incarceration in World War II.

That's still pretty much the sense that I get, even today, over fifty years later. The community institutions are broken down. For one, after the camps it was hard to rebuild, and when you did rebuild you had this other mechanism, this other dynamic of psychologically disposing of your own racial or ethnic identity. So I think that's gone on and on, and as Japanese Americans intermarry, I find that more and more to a greater extent. So I think it has definitely created a situation in which Japanese Americans from the generations past are becoming less attached to a geographical community, to a cultural community.

I think what you find, though, is that there are occasional pockets of people who come back to recognizing the value of having a cultural and ethnic heritage, whether they're half Japanese or a quarter Japanese; but they embrace the code of ethics or principles or culture.

You have, in this strange kind of way, popular Japanese culture becoming a little bit more popular in this culture. If you look at the anime type of cartoons, it just grabs the imagination of young people, not just Japanese kids. I talked to the owners of bookstores and only about 20 percent of the purchases of those cartoon books are by Japanese. There are other races among whom you find anime becoming popular; you see the reference to Harajuku girls by Gwen Stefani; you find the revival of old Japanese values in the films *The Last Samurai* and *Memoirs of a Geisha*. Those things become romanticized, popularized Japanese. In vogue. Whether that has an impact on Japanese Americans I'm not sure. Whether that instills pride in younger generations, fourth or fifth generations, to the point that they come back and find something about Japanese culture or Japanese American history, I think that's an unknown right now.

I grew up as an Americanized kid, and to the degree that I embrace certain Japanese things, I do it because I like it. There are certain foods that I love, there are certain aspects of Japanese culture that I love, but there are others that I could do without. The conformity—to that degree I'd rather be Americanized because that's how I was socialized. I respect that culture and respect what it means to be Japanese, and I think I'm living those with the American part and the Japanese part of me.

Changes in Race-related Issues: I've seen changes both good and bad. It's interesting obviously with the changing demographics that we have seen. When I was growing up in Gardena, the Asian Americans were predominantly Japanese, and that was in Los Angeles, not San Francisco. But over the years, with immigration reform, what you have is a panoply of people from Asia who are now taking major roles in this country's leadership—even sports and entertainment, almost all areas. I still think there's a glass ceiling, though. I don't think we're represented proportionately in the numbers that we have in our population.

The Glass Ceiling: For years I did employment discrimination cases, and in general what I saw the most was leadership positions where Asian Americans were stereotyped as passive, "nonleadership" types who were not able to command the respect of the subordinates. Yet many Asian Americans have a different style and they are terrific and competent and skilled. In some cases I was able to prove in hearings that their skills and their abilities were far better than the people that replaced them who were non-Asians.

The pattern repeated quite often is where an Asian American is in a position of leadership, has terrific evaluations, and yet the subordinate, a non-Asian, gets the promotion rather than the Asian American. I've seen that pattern repeated quite often.

With the changing demographic and the pool of Asian American leaders, surely that model has to change, especially with the advent of Silicon Valley in the American financial public scene, where we see Asians in leadership roles. I think that's helped a lot and changed the stereotype of Asian Americans not being strong leaders.

Hmong Community

Steve Thao

There are many layers to our communities. There's the Hmong that just came here, there's the Hmong that came later than us. I think for the generation that came in the seventies or even early eighties we probably tried harder to become Americans because there were so few back then. The ones that came a little bit later, they probably hold onto the traditions a little bit more.

Public Assistance and the Reported Backlash: A typical profile of a Hmong family is a mother with her kids who has no marketable skills in America, so they have to get on assistance for awhile. But if you look at the big picture of the entire community, a whole generation of men, fathers, heads of households died in the war. Tens of thousands men died and so what do you have? Very young men and boys and very old grandfather types, and it's hard to find a job when you don't speak the language or have any marketable skills. A lot of Hmongs were on public assistance, but I think that's changed for people like us who came early and are living the so-called American dream and working our butts off—but the perception does hurt us.

People look at us like we're only getting freebies because we're Hmong. It hurts us psychologically but the community is thriving. If you look at communities like Fresno, Sacramento, and Minneapolis,

Hmongs are becoming doctors, they're going to Ivy League colleges, they're doing very well, having their own businesses.

I attribute that to hard work within the family. I think people become successful because they either have their own drive or they have a good strategy put down by the parents. They'll push education. As with any community, Asian American or mainstream, it's all about access to education. That's how we come up in this world.

Cultural Mind-sets: In the Hmong community sometimes we have restrictions to the access to education. For example, in the early eighties there were a lot of young marriages. So a lot of young women got married and moved into the family and didn't get a chance to finish high school or college. It's taken twenty to thirty years for us to ease out of old cultural things that do not match with American society. You have to compare the differences between living in Laos and Thailand to an industrial country like America.

It's a constant battle because you don't know how much to give up and how much to keep. And some people hold fast to that. When you're eighteen, nineteen years old you have to get married. That's a traditional belief that won't die out. A lot of young women, even in mainstream society, feel that they don't have worth if they don't have a husband or family to call their own.

It's caused a lot of problems. What we're seeing right now, at the root of our problems, is families. In the early eighties you saw a lot of young people getting married for silly and stupid reasons. Now we're seeing a whole generation of those people divorcing left and right.

An Interconnected Set of Problems: You're seeing a lot of problems when parents divorce and kids don't have two parents in their households. You have young people in their late twenties and thirties and they're trying to relive their childhood and they forget that they have children they have to raise. So that just keeps the cycle going of no education, poverty, and perhaps crime.

I see that as one of the big problems, because during that time in the eighties when everyone came here we were so confused. They didn't look at themselves as Hmong Americans, they looked at themselves as Hmong living in America, so a lot of people just kept the old values and said this is our own community within America. We're going to get married, we're going to do this the Hmong way.

They realize ten to fifteen years later, Oh my God, we've made a mistake, it's not working.

I think the biggest change in the Hmong community is that women have come to understand they have rights. They should be able to do more and have more freedom. Obviously the Hmong community tradition is very beautiful, but there are a lot of things that are very chauvinistic and there's a lot of oppression of women.

That's the thing that causes all these other problems: if you're talking about gangs, if you're talking about crime, if you're talking about so-called murder-suicides or things like that. It all happens because people get together for the wrong reasons, and one person wants to leave and the other person doesn't want them to leave and then you have children involved who are the ultimate victims. So that's what I would put my finger on. That's based on cultural differences, the cultural acceptance of early marriages.

What happened in the early eighties was a very conservative tradition. If you find your son or your daughter with someone, a lot of times people force them to get married even though they don't know each other very well. Ten years later the two people realize they can't stand each other, causing harm to themselves and their children. So that ten-year forced marriage just created five different problems just because the family wanted to save face.

It's just my opinion. What I eluded to about saving face—it goes back to that family structure. You don't do things to shame your family—not just your nuclear family but your ancestors, your uncle, your grandfathers. You don't do things to shame them. You do things to augment their prestige and you go to school to make your parents proud. It's just your belief in your family.

It's a constant struggle. Different people within the community move at a different pace toward being what is called Americanized, or Hmong Americanized. There are people who are still very backward. I know a couple of twenty years where there are two wives because they are using the cultural excuse that it's acceptable, when it's really based on their selfishness.

I was at this conference at USC and statistics and research showed that second and third generations are going to have more problems than the first generation. And in our community that's scary, because we've had a lot of problems in the eighties and nineties and these other kids who were born in America are going to have more problems than us. Oh, my goodness. What are we going to do?

The Importance of Identity: I think a lot of it is identity. You don't have a strong sense of who you are and who you belong to. I went through that in my college years. I grew up in elementary school thinking I was American. In high school and middle school I was told I was completely different. In college I had to learn what my community was and I embraced it. For a lot of people that happens and they get into the community but they see all the bad stuff. They repel away and stay away from the community.

A lot of it is about identity if you're talking about kids growing up. If I have children, they're going to ask, Are they Hmong? If they go to a Hmong New Year, do they feel part of it? For a lot of the generation, they don't feel a part of it because they're very Americanized.

A lot of the Hmong celebrations are still very traditional, where a lot of the older people don't want to relinquish leadership positions and they are still doing things very traditionally, very old-fashioned, and they don't cater to young people, depending on where you live and how the community accepts you—in Wisconsin or Twin Cities or Fresno.

Leadership and the Power of the Vote: I would have to say that the older leaderships from Laos and Thailand still have the power. In Minnesota I think that's changing a little bit; you can identify who the leaders are. A lot of times it's military leadership—the people who were in the military, high ranking. It's all about legitimacy, if you have power or not. If an old guy who used to be a colonel has any prestige or power, it's because all of his captains respect that. That generation is probably ages forty, fifty, sixty. It's still very patriarchal and that's because it's still intact. We have to wait and see in another thirty years what happens. Will it be the sons of those old guys who take the leadership, or will it be people who come out of nowhere who will have actually done something and achieved something in the mainstream public realm or business?

Probably like the Chinese in San Francisco, the Hmongs understand the power of their voting block. In Minnesota there are many Hmong elected officials; there's a city councilman in Wisconsin, a Hmong city council president in Omaha.

In Minnesota, it's a much more progressive society than in an area like Fresno. So I think that the local government and the nonprofits have helped the Hmong progress a lot better and achieve more in Minnesota. I think in Minnesota they understand the power of voting. There are quite a few young people who have worked for major campaigns over there.

Language and Internal Divisions: Hmong people basically have two main dialects: there's the White dialect (Hmong Der) and the Green (Mong Leng). It's like comparing southern accents versus Midwestern accents, but there are spelling differences, tonal differences. Most times when state agencies print Hmong on brochures, they do it in White. Just recently, in the past two or three years, the state of Minnesota has been printing two versions, White Hmong and Green Mong. So that is a sense of division, in my book. I think the White Hmong has been more dominant, more prevalent because the leaders have been White Hmong. The spiritual leader or the leader of the Hmong, General Vang Pao, is White Hmong.

Perhaps you have your church Hmong and your very traditional Hmong, because you do ceremonies very differently. Your funeral

ceremony is very different. If you have your wedding, you do it differently, so that could be a division of what is considered Hmong
in the future. Are you church? Are you atomists? Do you do it the
traditional way? If you're Americanized, do you change it? So these
are issues that we need to talk about.

Gender Issues: That's probably huge. It's going to be happening in the next couple of years: to see and feel how much power men
and women should each have over the other—or do they have
equal say, or whatever? You have to understand there are a lot of
fifty-, sixty-, seventy-year-olds still alive who still hold fast to this
archaic thinking, that women are second-class citizens.

Interracial Marriage as an Issue? I don't know. I think that
will still be an issue. That's happening so much now. Families still
want their sons and daughters to marry Hmong, but I think that's
changing a bit since we're seeing so many divorces. They're probably a little bit more open-minded. I think with many Asian communities there's this racial discrimination concerning interracial
marriages. It's still looked down on. There's so much of it now;
especially here in Fresno, Sacramento, and the big cities. I think
it's happened so much that in the big cities people aren't surprised
anymore, as opposed to when I was growing up, you'd hear rumors
of someone marrying a white guy or Hispanic guy. It would be a
shock, but it's not like that anymore.

Two Decades Ago: The picture of Hmong Americans twenty
years ago—there's a world of difference. The majority of Hmong
people didn't really know English all that well. From 1996 to 2007
there was a gigantic gulf between the equality of the sexes and how
they viewed women. Back then it was all about males and young
boys. As for women, in my perspective, it was just that daughters
were just for marriage, and now I see a lot of progressive families
that value their sons and daughters equally, where they set aside
money for both to go to college.

Back in the eighties and nineties most of the people in college
were men, boys. The families didn't support women in college and

they were getting married early. Once they're married, their husbands weren't going to allow them to go to college. So there's a gigantic difference from twenty years ago. Today they have more prestige, they have more say.

From a Western standard we may look at it as a good thing. But some people may look at it as a bad thing, too. Here there are more divorces. Women are given more say and equality but some people use it as an excuse to do other things that hurt the family. There are many immigrant groups coming to America that say all the freedoms here are too much freedom, and it makes people abuse it. So some people might say it's been bad. They're a small minority, more of the traditional, I would say.

Hmong Holidays and Gatherings: The major ones are about the New Year. We don't have a set New Year. I'll just give you the landscape for us. July 4th was a humongous celebration for us—not because we all love July 4th, but it's a soccer tournament in Minnesota where twenty to thirty thousand people gather and have soccer tournaments, athletic tournaments, vendors selling stuff. A lot of young people look forward to that. You have your parties at night. It's an event; it's not a traditional Hmong event, but it's a Hmong soccer tournament.

Here in Fresno we have a long celebration from December 26 to February 1 that's supposedly called the Hmong International New Year. Probably about one hundred thousand Hmong come here.

During Thanksgiving you have the Minnesota New Year's celebration in St. Paul, and that gets a lot of people, probably fifty thousand every day. Also during Thanksgiving other towns in Milwaukee and North Carolina have New Year's celebrations; Sacramento has it also. It's not a Thanksgiving celebration, it's just a New Year's event and they hold it in a situation where there's vacation time for people. It's not a special time—the only special reason is because people have vacation and that's why they do it.

But it is a New Year's celebration. Some people dress in traditional Hmong clothes. They throw the ball, Pov Pob. It's also called a courting game. That happened back in the old country, where every New Year they throw it to a young lady and if she drops it she has to give you a gift. Or, if you drop the ball you have to give her a gift. It's a social thing. But the Hmong New Year is more than just that. It's actually like all mainstream holidays. It's very commercial. That's a time when people sell their goods, make a lot of money selling food, selling products. Then from Thanksgiving on to the end of the year various towns will have their New Year's celebrations. Chico, California, would have a celebration, some town in Wisconsin would have a celebration; there's no system or practice where they say I want to pick that date or another date. It's just whoever picks whatever date first.

There's no national organization or national consciousness that says, Let's do this here and there. There's nothing like that. How do they connect? Well that's the thing; they don't connect. Chico doesn't talk with Stockton, they don't say, What date are you doing it; they just pick a date and do it. And after a couple of years if their date overlaps with another one then they just kind of move it. That's the way it's done. Very informally.

Food: Traditional Hmong food is very simple—pork or beef cooked with hot sauce and rice. A lot of Hmong have comfortably adopted Laotian or Thai dishes as our own. Because there's larb, that's a Thai dish. Basically there's two ways to prepare it: if you go with beef, you just squeeze the blood out of it and eat it raw. That's kind of the hard-core traditional way. We have our county health department here, so it's not raw, it's just beef with various things in there. But it's mostly meat. Most people think of that when they think of the Hmong diet—larb, chicken, noodles. We're up in the hills and there's just simple food.

Clans: There are basically eighteen clans in the Hmong community. The clans are visible because of their last name; my last name is Thao, so that's one clan; General Vang Pao, he's a Vang, so that's one clan. A lot of our leadership is through our clans, so that's very important to our community. Minnesota, Sacramento,

Fresno, they have this organization that would be similar to that on a regional or city level. It's called the eighteen clan. So the eighteen clan would resolve any traditional disputes or dissolve any traditional marriages; if they don't want to go to court, they can bring it to the eighteen clan. They don't have any true power or legal power, but they do have the credibility of the clans behind them.

For example, if my father is about to see his uncle, and his uncle subscribes to the clan's decision—he's going to put pressure on me to accept it too. If I am sued and I lose, I can either decide to accept it or not. But my fathers or uncles would put pressure on me to accept the clan's decision. So it's really about how they did it back in the old days, except it's more formalized now. Minnesota is interesting because they have a legally binding aspect to their decisions now.

In terms of marriages, a recent development is that people want negotiators to have accountability for the marriages. When people get married they have negotiators for both sides, so it's the negotiator's job to meet with the fiancée's family to negotiate a dowry, terms of the marriage, and things like that.

For example, back in the eighties, a lot of marriages probably wouldn't have happened if there had been accountability. The negotiator would be like, Well, son, do you really love her? The son might say, We went out on this one date and we came home late and they just forced us to be married. So it would fall on the negotiator to have some sort of accountability to the match in case, after ten or fifteen years, there's a divorce and its determined that, Oh, you guys should (or shouldn't) have gotten married. It's going to fall on them.

There's also the dowry price in marriage. When or if I get married, there will be a dowry set from $3,000 to $10,000. Hmong Americans and older Hmongs like me, we look at that as a part of tradition. Some people look at it as payment for your wife. So that's going to be an issue. The man has to pay the wife's side of the family the money.

Let's say my girlfriend and I decide to get married. We talk to our parents and I have a negotiator and then she has one also. That's how you do it.

Because I grew up with my Christian background, I would do a church wedding and a traditional wedding. I would have to do two.

Hmong Wedding: A traditional wedding would be my party going to her house, where there would be negotiating while I sat in another room. They would negotiate, find a compromise, we'd drink to them, they'd drink to us, and that's how you do a Hmong wedding. That's the ceremony. I take her with me. Then she's married. There's just very close family gathered for this event.

Then I would have to throw a party for my family, too, and say, This is your new daughter-in-law. We'd have to buy a lot of food for her family, a lot of food for our family. For someone like me in my generation we would have to do the church and we would have to do the reception. I think that's how I would do it because I grew up in church and I'm Christian.

I think a lot of people who are not religious or not Christian would probably just do the traditional wedding and have a reception or party for their friends.

Sometimes it's tough navigating both because I have heard from friends and people I know who say you're not Hmong if you do things like this or that. If you have a Christian wedding or a Christian funeral then you're not Hmong anymore. I'm a little insulted by that because my Christianity is my spiritual self and Hmong is also my spiritual self, and I think I can mesh the two. Some Hmong people think you can't. As I said earlier, there are differences in funeral ceremonies and there are differences in wedding ceremonies. There are also differences in wedding ceremonies between Green and White too.

Churches: The big Hmong church in the United States is the C&MA, Christian and Missionary Alliance. They have big conferences every year and every four years they have gigantic conferences of Christian Hmongs, and it's called the Hmong district.

Almost every Hmong community in the United States has a C&MA church. There are Hmongs that are Baptists, Catholic, and all the other small denominations, but the C&MA is the largest one.

In terms of embracing religion, I think it's more psychological when people who are very traditional think that Hmong Christians are sellouts—that they're not Hmong anymore. In terms of true clashes, I don't know. I can't really conceptualize it; it's just verbiage. Some people genuinely accept Christianity, some people think, "Yeah, I got here because of the church," and maybe admit that in their spiritual soul they don't accept Christianity but it's a practical tool that got them here.

What It Means to Be a Hmong American: I don't know, I guess I just feel very fortunate to be a part of a small and special community. In my twenties I went to France and I met Hmong people there by accident. There's this ongoing myth that if you go to any city in the world and you find a Hmong person, they will take you in because you're Hmong. Because we have had thousands of years of persecution from the Chinese, from the Laotians, from everywhere we've gone to, Hmong people will help and love each other wherever they are. I found that to be very true.

Vietnamese in Maryland

Hoan Dang

I'm the president of the Maryland Vietnamese Mutual Association (MVMA). When the local government or state government wants to reach out to the community they will contact us. We're like one of the go-to organizations of the Vietnamese community, at least in Maryland. I've been doing that for the past seven years. The largest pocket of Vietnamese in the United States is in Orange County, California. And second largest is probably San Jose, third is Houston. The fourth largest is the northern Virginia/D.C./Maryland area.

Within the Vietnamese American community there are two groups. One group is doing well, very successful, and then there's the other group, where many have come over later—the second wave of boat people that are still kind of struggling. In Silver Spring where I live, there are some programs to support those who are in need. Oftentimes people just assume, Oh, they're Asians, they must be doing well, they don't need assistance. But many work multiple jobs and the kids are struggling in school. Other Southeast Asian communities are in similar situations.

We have a program called the Vietnamese Parent Enrichment Program that we started a couple of years ago. A social worker goes to parents' homes two times a month. We work with about twenty families in an area called the Red Zone, which is an apartment complex with a lot of immigrants. We teach some of the basics, like how to get their kids ready for kindergarten, and we work with the parents and try to teach them the value of education—just kind of help them get adjusted.

We've seen families with five kids who are struggling. A number of them are Amerasians. There are workshops where they get a dentist to teach the kids to brush their teeth, things that their parents wouldn't necessarily know how to teach them. Some don't have access to dental care because they don't have insurance. Just basic stuff that we take for granted.

I started out in this area volunteering. With the Amerasian Homecoming Act,[3] about six organizations in the D.C. area came together and formed this collaboration and hired a program manager who matched families with volunteers. She matched me up with a Vietnamese family that had a mother and four kids. No father came over. So I visited them about once a week, volunteering. I had to speak Vietnamese because they couldn't speak English, so that improved my Vietnamese greatly. I think the mother was not literate in Vietnamese because she was from the countryside, and the kids would get notes from school and I would read them and try to translate them to the mother and would help the kids with their homework.

I did that for maybe about six months after I graduated college, and in the process I met other Vietnamese volunteers. We got more and more involved and pretty soon I was helping another family. Then there was the Orderly Departure program.[4] Congress passed a series of acts which allowed political prisoners to come over with their families. These were people put in reeducation camps, former military people; the higher the rank, the longer they had to be in the camps—former civil government officials as well.

My aunt had a two-week-old baby when we came to this country; her husband was a lieutenant colonel in the air force and he was going to join us but planned to leave a few days later as he

Hoan Dang

wanted to make sure his parents were set. When we flew out the next day, Saigon fell and nobody could get out. Fast forward to 1990—he's coming over. He was in the concentration camps and under this program for prisoners their whole families got to come over, so that was another large wave of Vietnamese refugees.

I think they got permanent residency right away. These were families of former South Vietnamese officers. You hear of Vietnamese graduating as valedictorians and just excelling, like the woman graduating from the Air Force Academy. I think it's just the family discipline instilled in the kids. These were the former military officers, and I guess they probably passed on some of that discipline to the kids—also the value of education.

While they were in Vietnam in concentration camps doing hard labor for years and years, their children were not allowed to go to school. They couldn't get jobs either. They couldn't go to school and they couldn't go to work. So basically I don't know what they did. For example, my cousins had to go into business for themselves. My cousin who came over with the Amerasian family—two of the kids were Amerasian from his wife and he also had four other kids—was probably doing things like buying gasoline. They would add water to it to dilute it a little bit, then go to the market and sell it. They had to do things like that to survive—bicycled it to wherever and sold it. And that was that.

When they came they were young enough to still go to school. The oldest went to ninth grade; she did have some schooling in Vietnam because I guess my uncle wasn't a high-ranking officer. Now they work in the nail industry. Cosmetology. They do pedicures, manicures, and in Maryland they pretty much have a corner on the nail industry.

It's a very lucrative business. I think they do very well. I did some research because my organization helped start the Association of Vietnamese American Cosmetologists in Maryland. I estimated that 50 percent of the Vietnamese workforce works in the nail industry.

After asking around, I discovered they got started with a relative who didn't have a lot of education and wanted a job. They would bring her into the nail shop and have her help out; they found they could make a good living that way and more people went out. They kind of took over the market because apparently Vietnamese people have small hands and fingers and they can draw very small designs on the nails, so I guess there's some hand-eye coordination involved. I think the normal price is about $30 for a manicure and they can do it for $20 or $10. It's very cutthroat. Then they started getting into each other's businesses and competing against each other. So I think they kind of figured, We'd better stop this or we're going to run ourselves out of business.

My girl cousins, a lot of them, are in the nail industry. The boys are mechanics; they work in the garages. They make a pretty good living with that as well; one guy works for Acura or one of those dealers. The youngest joined the navy. He finished his tour, came out, and went to a tech school, and now he's an air conditioning/heating technician, doing well too. That uncle and his family came over in 1989.

Living Outside of Koreatown

Laura Jung

Laura's family lives in the Los Angeles area.

Koreatown[5] is a city on its own and it's part of L.A. County. There are restaurants and a lot of activities that take place, nightclubs for kids to go to—a happening place at night. A lot of recent immigrants go there because I guess they feel more comfortable there.

I think it is important to have a place like Koreatown. I think it's good for the immigrants to have some familiarity and also for second-generation kids to get to know their culture and to experience the food and the language without having to go to Korea. It's kind of nice to have that thirty minutes away from you.

Daniel Jung
(Laura's brother)

I really don't go to Koreatown except to eat. Koreatown in Los Angeles is like a city. There are Korean signs everywhere. If you wanted a haircut or a supermarket, pretty much anything you needed, you could get it in Koreatown.

Growing up, there were a lot of FOBs in L.A. (Someone "fresh off the boat.") When Koreans born in Korea come to the United

Laura and Daniel Jung

States, many still carry with them their ideas and values, which is good, but when they go out they just speak Korean with other Koreans and don't really get a chance to learn English.

They keep to their culture. Usually when you go to Koreatown they speak Korean to each other. But my friends, we speak English. We won't really talk in Korean. Their behavior and the way they dress are a lot different than me and my friends.

My mom would never let me go down to Koreatown to hang out, and when I did go, she told me to be careful and know who I'm talking to and just kind of be aware of surroundings.

I remember hearing stories about a kid in high school, that he shot a guy and was actually going to jail, and there was this big gang called the Korean Mafia. That was the story during senior year.

In L.A. there are a lot of Koreans that are superficial. They'll care more about what they're wearing and what they're driving than about where they live. I know this guy, he had a Mercedes Benz but he lived in the projects. I don't know about the thinking on the East Coast, but I know on the West Coast, in L.A., Koreans are always worried about how other Koreans might view them. You go down to Koreatown and you see Mercedeses and Lexuses and Hondas and it's always about what you're wearing and what car you're driving. My parents have never stressed that with me, so I don't really care about that.

Claiming Space

Shamita Das Dasgupta

Shamita Das Dasgupta is a founding member and director of Manavi, an organization dedicated to empowering South Asian women living in the United States.

Claiming space is very important: claiming space in terms of our bodies—there are more Asian faces, more Asian foods, more Buddhist and Hindu temples that have come up—and also symbolically, bringing in our ideas and thoughts that challenge the huge Western canons and philosophies. These are all ways of claiming space.

I always wear South Asian clothes, nothing else. I haven't changed, even now, and I won't. I was a kid when I came here and I wore jeans and stuff. When I came back into the community to work I made a very deliberate decision to change to South Asian clothing. This was mainly to let my community know that I'm one of them and they can't really dismiss me as a Westernized woman coming in and saying a bunch of garbage. This was a very deliberate decision on my part, to wear what I wear. And I won't go back anymore. I want to make sure that when I talk I do it in that language and that I look like them; that they recognize me as one of theirs and they don't have the opportunity to dismiss me. That I'm speaking from within them rather than outside on issues such as violence against women and race relations.

Assimilation: It is not location but the ethnicity that ties us together. You can see, for example, in Queens or South Jersey or the Newark area that there are these spaces that have developed that are completely South Asian. There are temples, lots and lots of temples, that are part of it, but more so individual families joining together and meeting with each other on the weekends. I think South Asians are very proud in terms of their own culture and language. They try to teach that to the kids. The second generation finds it's very important to hold on to that. They can find it in movies and dance and music and coming together as families. But that doesn't mean that they're not assimilating well. They are very successful outside in the larger community. I think one of the issues that's important is that they lead this kind of dual life. When they go outside in the larger world they are very adjusted and high-power people doing whatever they're doing, and they come home and they have their religion and their language and food and families that come together.

In terms of third or fourth generation, we haven't been here that long so we don't know. I think there is definitely an effort to keep the cultures going. I find that the South Asian second generation tends to do a lot of volunteer work, going back to Pakistan and Bangladesh to keep the tie going. The first generation, too—they keep going back and forth a lot more than any community I've seen, almost every year or every other year. I do see in the universities that there are Pakistani clubs or South Asian clubs, so there is absolutely a very strong need and effort in the community to keep it going. That doesn't mean that it's not changing or that there's no authentic culture, but there are these strong themes that run through. I think food is one, music, the way people talk, the way kids address me even if I go to lectures. South Asian kids will come up and call me Auntie, which is very important in our communities; older women and older men are given respect.

Arranged Marriages: I was married at sixteen, and I followed my husband to the United States because he came here to do his Ph.D. studies. I had completed about two years of college in India by then.

Our marriage was arranged, although I knew his family and him since childhood. Their family happened to live very close to my uncle's family. To this day, the majority of the marriages are arranged. In villages there may be a go-between; in cities you might find a go-between but if the families know each other, that's great. They might also advertise in matrimonial columns. Generally, the families get in touch with each other and see if the match is proper, whatever that might be. More and more in higher socioeconomic circles the prospective groom and bride meet each other after it's been worked out, but they have what I call veto power. They may just hate each other, or one party doesn't like it, in which case they can say no; if not, then it goes through. The parents take the trouble to see that the two are matched; there are all kinds of variables: education, socioeconomic status, class, anything you can think of.

Young people are okay with that because that's the way they've been brought up. I would still say, though, that there is definitely a shift toward more people getting to know each other and liking each other first, even though a majority are still arranged. That's how people were brought up.

The Other: I still feel my skin color and the way I look. I think this country is organized around race and "othering" people who look different than white Anglo people. So I absolutely have felt it and dealt with it—sometimes successfully and sometimes with anger.

I feel I am an American, but definitely would use a hyphenated "American," because I don't want to give up who I am, and perhaps so that other parts of my life are not lost or ignored. We have to recognize that we have multiple identities, multiple nationalities, multiple ways of doing things. The question of who is an American is problematic in itself, isn't it? Who is American and what is American? So in that sense I do claim a space, but I want to make that space complex and problematize it and make it as unique as I can.

Shamita Das Dasgupta (photo courtesy of Saptarshi Das)

I go back to India to do work there. I spend about three to four months there every year. Most of my family is in India. I've lost my mother but my father is ninety years old and he's still living with my brother and his wife. I feel a tremendous connection to South Asia and a tremendous connection to the United States, because this is where I've done my work and have my friends and my family and my home.

Values: Education is very important. Being close to family is also very important as is bringing up children who are honorable and good and nonviolent. The issue of justice is extremely important to me and my family. I hope I've imparted it to my daughter.

Bengali is my language, but I also speak Hindi. And I understand various other South Asian languages. My daughter was born here and when she was growing up we insisted she speak Bengali.

She kept the language, and now that she has two children she insists that they both speak Bengali. So both my grandchildren speak Bengali and German because their father is German. And I'm just amazed to see that.

For me, there is huge pride in being a South Asian, a Bengali woman. I see myself in these concentric circles: being a Bengali woman, a South Asian and Indian woman in the struggle for justice for our community. I see that as an issue of tremendous pride.

AFTER SEPTEMBER 11

Very Tough Times

Veronica Leung

Veronica Leung owns the restaurant Dim Sum Go Go in Chinatown, New York.

On September 11, I had the TV on. From the bathroom I heard that a United Airlines plane got hijacked. So I stormed out and saw on the TV the first building burning. I thought I was watching a movie. I stood there for a long time. After that I rushed down to Chinatown, to the restaurant. I remember they were blocking all the streets, not allowing anyone to come in. The only ones allowed were those with IDs who lived there. I didn't have proof. I owned a restaurant there, but they said I still could not go in. I was worried about my employees. They start at 6 A.M. and they were already inside. They didn't know what was going on in the streets. (Later I found out they had a radio on, so they had heard.) I could not go in and they were not allowed to come out. There was no way for me to get in touch with them. There was no phone line, no nothing. The policemen kept saying that I had to leave, so the restaurant was closed for three days.[1]

After the three days I went back. Everything was blocked, but we still had to open. It was really, really quiet. Initially, people were not allowed to come in. My customers told me that the first weekend they came down they were not allowed into the area. The second weekend, they were also turned away. The worst part was there was no phone service; people kept calling but we couldn't hear any ringing. That went on for a few months.

After the third week the people started coming in. That was the first weekend someone started coming in; then after that, they just came in slowly. At night, just forget it. It was like a dead city over here. It was very, very tough. Weekends picked up a little bit, but the weekdays were still really awful. For at least six months we were doing really badly. When I say bad, I think about three-quarters of the business was gone.

To this day, the head of Mott Street is still not open. And all the traffic on Chatham Square, where I face, has been rerouted. This hurts Chinatown. In those first months, there were no cars, no nothing. So that was tough. But, lucky for me, I have very good clients and they supported me. And I'm very grateful for that. It took about a year and a half to get back to a steady business.

For a long while it was scary. Everything was an unknown. When I say scary, I mean it was, "Veronica, this is it." That kind of thinking. I'm pretty lucky that I have very regular customers who, when they walked in and saw the place empty, said, "What happened, Veronica?" So I said, "Well, 9/11. . . ." And they said, "Oh, I'll have to come in more often. I'll bring my friends." That's how I survived, because they gave me more confidence, a kind of strength.

After six months, all the reserves were gone. One day they delivered the meat and they wanted money—cash. I didn't have money to pay suppliers, so they took the meat back. That was scary. It's like the mind is thinking, Veronica, this could be it. You need a miracle. I wasn't able to get any government help, I couldn't turn to anybody. So it was almost like a dead end. My miracle, as it turned out, was my customers—mostly European Americans, artists, entertainers. This restaurant is basically built through word of mouth. I am lucky I didn't have to lay anyone off. Whenever I could, I would pay the workers. I would make just enough to cover one payroll. At that time, I thought I wouldn't make it. I never worked so hard in my whole life—fifteen hours a day for three months straight, from 8:30 in the morning to closing at 11 at night. Even now, things are not back to what they were. On Park Row, they've closed the municipal parking lot, which many people depended on to park. They say they will reopen it, but they never have. Everybody complains about parking, and now when you get a ticket it's more money. And that has affected us a lot, too. So there are a lot of people angry with City Hall about all of this.

Looking back, things have been pretty tough. After 9/11 there was always something; in 2002, the stock market did poorly; there was the SARS scare in 2003; then there was the blackout. Right now I would say things are stable. September 11 has definitely made me stronger.

I started my restaurant in 2000. We have Cantonese food, and we specialize in dim sum. My parents were in the restaurant business all their lives. They did it in Shanghai and also Hong Kong and the United States. I was never in the restaurant business before then, but I grew up around restaurants.

I was born in Shanghai. My dad left Shanghai because of the communists. Dad came here first. One of the first Chinese restaurants in Midtown was the House of Chang. They went to Hong Kong to hire seven chefs to come here; my father was one of them.

I came to the United States in the sixties, as a teenager. We lived in Midtown. All I knew was A-B-C-D. Maybe not even twenty-six letters. They put me in ninth or tenth grade. I had a very good friend—we lived in the same building on Fifty-third Street. We would go to and from school together. That's how I picked up English. She was very, very kind—Mary Jane. Each time she heard a syllable, she would correct me if I didn't say it right. I'm very lucky that I had a friend who taught me that. I guess my first language would be Cantonese.

Eventually my family moved to Schenectady. I remember it was a small town, quiet, friendly. My dad opened a restaurant there. The customers were steady, and just like family.

There were three Chinese restaurants in town. I remember people loved to come to my mom's home to play mahjong after work. When she had her coffee shop in Chinatown, she made a lot of dim sum, so she liked to make all the snacks. While Daddy was playing, she was cooking, making midnight snacks. Basically, for Chinese, because of language difficulties, mahjong would be the thing to do—even in Schenectady.

I didn't work in the restaurant in Schenectady. But we would go into the kitchen and touch a little of this, a little of that. We hired workers from Chinatown, sometimes through friends, sometimes through an agency. They would go back to Chinatown about once every two weeks. We kept our culture. Every year on Chinese New Year's Eve we celebrated with the customers. We would do Chinese banquet-style food in the restaurant. There would be 170 to 200 people. So everybody came. It was a very good experience up there.

As for school, I had a really bad time of it. When I was in Shanghai, I was sick from age four to twelve. So it was off and on to school. When we left to go to Hong Kong, I had to learn how to speak Cantonese. By the time I figured that out, I was headed for the United States.

I am glad we left China, and I am very happy with who I am. For a fact, if we were still back in China, I would not be able to talk to you like this. I'm very happy with who I am, what I am, because I have dreams. At the time we left, we couldn't do whatever we felt like. I would probably have become a different person—what type, I don't know. But I'm sure of that.

New York's Chinatown: Getting Back on Its Feet

Corky Lee

Corky Lee recounts the days following 9/11 and describes the lingering effects of 9/11 on Chinatown.

After 9/11 I felt a strong obligation, along with many others, to try to get the community back on its feet. Chinatown was actually closed down for four weeks. The first two weeks you couldn't get downtown beyond Fourteenth Street, and then two weeks later they moved the boundary line to Canal Street. Everyone had to have a government-issued photo ID card to get into the area. People who live and work in Chinatown don't have photo IDs. It's a hardship because if you can't get to work you can't feed your kids, pay the rent, and so forth. There were, I think, over 120 garment shops in Chinatown before 9/11, and about 40 of them closed up within three months after 9/11.[2]

Those first few weeks Chinatown looked like a ghost town, desolate. It was very shocking. There was a military presence and a big police presence, too. They closed up Park Row from Chatham Square going south. Ambulances going to NYU Downtown Hospital couldn't go the direct route; they had to take an alternate route. They closed off Worth Street.

There is a guy down the street who owns a gift shop. He helped start the auxiliary police in Chinatown some thirty years ago. His son was in law enforcement and died at the World Trade Center. When they had the funeral about a week after 9/11, family members outside of Chinatown could not get into the area for the funeral. So he goes to the captain of the fifth precinct and says, "listen, you know I would like my family to come mourn for my son." Basically, they wouldn't let the family members into Chinatown on the day of the wake or the funeral to mourn for his son.

It was also four weeks without cellular phone service. Phone service! Which is quite vital in this day and age. Chinatown didn't have landline phone service for six months!

September 11 happened on a Tuesday; that following Saturday there was a meeting uptown—a lot of social service agencies gathered to figure out what they could do to contribute. I said if people could get to a phone to call Beijing or Hong Kong and say, "Listen, we're okay, we have hardships, there's no phone service" or whatever, it would ease the mental anguish. Here the whole world knows what happened but they don't know what happened to their friends and relatives and their loved ones in New York.

Among some people there was an indomitable spirit—that we'll rise, like the phoenix, the bird that rises from the ashes. It was a lot of self-reliance. They also depended on the federal, city, and state government. There were programs to try and keep the businesses here. People just pitched in. There was a guy who was a comedian and he decided to bring in some nightlife to Chinatown, because as a result of 9/11 hardly anything stayed open beyond a certain hour, mostly 10 o'clock. So he got some other fellow comedians together. They started in Asia Roma in the basement and soon outgrew the space, so they went to another place and continued there. Once a month they would do something on an entertainment level.

I know one guy who had just graduated from law school and he was working at LaGuardia Community College helping people get business grants. He read an article in the newspaper that said this Chinese restaurant couldn't get any funding. It turns out there were twelve different owners of this one restaurant and the application said that all the owners of the business had to sign or show up and fill out this form. He told them, "What you need to do is get an affidavit and have the other twelve people sign it and that will hold up in court." After they did that, the business got $75,000. That helped save the business; unfortunately it is not around anymore because of other concerns.

Population-wise, Chinatown is probably the largest community that suffered in the shadow of 9/11. Today Chinatown is still trying to get up from its knees. I think CCBA (Chinese Consolidated Benevolent Association) actually has taken a much bigger role post-9/11. They stepped up to the plate and allowed space in their auditorium for public discussion about the FEMA grants because a lot of the Chinese businesses and residents weren't getting any of the FEMA money. As a result, FEMA ended up hiring some bilingual people to address those needs and help fill out the applications. There was an allegation that out of four thousand applications from Chinese businesses only one hundred businesses got any money. And this was months afterward. So there is still a lot of resentment against FEMA because they should have come through just like FEMA should have come through in New Orleans. But slowly people did what they felt they could do.

They've held a couple of street events, such as Tastes of Chinatown, involving seventy to eighty businesses. They've done this once in the fall and in the spring. They would close off the streets in Chinatown and have some of the businesses who wanted to participate offer samplings of their food for a dollar or two. It was like an open carnival. At one point, they had a stage for performances and so forth.

It's been five years since 9/11, and there's more hope now in Chinatown than within that first year.

Within the South Asian Community

Shamita Das Dasgupta

Shamita Das Dasgupta talks about the impact of 9/11 on South Asians living in the U.S.

September 11 actually changed our community a lot, in direct ways. Several things happened: first, the South Asian community came into focus because the terrorists looked like us and many people thought we belonged to that community. South Asian women also became targets of other hostilities and stereotypes; women were beaten up. We are very distinctive looking, plus many wore clothes that became seen as belonging to the terrorist groups. I heard that in court the judges made comments like, "Oh, you're a sister of Bin Laden and you guys support Bin Laden," idiotic stuff like that.

The second thing was that many South Asian men were asked to participate in the Special Registration Program[3] because of security. The third was that many were put in detention—mostly men—without due process.

In Special Registration, men from Bangladesh and Pakistan had to go and write down their names and where they lived so people could keep an eye on them. If you were over sixteen years old you were supposed to do Special Registration. The federal government asked people to volunteer, but there was definitely a strong message that if you didn't volunteer they were going to do a raid.

One thing we found was that many of the men—even for a small infraction of immigration laws—were immediately put into detention or deported, even without notification to the family. Sometimes nobody knew where these people went and they would call from Pakistan or Bangladesh and say they got deported, because they couldn't even contact home. There was this family whose husband went in for Special Registration. He didn't come back and then the wife got a call from Bangladesh and he said, "I'm here; they put me on a plane." There was some irregularity with his visa—I'm not sure what, exactly. He couldn't come back anymore; that was it. So his family—he has kids and everything—didn't know what to do, whether they should go back.

Right after 9/11 most of our energies and work went into those kinds of issues instead of violence against women, because we wanted to make sure that these men didn't disappear, given what was going on in detention. A group was organized to be outside these Special Registrations, so when someone went in they would write down his name and make sure he came out and checked off the name so at least they knew how many were going off and disappearing.

The community was totally frightened. Nobody trusts the police anymore, nobody trusts any sort of outside resources anymore because it comes with a price. So 9/11 has had a major impact in terms of individual liberties as well as state-sponsored liberties.

There's a sense of a tremendous injustice within the community that a country that continually talks about justice does that to its citizenry and to human beings, violates their human rights. I don't blame them. I'm very horrified that happened and that this has been going on. We have to recognize the racialization and class issues in this. Does it make the country safe? is the question. I don't think it does.

I know that many, many women who wore anything traditional wouldn't go out of the house after 9/11 for a long time. Many just gave up. A friend of mine—she wears South Asian clothes—was stuck in California when 9/11 happened, and there was such hostility that she had to go buy clothes, a pair of pants and shirt, just to travel back. People can be called out of airport lines all the time. After 9/11 I just assumed I would be called out, and every time I traveled, I was. Every time.

III. Journeys and Passages

PASSAGES

Reconnecting

Naomi McWatt

Naomi McWatt talks about growing up as a child of a Japanese mother and an African American father and about her journey in reconnecting with her mother.

I was born in Yokohama, Japan, in 1948. My father was a sergeant in the U.S. Army so we lived on the base. I remember going to school in Japan. It was pretty nice. The people who lived on the base were families like myself. There were a lot of mixed children; people were traveling like my father. I spoke a few words of Japanese here and there. I lost that because my mom and I were separated after we came to the United States and I grew up with my father and stepmother.

My father tells me that I really didn't speak English until I started to go to school. Once I started school I began to learn English. I don't remember that, of course. But he told me I spoke fluent Japanese. And I kind of regret that I don't have that anymore. It seems like we were middle class. I remember we had a maid who was Japanese and I guess my father could afford that because he was in the military. I remember visits from my mother's family. I remember having a lot of pets—parakeets, fish, turtles, a dog. I remember being pretty happy in childhood. They were happy years.

It was different when I came to the United States. I was seven. We went to California where my father's grandfather lived. Then we settled in Colorado and Kansas because my dad was moving around a lot. It was still okay because the kids that lived where we lived were all sort of mixed-race or from other countries and so there was really no issue about race or anything. Not at that time.

My father and mother separated shortly after they got here. She just decided she wanted to leave one day. My father was kind of abusive and she didn't really speak English. Maybe one or two words. She didn't have any experience for work. I guess she just didn't want to be here anymore. But she later told me, because we did find each other, that she felt I would be better off with my father because she couldn't really provide for me. So she left one day. And I never really cried over it. It was just this hole in my heart that I didn't really understand.

Florida: My father called his ex-girlfriend—she was his girl-friend before he went to Japan. He asked her to come to Kansas to take care of his daughter. So she did. And it's really strange because she was so unlike my mother—but I had an immediate attraction to her. She was just very warm. And she took me back to Florida with her. She raised me from eight years old. My father didn't come with us at that time. He was still in the service; he traveled to some other states and I think he may have gone back overseas before he finally retired and came back to Florida. So I was really raised by my stepmother until I was eighteen.

Initially it was great because she was just so sweet and wonderful to me. I felt safe and wanted to be with her. The problem really started when I moved to Florida and I found I was different. My neighborhood was predominantly African American, and there was just no one around in these small towns in Florida who looked like me, who was mixed. So I had a lot of problems in school with the kids. I cried a lot. You know how kids are. They pick at you because you're different. They talk about you, call you names. They called me Jap. And half-breed, which really hurt me. I was young and I had never really experienced that before. So I really had a hard time with that. For a long time it made me feel really insecure.

Naomi McWatt

I'm even getting little shakes talking about it. Sometimes I didn't even want to go to school. I would come home crying. And my stepmom would feel for me but she was the type of person that felt you had to fight back. But I wasn't like that. So it was difficult. This was in a small town called Bunell. I think it's like twenty-three miles outside of Daytona Beach, Florida. Friends? Yes. Growing up, I had friends. I would do homework sometimes for girls because I wanted to be their friend. But now, as I look back, there were some people who really did like me. Others just didn't because of differences; they just didn't understand. The boys liked me, yeah. That was no problem.

I don't remember my father being part of my life much. He may have come back once—he was still in the service. When he

retired I was already in New York and had moved away. All I could
think about when I graduated was I couldn't wait to leave.

In Florida I was too busy trying to fit in. I felt sad—not all the
time, but there were lots of times I felt sad, which I didn't understand. Later I had to seek some help. I never really grieved about
my mother and the fact that we were separated.

Reconnecting: Sometime in my early twenties I started to an-
alyze it a little bit more, and I talked about it more, even though it
was just to a close friend. But I didn't really put the pieces together
and feel the mending of that hole until my mother and I found
each other again.

I had a friend that had a relative who was a detective. And he
kept saying, "Why don't you look for her? Give me the paperwork.
I'm sure we can find her." I didn't want to do it because I think I
was afraid. I finally relented. It was within four months—he lo-
cated her. He called me and said, "I found your mother and she's
waiting to hear from you." I got kind of angry because I thought he
was teasing. And he was like, "No, I'm serious." It turns out she
was right where we had lived before, in Colorado. She was somewhere else for a while but she went back to Colorado. She had
been living there all those years. I called her and I still didn't really
believe it was her. She asked me a question about a scar I had on
my leg and then I knew it was her. I was so thrilled. I can't describe
it: very, very happy. No anger. All I wanted to do was talk. And we
did. We talked a lot over the next few weeks and months and we
just called and talked a lot. I had to have already been thirty-five at
the time.

She didn't have any more children. She got married. She said
that she thought about me all the time, wondering how I was. And
I told her I thought about her, too. And she paid my stepmom a
compliment and said I had grown into such a wonderful woman.
Just basically catching up—like how many kids I had and things
like that. But somehow we never got together. I don't know if she
was afraid or I was afraid. Even when I said, "Oh, I've got to send

you something," she would say no, as if she didn't deserve it because she wasn't there for me. So we never got together. We just talked, exchanged photos, and sent each other things. But we never saw each other. And then she passed away. I hadn't heard from her and I told my girlfriend I thought something was wrong. So she said, "Why don't you call?" And I did, and the phone was disconnected. So she encouraged me to call the police and I did. The police went and I found out from a neighbor next door that she had passed. I think I called her around Christmas and she had passed around Thanksgiving.

I think we communicated for probably three or four years. She died of kidney failure. I don't know why she didn't want me to know. But the friend said she went to the hospital and she decided she wanted to go home. I'm sure she had an opportunity to call but she decided not to.

I wish I could have seen her. I don't think about changing anything except that. I do wish I had insisted on flying out there. But I am grateful that we did connect. It could have been a few years later and I would've tried to find her and someone would've said she passed already. So at least I had that.

Was there anything striking in reconnecting with her? Just that the past didn't really matter. You know how some people like to rehash things, like "Why did you do this? I'm angry and stuff." I didn't feel any of that. We reconnected and just started out from where we were. I've often felt that who I've become has a lot to do with my background. Even if I didn't grow up with my mom, I think I already had that foundation that I was able to carry with me. When I'm asked on an application, I say I'm mixed—half Asian, half African American.

Do I ever want to be anyone other than who I am? No, I don't. If you see me or look at my house you can see that I do really lean more toward the Asian. I have a lot of Asian influence. I enjoy it. Japanese is my favorite food. When I got to New York I just decided one day I wanted to go back and try Japanese food and that was it. I don't know if the taste buds came back or what, but it was wonderful. That's all I ate when I was with my mom. That's all she knew and that's all she cooked.

When I went to Florida I ate southern food, which I enjoy. At first it was hard for me to get used to. My stepmom had to say to me, "Why don't you just try it—you'll like it." Like collard greens and sweet potato. I ate it and it was wonderful; at first I didn't want to try it but I did.

My life would probably have been different if I had stayed with my mom. First of all, I would still speak Japanese to some extent because when I spoke to my mom after all those years I could tell that she didn't really speak English fluently, but we understood each other. She still had a very strong accent. When she left my father, she found other Japanese families—she worked in a Japanese restaurant. That was comfortable for her—I understood that. So there would have been a lot more Japanese influence in my life. I'm not sure how I would've been treated; it may have been the same as what I experienced in Florida. Mixed. I was used to feeling this, because you do feel insecure—you know, your mother leaves you. Maybe that was an issue for her. Maybe I was too black.

I really didn't care about any of that after we connected. I was just happy that we could. I felt that hole in my heart getting smaller and smaller. It was a wonderful feeling. Every time I saw movies about the same kind of situation I would just cry. I could relate to it. You know—with people not having a mom around. And even though I had a stepmom who was wonderful and raised me and I never wanted to hurt her, this was just something I had to pursue.

My mother seemed delighted to hear from me. When the guy said, "I'm going to call her and have her call you right now," she was sitting by the phone. She was happy that I wasn't angry. As you get older you understand things that you didn't understand as a child—what makes people do what they do. She had remarried a white man who was in the service, too. She spent her life working in a Japanese restaurant after she left my father.

I wrote to one of her brothers in Japan after she passed away. Her neighbor from next door gave me the address. So I sent a letter and a picture. He had his son write back to me because he said he wasn't very good at it. He recognized me right away from the picture. I often tell my kids that before I die I would really like to be able to take them to Japan to meet what family I have left there. So they can see where I was born. I don't know if it's going to happen but I think about it sometimes and it would be wonderful. I have two daughters. I don't have any siblings, so God blessed me with eight grandchildren who make me very happy. I love who I am. They love Nana. The youngest is a little girl named Maoki. My daughter picked that name.

Family: I think they all love the idea that their grandmother is part Japanese. I ran across some old photographs and my daughter was just so thrilled to see them. I found one of her great grandmother—my mother's mother—a picture of my mother, one of her brother, and some old photos of myself. So they like to talk about it on occasion, the grandkids too. I tell them I have some Japanese in me. "It's cute," they like to say.

My mother's last name was Fuji. My father told me that when he was in Japan he went out one night, met her, and I guess he fell for her. In all of this is also the love story between my father and my stepmom. He was engaged to my stepmom before he went to Japan. After he met my mother, had a child, and married her, he brought us both back to the United States. After his wife left, he called his ex-girlfriend and asked her to look after his daughter. Even though she had been hurt, she agreed to take care of me. My stepmother loved me and raised me. I was her only child. I owe so much to her. Years later, my dad finally married her—at my insistence—after he retired.

Being raised during that period of time, I often thank my father because I don't believe I would've done very well in Japan. There were a lot of soldiers who didn't bring their children back. Even though I had a hard time, I believe it would have been worse there.

From what he told me, he wasn't going to bring my mother. I said, "No, you can't leave my mother. You have to bring my mother too." I was seven. So we came together. So I thanked him many times. Not that I said that to him—but as one grows older one thinks back to those things. My mom was in this country about a year, then left him. I feel my dad did abuse my mom for I don't know what reason. She was not very aggressive or outspoken; she just came here and was in a strange country. So I really never had that conversation with him, but I know he did because I would hear yelling sometimes at night. All in all, though, I thank him for bringing me back to this country.

Asian or African American? Growing up, I felt that being a mixed person—neither totally African American nor Asian—created a sense of feeling lesser, because of the way I was treated. I don't feel that way anymore. In some cases though, it felt as though it was an advantage. I guess I hate to say it this way, but when I first entered corporate America I felt that race had an impact on how people saw me. When I first entered it was mostly whites. There were very few African Americans. I started working at Chase; that was my first real career. And there were very few of us. At times I even was referred to as Japanese as opposed to being black—at some points it seemed to be an advantage. I'm not saying I wanted it to be. But just in terms of the way people treated me, it worked in a positive way for me.

Right now I'm doing consulting work for companies which are developing and managing low-income affordable housing in the communities. For years I was in the real estate business. Since 1992 I've been doing property management work in the nonprofit arena, mostly low-income. I have about twenty-five years experience overall in real estate.

I've gone through some rough patches but I've learned from them. I believe that being an only child and going through the things that I did made me stronger. It gives you this drive that maybe you wouldn't have if you didn't have those kinds of circumstances. I'm sure not everybody would feel the same way, but when you're viewed as different and you always have to prove yourself, it does drive you to do more.

I believe there has to be something inside. I don't know where it comes from; it's just something there to assist you. I was alone and I was a loner and I felt I had to fend for myself all the time. That's how I live my life. The only thing that I had to fight through was this—call it a coldness—shutting myself down to protect myself. I guess that's because I didn't have that connection to my mother after I was eight years old. I just felt alone—whatever happens there's nobody there for you. My father wasn't there, Mom was gone. I had my stepmom but there was still that emptiness. So, through life, every time I connected with someone I protected myself. And sometimes I felt real cold, and I didn't want to be that way but I guess it's a barrier. I don't know if that has anything to do with my being mixed at all—just that this was something I thought about.

No one would ever say I'm Asian. But there are times when I've had to fight that other part, where people say, You're not really African American. You don't even have any African American stuff in your house. I felt I really had to defend that part. And the Asian part, I just feel it comes. That's who I am. I'm a combination of both. I am proud of who I am.

Marriage

Gita Deane

Gita Deane was born in India and arrived in the United States in 1979. Along with her partner, Lisa Polyak, Deane is lead plaintiff in a suit filed in Maryland challenging a 1973 statute prohibiting same-sex marriage.

I am a learning specialist. I work with students who have learning disabilities and provide academic learning adjustments for them while they're in college. I did that at the middle-school level for many years and now at the college level.

Lisa's a chemical engineer and she works as a civilian federal employee for the Department of Defense cleaning up air pollution situations that are associated with the army. We have two daughters: Maya is ten and Devi is seven. Devi is the Indian word for goddess.

I came to the United States in 1979 to attend Trinity College in Washington, D.C., which is where I met Lisa. I was not out to myself at that time, and Lisa and I didn't really have a relationship until the end of my sophomore year. I remember I was a very shy person at the time and I found that very difficult to negotiate. Also, this was the first time I was in a country where I knew that if something happened to me, everybody in my family was an ocean away.

My grandparents are from what is now Pakistan, but they were Sikh, so they wore a turban. My grandfather converted to Christianity and they live in what's now the Punjab. They lost their farm during the partition of India and Pakistan. They moved to a place close to Bombay but four hours away called Pune. And that's where I grew up until I was fifteen.

The ACLU: The suit was filed in July 2004. We're not at all politically active. Probably the most politically active thing I've done was to write a check to an organization. I had never been to any rallies. But we belong to a group in Maryland called Families With Pride, and there was a phone call from Equality Maryland (a civil rights group for the lesbian, gay, bisexual, and transgender [LGBT] community) to the Families With Pride group asking if there were families who would testify in Annapolis against the proposed state constitutional amendment to disallow same-sex marriage?[1] So Lisa and I thought, Okay, we can go tell our story and say why the Constitutional amendment would be bad.

After we testified, the director of Equality Maryland met us and asked us to do a town hall meeting at Johns Hopkins and other speaking engagements because, he said, "You guys are great spokespeople and you've been together for a long time." Actually, next week is our twenty-five-year anniversary. He said we were the couple that needed to speak out in Maryland on this issue. He started asking us to do different things and do little press interviews.

Because Equality Maryland and the ACLU together were looking for the plaintiff group for the Maryland case, he suggested that we be put in that pool. We had to write up our personal story and send it to them. I believe five hundred couples sent in their stories, out of which they chose nine couples.

Initially I was quite resistant. I am not a very public person and it was very hard for me. And because I have children, I didn't really want anything to be a negative force in their lives. My whole focus was on my need to have protection for my children.

We talked extensively with Ken Choe, who is the attorney on this case from ACLU national: What will this mean for my children's lives? What would this mean for our lives? Basically he said the plaintiffs are not the people that get targeted because it would look really bad for the opposition to target plaintiffs. So reluctantly I said we'd be one of the many couples in the lawsuit.

When the couples met as a group, we all had to tell our stories. Afterward they approached us and said, "Will you be the lead plaintiff of the case?" I was like, Oh my God! Because that's the name that everybody knows and the face that everybody knows. Just as in the Goodridge decision in Massachusetts[2]—I don't know the other plaintiffs but I know the Goodridge name because of the case. So they gave us two weeks to think about it.

Every night Lisa would ask, "So what do you think?" I would say, "I'm not ready yet." It was really hard for me to be out that publicly, particularly because of my children. It's one thing when we make a decision and it comes back at us, but as a parent it was very hard to take that extra step. But, as Lisa said to me, our silence will also make them pay a price. They'll pay a price if we speak out, but maybe we'll move this discussion further for them in their future life. That made sense to me. And we have shielded our kids. There are no pictures of them anywhere and they're not in the press when we talk to the press. They know what's going on. We talk with them in age-appropriate ways about it.

It's been shocking to me that my family has been so wonderfully supportive. My sister and her husband are both Indian—he is very traditional; their children are teenagers; then there is my brother and his wife and their kids and my mother. It was a shock to me that she completely supports us 100 percent and has sort of taken this journey with us.

I really do believe that love can be unconditional and it's not about your kids having to be a certain way for you to love them. As a parent you just love your children and you go on a journey with them that's always an adventure and nothing you'd expect. And I hope that I'd have that courage to do that with my children—take a journey I'm not comfortable with or not know much about.

When Did We Out Ourselves? When we got pregnant. That

late, really—to everyone. When Lisa was pregnant I came out at work. And when I was pregnant she came out at work. Even when she was pregnant she didn't come out—she just said, I'm going to have a baby and I'll be taking so much time for maternity leave. It wasn't until I was pregnant that she told the people she supervises that she would be taking a month of maternity leave because her partner was having a baby. That was the first time she said those words. I think the first time around, when she said she was having a baby, they just thought that she'd gotten knocked up, and Oh no, she was having this child unexpectedly. So that's really how we came out—when we were pregnant. We had promised ourselves that with our children there would be no secrets and there would be no such thing as having shame. We didn't want them to have shame about who we were. So that was a big motivation for us to come out.

Starting a Family: It was very important to us that our children be multiracial, because we're a multiracial couple. I always feared that if I was walking around with a white child they would think, Oh well, she's the nanny. It was important to me that my heritage be reflected in my child. Lisa carried our older daughter, Maya, and she had a Southeast Asian donor. Maya has my color and my hair, and most people think she's my kid because Lisa is so blonde. I carried Devi, but I had a Caucasian donor. Since I think the darker genes are more dominant, they both have darker hair and darker skin, and are beautiful and wonderful kids. That's how we started our family.

The most important thing is that we be legally recognized as a family because that entitles us to so much more protection for our children that we don't have at this time. We do have in the state of Maryland recognition of second-parent adoption. Lisa and I cross-adopted the children. I adopted Maya and she adopted Devi, so we are legal parents in the state of Maryland. But if we were, say, in Virginia, which is not friendly to our type of family, and my child was hospitalized or we were in a car accident, it could very easily be questioned or challenged that I have any legal relationship to Maya.

It's that kind of thing that's very terrifying. Before we had the second-parent adoption statute, the pediatrician that we were going to made it very clear to both of us that I could not bring Maya to her well-baby visits, because she got her shots on her well-baby visits, and if she had any reaction and there had to be medical decisions made, I couldn't make them because I was not parent or guardian to this child. I was a stranger.

We didn't adopt right away because it was so expensive. We decided once we had both kids we'd do it at one time. So Devi was six months old when we did the adoption, but Maya was three. One thing that is always in the back of my head is if something happened to our kids and we were not in the state of Maryland, what would happen? The other piece that is always in the back of my head is what if something happened to one of us and, God forbid, that person's family doesn't feel okay about our relationship and tries to get custody of her kids? It's happened to friends of ours, where the family tries to take custody of the biological child that's connected to that family. That always worries me.

There are simple things, like we can't all share health insurance. I can't be on Lisa's health insurance plan. When I worked part-time I had to buy my own insurance, which is so expensive and is only for catastrophic situations. For other families it's not even a question. Whoever the parent is that stays home gets insurance from the parent who is working. Lisa carries both of the children on her insurance; that's why we rushed the second-parent adoption, because Devi had a lot of health issues and I had very bad insurance.

So these simple things started to become an issue: retirement, inheritance, all of these things where you have to pay extra taxes— for example, on the inheritance; and a house that we both acquired

Gita Deane, daughter Maya, and Lisa Polyak

together, but it's looked at as half Lisa's and half mine. And so forth.

I tell the girls that no matter what happens we will always be a family. We all love each other and we all take care of each other, but the most important thing to me in this litigation is that we be legally recognized as the family that we already are. And that would give us access to so much of the security and safeguards that other families have.

For many years I was buying insurance as an individual. Then I went and talked with the president of my college and explained to him that I worked part-time but can't be on my partner's insurance. I have just been amazed at the goodness of people. I talked to him in August; on January 1 he offered insurance to part-time employees, which they have never offered before, and included domestic partner coverage, which was also unbelievable. So that has changed for me as of last year. But again, we rely on the goodness of other people to do these things and not on the law. So if you meet up with somebody who doesn't want to let you into the emergency room where your child is sick, you're really in no position to challenge it.

I was never brave until I had my kids. For me that was it. For different people it's a different journey. I know I'm completely a different person now than when I didn't have children. I can be brave for them because I need to make sure as a parent that I do everything so that their life is better than how it might be if I just kept my mouth shut.

Immigration Issues: If I had to do it over again, what would I have changed? I would've had children sooner. Because they really made me a better person. They made me have more direction in my life. But unfortunately we couldn't have children sooner because I had terrible immigration problems. Since I couldn't marry Lisa and she couldn't sponsor me, it took a long time for me to become a citizen. It was a very stressful, tedious journey to that point. We waited until after I became a citizen. A year after that, Lisa got pregnant. We knew we were on that road and we wanted it to be the next step.

In 1989 I got a deportation letter. I lived here illegally. We then went to search for an attorney and found a very nice, ethical immigration attorney, because most of them aren't ethical. He basically made it so we could have a payment plan and we didn't have to come up with money upfront—the thousands of dollars which the others wanted—and we started a legal process for my coming into the country through an immigrant job. I had to get labor certification. That takes a long time because basically your employer has to show why no U.S. citizen can do that job and what unique qualifications you have for that job. Then they will sponsor you.

Once you get labor certification, the paperwork moves to the

U.S. Immigration and Naturalization Service, which approves it after an interview. But since I was illegal I had to leave the country and have my interview in India. So I left and went to the U.S. Embassy in New Delhi and had my interview there.

I also had my medical exam there, which was quite humiliating. They have a list of medical personnel that they can send you to and they're not always the best doctors, but they're the ones that are on the list. You have to have an AIDS test and a TB test, and once you get a clean bill of health you take that to your interview at the embassy. They tell you to come back in the evening and they'll have your packet ready, and if you get the packet you can go back to the United States because that packet is how they process you into the country. If this didn't work that was it.

Once you get to immigration at the airport they pull you into a separate room and take your picture for a card which is your green card; it has both your picture and your thumbprint on it, with all these official numbers. And they laminate it. Then, if you've been a green card holder in good standing for five years, you can apply for citizenship, which is what I did in 1994.

How often we sat and said, "If only we could get married," because it was a very, very torturous process—because of the money and because I was not out. I had to tell my mother that I needed this money for this process but not with the same urgency that I really felt. I couldn't really pour my heart out about it—how this was the biggest thing in my life and if it didn't work I would not be able to live. I don't know what I would've done.

We talked about Lisa going to India, but I don't know what she would've done there. We were just in our first jobs. I'm sure she would have gone. Or we even thought, Could we go to another country? It was funny because we knew nothing about this. We would call up attorneys and ask if there was any country in the world we could go to and get married. We were so naïve. And they said no, there was not. At the time there was not. They said that even if we did, it would not be recognized in the United States.

There are several countries now that recognize gay marriages, but not back then.

Identity: A press person asked me how long have I identified myself as a lesbian. I have to tell you honestly I never could really identify that way because of the pictures I saw of people, especially in the seventies and eighties—pictures in the media of people depicted as lesbians but who didn't look anything like me and didn't act like me. I felt like, This can't be who I am—they aren't who I am, so I'm not a lesbian. I'm just in love with this particular person. If it wasn't this person it wouldn't be another woman.

It's been interesting to me to find that there are so many people who never felt that they could communicate with the LGBT community because of the pictures and stories the media put out there. The stereotypical images—I never felt like I related to that.

I think that has changed tremendously in the past ten years. Since I have come out, I have so many Asian women who have come out to me and said, "Thank God you're out there." Now I don't feel that this can't be who I really am. I've heard these horrible stories about some people who have no contact with their parents or who are not out because they feel like they will lose their family.

In some ways I wish there had been somebody for me that I could have identified with to make my journey a bit easier. But since there wasn't, I'm happy that I'm that person for other women who are looking up and saying, Yeah, there is somebody.

I wanted a lot of the things that these young women want. I wanted a partner for life and I wanted children. From the very beginning with Lisa, no matter what we did with our lives, I had to have children.

I think that we were chosen for this lawsuit because I was from a different ethnicity, to show that this issue does not just affect Caucasian Americans but is an issue for a very inclusive community and a very diverse community.

I feel bad that neither Lisa nor I could really say that we did this lawsuit because of our love for each other—because we never felt worthy of doing this for ourselves. But once we had children, once Maya came into our lives, it became so clear to me that I wanted the world to be a little bit different for her. I was able to then put my foot forward and ask for things for her that I had never felt empowered to ask for myself, because it was my child's life. I never really understood that until I had a child. It's a revolutionary thing; at least it was for me.

Whether we win or lose at the high court, we have moved this discussion forward, we have become visible. We will have shown people a little bit of who we are and hopefully they will deal with compassion in terms of other LGBT children growing up, and also our children, even if the law doesn't change. That's really the focus: that the world will be kind to my children and not be cruel to them because of who we are. That's really where I get my strength. It's really interesting that our kids in their own way sort of know what's going on and have their opinions about it.

Asian Pacific Islander LGBT Community: I got an award from the Asian Pacific Islander group that is the LGBT group in Washington, D.C. It's a pretty large group under that umbrella. There's an Indian group, a Korean group, a Japanese and Chinese group; they gave me an award for my participation in this lawsuit this past summer. It was the Pride and Heritage Award.

It's just amazing how small the community is in some ways. I got a phone call from a woman in Washington State—she and her partner are both Indian and were plaintiffs in a lawsuit in Washington. She wanted me to come to a conference she was doing in San Francisco for the Asian American community. But I didn't have care for my children so I didn't end up going, but through her I realized that this network is nationwide and all these people are connected.

That blew me away. Really blew me away. I thought that I was the only one. When I went to this event in Washington, D.C., there were over one hundred people in the room and many of them identified themselves as gay or lesbian. I thought, Where have I been living all this time? It was just amazing to me.

There's a group of Indian and Pakistani and Bangladeshi women that meet on their own. I hooked up with some of them by just chatting about our experiences. Some of them have partners in India and own property with them. Because there aren't any laws in India, if you own property with them you don't have the same issues that you have here because it's just assumed that you both own the property. So it was very interesting to learn about so many people in the Asian community that are gay and lesbian, and that they have deep connections to their home country or country of origin.

There was a woman I met at the University of Maryland who was married in India and then came out and left her husband, and she still has a good relationship with the in-laws. When I heard that story, I was like, No way—they didn't kill you? Because I just know that in India it can be a very difficult struggle for a woman. And she said no, she's from South India—she has a good relationship with them and she has a partner and her partner lives in India and they own property together, and she goes back and forth and the partner comes here. These stories are just unbelievable to me. I just never knew—I thought I was the only one.

How have I changed since the lawsuit? I talk a lot more. I was really traditional. I remember growing up thinking, Okay, girls don't always get their opinions. My grandma would always say, "You have very strong opinions, and you have a temper," when I was a little kid. She said, "Men don't like that, they won't put up with that." So I was sort of this person that went along with almost anything. Never really articulated my opinion and was very quiet. Even my college friends tell me how quiet I was and that I never said anything. They always thought I was so shy.

So one of the biggest things for me is I talk a lot, but that's not the only thing. The other thing is I've come to understand that if you don't speak out you really can't move forward. If you don't tell your story, you can't act, and you can't get what you need. And it came to me very late—almost when I was forty—but that's the biggest change for me now, that I learned to ask for things I need and to say things that I agree or disagree with.

Do I have any thoughts about which way my daughters would go in terms of their sexuality? Oh my gosh, no. They are who they are. I just feel like we birthed them but their spirit is their own and their journey will be their own. And I hope that I am supportive of them no matter what their journey is. I mean, both Lisa and I support our kids and want to keep them safe and healthy. I think the thing I worry about most for my children and other children is drugs and teen pregnancy. Those are the two things I would like to keep out of my children's life. Not that they're headed in that direction, but just looking at the culture that surrounds us, those are the two biggest things I worry about for young girls. And particularly for mine. But whatever their journey, I just hope that I can be loving and supportive unconditionally.

Indian Culture and Gay Discourse: There are a lot of films coming out of Bollywood now that have the story of lesbians. Lisa and I have watched every single one of them. It's just been amazing, but unfortunately several of those movies have not been allowed to be shown in India. Like they burnt the movie theater where they tried to show one of them, specifically the movie called *Fire*. It's about these two daughters-in-law who end up in a relationship and leave the two brothers that they're married to. They're living with the mother-in-law who discovers the relationship. It's an amazing story. There have been several other such movies.

Some of my high school friends from India have Googled me and have been contacting me and said, "You know, we found out you're in this lawsuit. We think it's wonderful that you're with somebody and you have a family and you're happy," which surprised me to even hear those words from people that I knew more than thirty years ago. My sister goes to India every year and she says that the climate is changing tremendously. At least in the big cities people talk about it. There are places that are now bars in Bombay that you can go to, and there's been a scandal with one of the movie stars that's been on the front page of *Stardust* magazine, that she had a lesbian lover and that's why her husband killed himself. But there's discussion. So I think that things have changed and are changing.

I don't know what will happen in this case in Maryland, but I am hoping that we will be successful. But even if we aren't, I'm going to look for that silver lining, that at least we got this far down the road and somebody else will pick it up at some point and move it further. I think that it will get better. I hope it will get better in my lifetime.

Note: As of September 2007, Maryland's court of appeals upheld the state's ban on same-sex marriage.

Being Asian, Being Gay

Albert Lee

Albert Lee talks about aspects of self identity.

Do I see myself in any Asian context? It's a factor, but it's just not something that I have to think about very much because it doesn't come up in my work or personal life. I think part of it might be the fact that I'm gay and I think that has always been a much larger struggle for me. That was an issue I had to tackle more, and where I had more resistance—being gay rather than being Asian. Being Asian was never really a problem. But being gay always was a bigger problem that I had to cope with—being gay, eclipsing being Asian, and sort of my mind space. Growing up in Kentucky as a minority was something that was a huge obstacle to overcome. But I don't really dwell on the past very much.

I was in the closet for a long while. I always knew I was gay from the moment I hit puberty. I mean, people don't assume you're gay, so you have to come out. So I kind of hid it from them for a long while. And that was very difficult.

I remember I was partially out of the closet in high school—then I went back in the closet my freshmen year of college because there were several people in my hall who would say these awful antigay things. What was really ironic was later, when I came out, one of these people who was very antigay actually became one of my best friends. People will say a lot of stupid things when they don't think the object of their scorn is around to listen.

Coming out is a constant process—it's not like one event. Every time you meet a stranger they might assume that you're straight. Depending on your mannerisms or whatever, you're going to have to come out to them all over again. When I went to Princeton, no one knew me there. For all they knew, I was straight. So I had to find an opportunity and I had to build up the courage to tell them, "By the way I'm actually gay." Otherwise you're just sort of hanging around with these new people that you meet and you change jobs and you go to a new job and someone's just sitting around saying, Oh, that faggot this, or whatever. They don't know that you're gay so you're just going to have to come out. Then again you have to find the appropriate moment to do this. So it's always challenging. Say you're working on a new project with someone and you're putting together a PowerPoint presentation—you lean over and say, "Oh, I'm gay." That makes no sense.

As for dating and being Asian—I've certainly known a lot of other Asian gay men that have very deep, complex feelings about it. I think there's a lot of, frankly, self-loathing among a lot of Asian gay men, because I think a lot of Asian men ascribe a larger meaning to rejection and it becomes a rejection of them as an Asian in particular or that someone isn't into Asians.

There's also this term called "rice queen," which is someone who is non-Asian who prefers to date Asian men exclusively. A lot of guys have an issue with that sort of thing. I think in some ways it's the same with some of my Asian female friends. But I think with Asian gay men it seems to be more pronounced. So that's always been interesting to me.

Attraction is a very difficult thing to pin down. I don't think anyone can justify or explain precisely what they are into. Once you get older and have more dating experience you kind of connect the dots and say, I've dated some very physically attractive people but they were not really great relationships at all. And you understand how less important that becomes. You become a little bit more mature: I don't have to date someone just to impress my friends, or to say, "Look at this hot person I'm dating." Just things like that.

As far as work goes, it's definitely not an issue at all. Being gay has become easier socially and culturally over the past decade, absolutely no question. Visibility in terms of gay people in, let's say, television and the movies plays a huge role and has encouraged people to come out. I think that's one of the reasons a lot of gay activist groups promote the idea of coming out of the closet. I read some statistic in an article last week that 70 percent of Americans polled personally knew someone who was gay. And when you know someone who is gay, you are less likely to throw out generic gay-bashing terms.

Parents: When I came out to my parents, we didn't speak for several years. It was hard for them. They grew up in Korea—it was practically a Third World country then—so they're old school. And certainly being in the South certainly doesn't reinforce any progay beliefs. But at the end of the day I think they love me and care about me deeply like any parent would, so you know they're trying to understand. It's not something we talk about. But I have to be honest with you—if I were dating a girl, I don't think I would talk about her very much with my parents either. I mean, my sisters are both straight and they don't really talk about their dating life with my parents. It's like you don't really open up about your personal life, at least with my family, in that way.

JOURNEYS

Adopted, from Seoul to New Jersey
Karl Ludwig

Karl Ludwig, adopted from South Korea at five and a half years old, arrived in the United States in 1975. "I barely spoke English. My mom said my only English saying was 'I'll have a coke.'"

I very vaguely remember the days in Seoul. They seem like what I would describe as black and white, from an old movie. Like old photos. My images of those days were like of a green grass field, a big watering can or bucket, some dogs running around, straw huts, a bridge, stuff like that.

I think my father was an American soldier, a GI, so I don't remember him at all. I believe the only glimpses I have are of what I would call my grandfather and grandmother, who raised me. I don't have a visual recollection whatsoever of my birth mother.

A lot of people don't really know whether I'm of Hawaiian descent, or Asian descent; but I go into a Korean restaurant and people will look at me and right away say I'm Korean—I'm only half Korean—and they've honed in specifically on that. I don't speak Korean, I just know how to say hello.

Memories Upon Arrival: I remember a big house with a big family. There were 4 children—two of us adopted; two, the son and daughter of the Ludwigs. It was a large house in a nice neighborhood. From day one I knew—I remember someone telling me—that you're given an opportunity to succeed or do well, more so than I would have in my natural country in my natural environment.

I think my grandparents said that if I had stayed in Korea I would've been picked on because I was kind of considered a half-breed—like being American, an Asian American. I was pointed out as a minority too, because I'm part Asian. So it's kind of weird but I think I got to be a little bit more accepted and it was a little bit easier in America.

I believe my plane arrived at JFK airport, and I was picked up by Jay and Joan Ludwig. Throughout the whole process when you are selected for adoption, they take a picture of you, and the family from the American side can say, "Well, we elect to adopt him," and then they're brought up to speed on my progress through a foster parent or a guardian. What Joan always told me was that after the birth parents decided to place me up for adoption they put me in a foster home for I guess a year, and then I was adopted.

I grew up in Morris County in Kinnelon, New Jersey. I spent pretty much my entire life there until I was seventeen or eighteen, when I graduated high school and then moved out to go to college. It was funny because when you're growing up you don't realize what you have. We always complained as adolescents that it's boring, it's quiet, there's nothing to do here. Now that I am a parent I kind of miss that—I want that for my own family.

Kinnelon was fantastic. I really enjoyed it because there was a suburbia where there's a lot of stuff to do and there's a movie theater right there and a lot of places to go. It's a great school environment, with sports and everything else. I can honestly say I felt like I had a great opportunity for every success.

Kindergarten: I was five and a half and barely spoke English in Mrs. Brown's class. It was like taking someone and throwing him into a completely alien environment. Not understanding the language, not speaking it—with English as a second language, it's kind of a sink or swim theory. You are surrounded by people who do not speak your language so it's kind of difficult to communicate. I think that's why you try to stress or focus on symbols or other ways of communication, with hands, sounds, smells, pictures.

My mother told me it took six months of being completely immersed in the language—by then you tend to understand a lot. Television helped a lot, sitting in front of the television after class, *Sesame Street*, just the little cartoons on Saturdays.

You can sort out some things but you're completely like a newborn baby. You are dependent on the people around you to teach you everything in terms of food, water, shelter, clothing, the fundamentals; everything from right to wrong. Not only am I completely immersed in the family but with school it's a different environment and there I'm also completely dependent on everybody.

All the time it was kind of awkward dealing with it. But once it's a handicap and you see it as a handicap and you grow up with it, then you can turn it into a strength. So it's kind of neat when you look upon it that way and say, "Well, this is me, I can't really change who I am." So you are going to gravitate toward people that aren't going to cut you. Growing up in high school I had great friends. I had great neighbors too. Because I remember the first day they were always very nice.

The crowds I hung with in school were mostly white. The high school I went to at that time was maybe 5 percent minority, including Asians and African Americans, so it was like 95 percent white, so even growing up all my neighbors were white.

As far as wanting to learn to speak Korean, there's always been that desire. Growing up in high school I always was curious and fascinated with language. So I took Latin, I took French, and Spanish. To this day I speak more words in Spanish than I do in Korean or Chinese. But I worked in a Chinese restaurant so I picked up a few phrases there, and I guess it has always kind of been my dream to learn Korean again and to go back.

So Many Questions: In terms of ethnicity, I consider myself Asian American. I like to teach my kids a little bit about my family history. My only regret is that I wish I knew more about it—my background and genealogy. And even medical issues too. There are so many questions, so many areas.

It's a little depressing in America—where you can go to a horse show or a canine show and can even trace the animals' breeding down to so many hundreds of years. I've always wanted to do that about my family because it's just a way for me to honor my past and learn from it, as well as I can say to my children or their children— my grandchildren—"Watch out for cholesterol because there's heart disease that's been in the family," or breast cancer or something like that. Even traits or appearances—like I'm half Korean, half American, and my wife is a redheaded white American, yet we have two offspring who are almost blonde haired, blue-eyed. So the question then is, was my father like that? Was my grandfather like that? Who does he or she resemble? So it's pretty much where did he get the blue eyes from? If it was just my wife and I, some of those questions never would have arisen. But now that we have kids, it's like, okay, now there are more questions. Like where does he get that stubbornness from? Where does he get those blue eyes from?

Then there are questions about profession, education. What were my mother's and father's professions? What did they do? Like if they were a nurse or military. They could then give me feedback on why I chose the career path I did, or my personality. Why I am the way I am. If there was mental illness in the family, it would be good to know that too. Even physical characteristics, mental characteristics, emotional characteristics, psychological characteristics, everything. I've thought about going back to Korea and maybe trying to trace genealogy and roots, but it's just a huge undertaking. It'd be like trying to find a needle in a haystack.

I did try to access the adoption records with consent from Jay and Joan. I contacted the adoption agency and they were able to help me out a little bit. The adoption agency got in touch with correspondents from Korea, who sent me a letter saying my birth mother had passed away. But it's on letterhead, which makes you think, Well is that real or is it just someone's conception or what someone wants me to know? So there's always been a blank or a void there.

I'm very thankful, I'm very blessed to have the opportunity to be adopted because I know there are a lot of people who aren't, and they're less fortunate than I am. So I like to take time, especially around November (the month I first arrived in this country), just to reflect on what my life could have been had I not been adopted.

But it's kind of hard to reflect back on that because I'll never know what I could have been. I definitely have more appreciation for what I have because of the opportunity that Jay and Joan gave me. I look at it in the physical aspect, but then I take the emotional aspect of it as well as the psychological aspect of it and I always think, What would it have been like if I had been able to make contact with the birth relatives, if I had ever contacted my father? It would be kind of neat to fill in those voids, too. Those empty spaces.

I'm 95 percent sure I never will be able to, but there's always that 5 percent hope. So it's almost like being in a divorced family, where the father's gone to the right and the mother's gone to the left. I've always though of Jay and Joan as my natural parents and that's the firm foundation on which I grew up. But the left side of me says, Is my real father out there? Did he pass away? What is he like, is he poor? Is he homeless? And if so, can I help him out? And my mother too, who has passed away; she was Asian and I've been trying to track that down too. But am I ever going to get the opportunity? I doubt it, but the interest and curiosity is always going to be there.

Choosing a Career: In college I wanted to pursue a medical career because I always loved little kids and I wanted to be a pediatrician. During sophomore year I was taking a lot of science and medical courses, but I didn't know if I could afford medical school. I looked at the military and then law enforcement. I graduated in criminal justice, thinking I could go for law enforcement to save up for law school. So right out of college I got into law enforcement and I've been there ever since. I'm a police officer in Sussex County, New Jersey.

Karl Ludwig and family

I have to believe that's part genetics. Since my father was in the army and that's how he met my mother—or that's what I've been told—maybe that's one of the reasons I chose the path I did. So sometimes when I make a decision like that, maybe it was more profound than I thought or realized.

Maybe if I had to do it all over again I would choose to be a fireman. Or there's always that college role too, where I wish I had gone into the military. The uniformed services—just seems like there's what I call a constant echo.

Do I find it difficult being an Asian American police officer in a basically white suburban town? Yes and no. They respect the uniform and I think we're going to have problems no matter what ethnicity. But I find it advantageous when we do come across minorities and they see I'm a minority; so I look upon that as a helpful instance and not a hurtful one.

People look at my résumé and it says Karl Ludwig—and they're thinking, That's possibly a German name, especially with the German spelling of Karl with a K. Then I show up; some people look at me funny and say, You're a Ludwig? So it's always interesting. I'm used to it now just because of the comments and the looks. I mean, it's not awkward, it's kind of like a good icebreaker; or people look at me and think, Well, you must not be full Asian. Well, I'm not full Asian, but being adopted, I don't know if I'm German or not.

Do I find myself gravitating to my Korean heritage? At times, yes. I find it to be almost cyclical. Sometimes I gravitate toward the food, the dialect, and everything else, and there are times when I have the same routine of going home, watching the kids. Everything else, like researching my background, I have to kind of step away from because of my family life and the daily grind.

That 5 Percent: I'm definitely a happy person. I like to make other people happy and laugh and joke, I'm 95 percent fulfilled. Growing up I felt more unfulfilled, but now that I have a family of my own, I feel like okay, this is my path, these are my kids and I want to raise them as best as I can and give them every opportunity I was given. But there's that 5 percent that's unfulfilled: where's my genealogy, where are my roots with my medical history, what did my father look like? There will always be questions that will be unanswered that we never may be able to deal with.

Kristen (adopted sister from Korea): I think it helped a great deal to have Kristen. I looked upon her like a big sister and was able to lean on her. We compared and contrasted, like, Growing up, did you notice this, did you notice that? We talked about family: Have you tried to get in touch with your family and have they tried to get in touch with you? Your friends, do they notice this about you, do they notice that about you? She was a great support that way.

Did we ever ask each other why we were given up for adoption? Yeah, we've talked about it and I've talked about it with my friends. In college I had a friend who's Korean and he's adopted too. I guess we narrowed it down to affordability, economics, opportunity.

In terms of economics, my parents couldn't afford me, so I was given the opportunity to receive or get a better life in the United States, given how society would look down upon me because I was part American. So my sister, Kristen, and I always talked about that and admitted that it was probably better.

Am I able to understand it more, as I get older? Yes. And do I look upon it as a small child who doesn't understand the concepts a grown-up would? Is there still anger there? Yes. A little bit. I'm like, How can you give up your own blood? Why couldn't you make it work? Why couldn't you get a second job? Or if I was five and a half, I don't know what child labor laws were then, but maybe I could've tried to help raise money for the house, shine shoes or something. But maybe they didn't want that type of lifestyle for me either. It's a full gamut of emotions and issues and topics.

I think growing up there was more anger, but now with a family of my own I can understand why, but it's hard because I have a daughter who is six years old and, having raised her for her first six years of her life, I look at her and say, Can I give her up? Would I be able to put her up for adoption? Given the financial situation I am in, I of course say, No way, hell no, I'm not going to give her up, nothing can take her away from me. But growing up in a grass hut, with barely anything to eat and possibly tattered clothes, possibly, yes. I think it's understandable.

Am I scathed from this? Yes. But I'm living my life in a positive light because I was given an opportunity, and now that I have a family of my own I want to give my kids even opportunities that I never had growing up. So I look upon the future with hope but I also want to remember and honor the past.

When my kids get a little bit older I want to say, This is why you should appreciate the finer things, because your father grew up in hardship. Right now I haven't told them much because they haven't been asking. But there was a gift that I had brought to my mom and dad from Korea that I believe my grandfather had made and it was a straw house that had a little light bulb in it and you plug it in and it's like in a fish tank or aquarium. When I moved out and bought my first house, Joan gave that to me as a housewarming present. She said it was symbolic because it was the first present I had given her and it was a house. So now here's my first house and she said, I want you to take this back and hold onto it. I thought it was kind of neat because it's always been reminiscent of where I came from. It's very fragile. I can't put a price tag on that. It's worth more to me than a Rolex watch and it was handmade. So I look at it as a gift that I'm going to show to my kids when they inquire about where I came from and what happened. It's a great tool for learning and for saying, This is why I want you to appreciate everything you have today. We haven't gone down that road yet but I think in the near future we will.

Growing Up: I loved having a big family; Christmas was fantastic, dinners were great. Even sports. We were quite different. The oldest was twelve years older than I am, so growing up on that type of scale was a little bit different. But it was great. Growing up I loved having a big family and now I have a big family; I have four kids.

At home with dinner and breakfast, my mom and dad were fantastic. Some of the things they did I wish I could do for my kids but I can't because of my schedule and my hours.

In first grade we would have show and tell, so I would have my mother bring something in if I forgot it, like my pet cat, and all my friends would be like, Why does your mom look different than you? Why is your mom white and you're Asian? So it was interesting.

It was definitely as ideal a family as possible. But then there were outside circumstances that would happen—that I'm adopted and I can't deny that and I can't escape that. So it was kind of a neat embrace.

This all definitely defines me in terms of who I am and it forces me sometimes—once a day, sometimes once a month—to take a look at some of my reactions as to why I do some of the things I do, or why I look the way I do. Or why I answer some of the questions of my kids the way that I do.

I told you I have four kids—one is a newborn and he's only five months old, so everyday we're looking at him and wondering what his hair's going to be like, or his eyes. The firstborn, she looks Asian. You look at her and she looks a lot like me; you can tell she's Asian. The next-to-oldest and the third youngest, you look at them and he's got blond hair and blue eyes and she's got light-brown hair and hazel eyes so, the oldest asked me, "Well, why are they different? Why do I look like you and they don't look like me?" So it's just interesting the questions that they come up with, and we have to talk about adoption and about how you look like I do, and they look like the mom, and we don't know what my dad looked like, or my mom looked like. So just in terms of family or societal dynamics, there are pretty interesting forces that make us take a look at and accept each one of us for who we are. It's kind of neat that way.

Racism in Dating? I felt it strongly three times in my life. I was dating a girl in high school and we were over at her house for dinner; you could just tell when there's tension in the air and over dinner conversation, in close proximity, there was an unkindness— kind of like an elephant in the room where you feel unwelcome or unwanted. And after dinner the father politely excused himself and I was asked to leave the house. I said okay, and I asked why, and he said "It's my house, I don't have to give you a reason. I want you out." So it caused a lot of tension, a lot of heartache, and it was kind of sad. But I honored his wishes as I was in someone else's house and I left. I talked to the girl two times and she was like, "I'm not allowed to date you anymore." So I said, "Okay, if that's how you feel and that's what you want to do, fine."

She was Italian. And American. Actually both of them. I had two girlfriends with similar type instances, one in high school, one in college.

The third situation, she was Irish and said her father didn't want her dating me anymore. So I said, "Okay, if that's how you feel, if that's what you want. But you're over eighteen, you're able to make your own decisions." But she said, "Well, I don't want to go against my family," so I said, "Okay, I understand that too." She was twenty-four and I was twenty-four, something like that.

I dated two Asian girls that I can think of; one in high school and one in college. Actually it was the complete opposite with the parents. They really liked me a lot and she said, "My parents love you—they love you more than me." Things were going good but it just didn't work out.

Religion: I'm Episcopalian and I'm raising my kids to be that way. I've always wondered, Are we always a product of nature or nurture, are we part of our environment? If I took a Buddhist monk's baby and raised him Catholic, would he convert back? Would he have the opportunity or would he be happy in their religion? I'm happy with the Episcopalian faith and celebrating Christmas and I believe in Christ and everything else. Baptized, raised, and confirmed.

I've always thought, Okay, I was raised as a Christian. I can't say that religion was a part of my life in Korea, but it always made me wonder how come I'm not a Buddhist or any other type of religion. So it was interesting in terms of the parallelism or just thinking about it. It has led me to a deeper belief or appreciation of religion. It's another avenue I think about, maybe go down that path later on in life, or research it when I have more time or when I'm retired.

Do I remember my name before it was Karl? Yes. It was Jung Suk Lee.

I have a wonderful family and wife and house to be thankful for and a career and education. So I'm definitely blessed in all those aspects.

Found

Kristen Houghton

Kristen Houghton, adopted older sister to Karl Ludwig, arrived in the United States from Seoul in 1969 at age six.

About a good ten to fifteen years ago I got a call from my mother, Joan. The adoption agency, Welcome House, had reached out to me because I had a stack of letters from my biological mother. First of all, I didn't know what they said, they were all in Korean. So I had to run down to my dry cleaners, and I was like, "Michelle, can you translate these for me?"

The letters were very sweet. They were basically explaining to me why she had to do what she had to do. And it's sad because, well, she was married to a North Korean soldier, and there was the war, the whole works, and he died. The North family did not want anything to do with her because she was from the South. So she was pretty much kicked out with four kids on her own and tried to survive postwar and no husband to speak of and you know how women's rights are. It wasn't that good in Asian countries. She had to make a tough decision. I was the youngest so she put me up for adoption.

I remember her telling me I was going to be put up for adoption. I remember running away from the orphanage, I remember them cutting my hair. I had really long hair and they're afraid of lice and all that, so I ran away. And I ran away several times from the orphanage. I was very unhappy. I was probably around five.

I actually stayed with my biological family until Joan and Jay had identified that they wanted to adopt me. And at that point I was put into an orphanage. Just to prep me to come over. So I pretty much stayed with my family until I was flown out.

Jay and Joan Ludwig. I met them here at the airport. I cried for almost a week; didn't eat for a week. It was a big adjustment. I remember the whole flight over. I was the oldest so I kept myself occupied by taking care of the babies.

When I landed here it was reality. I was very, very sad. I didn't know anything, I couldn't even communicate with them. I didn't understand English, they didn't understand Korean. The transition was very tough. My mother was a schoolteacher, my father was a dean at that point. My mother had the winter break off, and come January 3 I was put into school. So I only had a week of transition and it was really tough.

My God, did I miss Korean food. I still do. I couldn't eat anything they gave me. It was such a drastic difference from what I was used to; even utensils. All I wanted was chopsticks and there was a fork and knife. Even sleeping was different; we used to sleep on mats on the floor. I fell off the bed a couple of times until I was used to it. It's little things like that you remember. I remember falling out of bed and the only way to keep from falling out of bed was to keep one leg out off the bed, so I knew that there was an end to it.

It's not like I was baby. I had experienced quite a bit and I wanted to go back to it. I held on to that for the longest time until I said, This is my life, I gotta accept it for what it is. And that made a big difference.

I remember being in tears. It was just tough. So when Karl came I tried to help as much as I could.

There was this one girl, after a week or so, she made my school bearable. She befriended me and it was something I really needed. She's still close to my heart. We had sleepovers. I started getting into the fold of the United States and the cultural change and all that. Initially weeks went on and I had pretty much stopped eating, couldn't stop crying. I'm sitting in front of the TV watching Lucille Ball and the chocolate factory episode—you don't need to know English to understand that—and that was the first time I started laughing. I still remember that. Then I started eating, so it took awhile—probably several months—but it happened.

I came to the United States to a family I knew nothing about and was thrown into school. So I had two very different elements going on at the same time. I didn't really have much of an adjustment to home life before I was put into school. So it was just kind of too much.

Mom and Dad did their best and I know they did. My mother and I have had many bouts of disagreements over anything and everything. But we worked things out a lot. My mother is the focal point of the family—whether it's strong or negative, she's the focal point. My dad, at home he was kind of in the background. My adopted sister and I (she's three years older), we do not get along, we never will. We had thirty years of trying and we finally came to that understanding. We have very different thinking patterns. Some personalities are never going to meld. We've grown up trying, both of us.

Karl (adopted younger brother): Karl is a great guy. He and I, that's a friendship we've always had, and I remember it from day one. He wanted to speak to me in Korean and I didn't know a word of it, so there was a tremendous amount of frustration in the beginning because I wanted to comfort him. But we worked through the language barrier and he and I are very close. I am six years older than Karl, so I was around twelve when he arrived.

We went through a pretty rough time and I helped him adjust as much as I could. He added to my life because he became a very good friend. He's not just a sibling. As we've gotten older he's become my friend. I think he and I will always be close.

Reconnecting: I remember my older sister in Korea telling me, "Don't worry, no matter what, I'll find you." So when I got here I was like, Please, please find me. My oldest sibling—I remember very clearly—I loved her and I knew she loved me. It may not have been ideal financially and everything else but I knew I was well loved. So it was sad.

She found me, eventually. She took my biological mom and went down to the adoption agency to have the file opened. She knew I was eighteen and they knew they couldn't contact me until I was of age. So as soon as I turned of age they had their adoption agency contact this adoption agency—it was on-going back and forth—there was all this red tape.

They found me when I was thirty.

I'm still having issues with it. I don't know if it's because I feel abandoned. You know what it was: after I had been here ten, fifteen years I knew that my life over there was gone, I had to let it go. It was more of a peace of mind kind of thing, instead of constantly hoping that we would connect again. I finally let it go. So with that in mind I had a hard time reconnecting to it and still do. My sister writes me on a regular basis. I've e-mailed her a couple of times, which was an emotional chore, an absolutely emotional chore, and I can't continue doing that. It broke me. It really did.

I don't know why but I remember sitting there in front of my laptop typing away and I was in tears. In tears. I'm having a hard time making that connection. I've written them a couple of times to let them know I'm fine, here's a picture of my husband, my baby. And I almost wanted her to say, "Let it be, I'm okay, you're okay, let's go on with our lives." I think it has a lot to do with my promise to myself to let go of my past. So that's where I am.

It's not like they won't let go of me but I don't know what part of me they want, because the part of me that they remember has long gone. I can't even communicate with them. I can't speak Korean; that's one thing I regret because it's quite embarrassing. They start talking to you in Korean. So I don't know, I'm still coming to terms with it. My life has been so busy that I'm having trouble just focusing on it. Many of my friends have said, "Go do it." I can't get myself to.

My mother is still alive. She has some heart conditions. The last e-mail they sent me they asked, "What's going on, where are you, we want to see you and we want you to come visit; we will visit you." I'm having a hard time with that kind of commitment. That's the next level they want to go to and I have explained to them it's all very emotional for me. But they responded by saying, "I want you to come."

I'm not sure if I want to go there. Not because I don't love them—as a matter of fact that's probably the biggest barrier. Because I've created them as being my memories and God knows human beings are famous for disappointing you on those expectations.

My siblings trying to contact me—I'm afraid of the emotions that might come back. I'm afraid of the anger that might come back. I've squashed it down to nonexistent. I'm just trying to survive at this point.

This is sad because Karl was very excited when this happened; he said, "I want to find my parents, I want to find mine." But it doesn't always work out the way you really want it to. His didn't turn out as he would have wanted it. His mother had passed away and his grandfather whom he remembered had passed away.

Life's Destiny: I have thought of that quite a bit. If my father had survived I would have been in North Korea right now. Yes, that image stays right in my head. My life would have been a lot worse. Women's rights in Asia just aren't there. I wouldn't have been as well off as I am right now. I'm not that well off but I have opportunities which I'm pretty sure I wouldn't have gotten over there. So destiny has a way of working itself out through the tough times.

Am I glad this move was made for me? That's a hard question. Again it goes back to not looking in the past. It's been made. I'll accept whether it was destiny that brought me here or pure luck. It's not a matter of rethinking how my life would have been. This is how it is.

I'm happy as a human being. I love my husband. I love my three children. If what happened didn't happen, I wouldn't be where I am. I'm a manager of volunteer services and customer service at a hospital in Summit. When I was growing up I wanted to be an architect. But I didn't go to college. Concepts were no problem. Math came very well to me. It was actually the reading. I can't phonetically sound it out. If they can read it to me I can put it to memory.

Memories of Korea: I remember living very well-off and I also remember living poorly, very poorly. You could tell. It really was both. It seems as though my biological father was affluent and we lived a very good life until she and us got kicked out. We were literally probably living on the streets at times. There are things I remember, strawberries, soldiers, high-heels made with rocks. We must have lived at one point near an army base and they used to get us strawberries and Coca-Cola. So there are a lot of memories. I have probably put them in the back of my mind. As I've gotten older I've gotten more comfortable talking about it. I remember we wanted high-heel shoes so we used to stick some rocks up underneath our shoes and walk. I had two sisters and one brother. I remember my sister saying when you go over to America to marry a blond. Because that's American. I did. I don't think it was conscious but that's our image of an American. Caucasian, blond hair. I used to call myself by my old name, which I can't even remember.

There was a social worker who used to come visit me and I got very attached to him. He was Korean, from the agency. I wanted to keep a hand in my other life—in being Korean and having anything Korean. Mom and Dad, we used to go to some of the picnics. The Welcome House picnics with other Koreans, but it was very limited.

Would I have gone to Korean school? Yes, if it was offered to me. But when Mom and Dad went through the adoption agency they were strictly ordered to sever all connections. That's what they did. In retrospect even my mother said, "I wish I could have

Kristen Houghton and family

sent you to school to keep up with the language." And to this day I would still like to learn. My dry cleaner, who's Korean, asks, "Any more letters, any more letters?"

I probably was in my mid-twenties before I understood the politics and felt fortunate about being here. I was in my own little world for the longest time. I have no regrets. I know I'm better off than so many other people. And I know my mother and my father did a damn good job. We have our obstacles and we're as dysfunctional as everybody else.

Will I ever go back to Korea? I don't know. Is there a desire? Maybe, but I don't know where to start, and it's not like I'm in denial of my past. When I came over here this was all foreign to me. It would be reversed if I went over there, it would be a completely different world. I told my children I was adopted. They totally understand that I was born in another country and Joan and Jay are not my biological parents but they're Grandma and Grandpa.

My family, my immediate family right now, means more to me than I could ever imagine. My children, I could never imagine giving them up or having another life without them. I have a better understanding of my biological mother's perspective now that I am a mother, and the heartache she must have gone through. Which makes it hard because I want to ease her heartache, yet I'm having a hard time passing through that.

I'm so glad I know what happened, that they tried to track me down after all these years. I was glad to let them know I'm doing fine, I'm married, have three kids. But I couldn't take the next step. I still can't.

Do I feel vindicated that they found me? Yeah, because my sister kept her promise. The heartbreak I'm going through about not taking the next step is just killing me.

She ended up being a nun.

It's hard to go back to a life that I guess I miss so much. But I'm grateful for the life I have.

THREE GENERATIONS

Of Personal Challenges and Triumphs

Ark Chin

Ark Chin arrived in the United States at age ten, in 1934. He talks of growing up and his relationship with his father.

Being Chinese. I felt that the value of that could be transmitted through the generations. We told our children and grandchildren when they were growing up, You guys are the luckiest people in the world and the reason is that you can look at the Chinese culture and the Western culture and you can choose the best of each to live your life by. Then we try to be role models not by being conscious of being a role model but by living our lives that way. It's bad to keep telling people that you ought to do this. I resented my father very much growing up. He would say, Why aren't you like that? But I did not challenge him.

First he opened with the phrase, You're no good. Then he'd berate you for not doing the right thing. The right thing was that you were supposed to clean up the restaurant before you do anything—before you go to school. But I always loved to read the paper a little bit and he would always catch me. Then he would give me hell. So anyway, it wasn't until toward the end of my college days that one day I went to Aberdeen to consult with him on something that was of consequence, that he shocked me. He addressed me in my Chinese name and said, You fought in the war and now you're a college man so you're better educated and have much better experience than I have. You should make the decision. I was in total shock! Our relationship changed there and then.

What's the relationship between a man and his Chinese father? Well there's certainly respect and there's also a sense of fear. Because in China literally they had control over your whole life. So one just did not challenge his father or speak to his father very much. It's just one-way communication is what it was. He tells you and that's all. To survive you had to understand that and not challenge it.

Did I know my father? In the sense of knowing what drives him. Everything you wanted to do you had to ask for permission. For instance, going to my high school football game: that was intolerable to my dad. If my dad was maybe halfway accommodating to me, maybe considering allowing me to go, his partner would needle the hell out of him, and he never heard the end of it from his partner. Because to the partner I represented a grunt that does work for nothing.

To start out, dishwashing—in those days it was a big tub, I couldn't reach the bottom so my dad brought me an apple box so I could stand up and reach the bottom. I was ten. Then I was the busboy. As I learned English I became a waiter; meanwhile, I was also the vegetable preparer, and I had the job of cleaning up the restaurant in the morning before I went to school. My day used to go something like this: clean up the restaurant, go to school, and then sneak in some time at the library for reading. Then I would go to the restaurant and start working, wait on tables and then about 8:30 go to bed. At 11, wake up so I could help with the late restaurant trade. In Aberdeen the taverns are jammed until closing time which is around 12; after which they want to have some food to eat. That was one of the reasons why I was so frail. My sleep and eating was so irregular. The service did a great thing for me. It put me on a regiment of physical exercise, fresh air, hard work, filling food.

All that time my mom was in China. She couldn't come so once in awhile I would write letters to her. I had four years of school in China so I was passable in reading but as far as writing there were many words I had to look up in English. I had an English–Chinese dictionary. The letters were always very formal sorts of things. You address mother, "Great woman, I'm a son at your need." I didn't see my mother until 1947. Thirteen years.

Returning to China: The reason I went to China was that my grandfather had retired and he said, I want to go home, and going home was China because grandma was there, the house was there. He could look forward to a very comfortable retirement and enjoyment of life among his peers. My father said to me, Ark I want you to take grandfather home. This was the summer before 1947. I said, Dad, I think you should go. You haven't seen Mom for thirteen years. He said, Look, all through these many years of owning the restaurant we never made much because Aberdeen was so poor economically. Now the times are still good from the war days so he said, You go. See, in those days if you left the restaurant to go back to China you didn't get any part of the profit. It's no share. So he says, If I go I lose all of this money.

But before I went he sent my mother a letter saying under no circumstance are you to allow your son to be married. Because he understood the village culture. In 1947 I was twenty-three years old and in those days that's old for not being married. So I agreed to take my grandfather back because we couldn't afford to fly. We took the steamship and it took twenty-one or twenty-two days to cross.

The very first day in the village it was hot. I remember we were eating dinner out there in the alleyway and my grandmother says, Oh, here's my grandson, a fine-looking young man, twenty-some-odd years old, there must be many girls who are attracted. So she said, We oughta send the matchmakers out and I said, Grandma, I'm not here to get married because I haven't finished school yet. But each day we went through the same thing, the same song and dance. I wasn't bending so she started working on my mother. My mother had suffered through a great deal during the war, being in occupied

Japanese territory. She was like eighty-some pounds and five-foot four. She would sit in this rattan chair with a soft cushion for no more than ten minutes and she'd have to get up because it hurt her so much. So now on my mother, grandmother would use reverse psychology—Oh I have such a fabulous daughter in law who is so concerned with her son's education that it's alright to deprive her of grandchildren. That would be my great grandchildren—it's alright, you know.

I could see as soon as I left China to go back to school this would be a constant matter that could easily affect my mother's health.

So I said, Grandma, I will get married under some conditions. She said, What are they? And I said, Well, the girl must have a high school education. Now remember back in 1947 in rural China the odds of anyone even going to junior high weren't very high. And I said this is someone I'm going to sit across from, for a long time so she has to be a beautiful woman. Then the last condition was that I absolutely insist the choice be mine. But my grandma upon hearing I wanted to get married couldn't care less about the conditions. We went through this whole charade in the village of getting résumés and interviewing potential brides. Not getting any place.

I went out to Hong Kong to book passage back because I wanted to start school again in October at University of Washington. When I was out there this uncle—my distant aunt was married to a fellow that was a graduate of University of Illinois and he had opened up an electrical equipment store in Hong Kong selling telephones and X-rays and what not. So he said I heard you're being very picky. I said, Oh, come on, get off my case. He said I know just the girl for you. She's beautiful, she's going to college. I said, No, I'm going back to finish school. So he said it can't hurt for you to meet her. I said, No—if I say no she loses face, and he said, Oh, we in Hong Kong are very modern. You just go have tea and if you don't like each other, fine, you just walk away from each other. He finally got me to agree to go meet Winnie. That's fifty-eight years ago. That was it. I was so enthralled. After a number of months of courtship I said to Winnie I'm going to transfer here for a year so you can get to know me better. I had originally intended to remedy my deficiency in Chinese by going to study civil engineering and Chinese. When I went to visit the dean of the civil engineering department he said that didn't make any sense. He said UW's college of engineering is so much better than ours. He said, You go back, get a master's then I will hire you as an instructor and you can learn your Chinese that way.

Well, it was a number of months later that Winnie and I got married. We have six children.

Journeys of Self Discovery

Candace Chin

Candace Chin, daughter of Ark Chin, born and raised in Seattle, is in her fifties. She talks about her relationship with her parents and her journey to China.

Growing up there was just a huge dichotomy between Chinese American on the outside and Chinese American at home. At home we were Chinese. It just didn't always jive with what was okay on the outside. Example: Everybody was always going over to other people's houses and having slumber parties. My parents really didn't see the need to socialize because the family is the home and the hub of everything. I remember my mother saying distinctly, Your family is here. I had these mixed messages that I couldn't reconcile. This is where your family is. It's not those people, they're not going to help you when you need help.

Basically most of my friends were Asian American and we talked a lot about our problems having Chinese parents, like some things that Caucasian Americans were allowed to do that we weren't allowed to do, such as dating.

I was never allowed to date someone other than Chinese. I had a boyfriend who was Jewish. I didn't think about color, I didn't think about religion, I didn't think about this dichotomy. That's how I sort of developed this belief system that we really cannot judge people based on the color of their skin.

When I married a non-Chinese, they disowned me. It was hell. I met him in Seattle. We were working as camp counselors for disadvantaged youth. My parents did not approve. They tried to talk me out of seeing him. I was very honest and I tried but I couldn't do it. So I chose to marry him even though I wasn't quite ready. No one came to my wedding. My grandparents were still alive and they loved me in spite of it. They couldn't come but they supported me.

So for three years I was dead to them. And then my grandmother told me that I had to write a letter because I got pregnant with my first daughter, Hannah. It was sort of up to me to mend the bridges. They came over and it was the most awkward time. We played bridge and the uneasy truce happened.

My husband and I divorced after fifteen or sixteen years. The youngest was four and the oldest was 11 at the time. We had four wonderful children together.

With my parents it used to be a paradigm of right and wrong, black or white, there are no grays. But it was always my claim that there are more perspectives on a situation and more gray areas. You can't just say black and white because that precludes possibilities for collaboration, and that's the situation with my parents. Black or white. You're married or you're not. You love him or you don't love him. You love him or forget you.

I understand from being in China we talk about thousands and thousands of years of an evolution of a mindset and a way of looking at things. They don't call it middle kingdom, center of the world, for nothing. So what I came to understand is that they cannot help viewing things through that paradigm of black and white, either, or.

Understanding that they cannot see it in other terms allows me to say, okay, they did it because they believed in my best interest, that it had to be this way. And yet a part of me still says, Aren't my children living proof that even though they're mixed and even though I'm divorced they're some of the most amazing human beings—they are balanced, and kind and passionate—and they want to know about their cultural past? The oldest, Hannah, is thirty now, Libby is twenty-eight, Susha is twenty-five, and Weston will be twenty-three.

What I also understand about a paradigm is you can change it if you want to change it. I just finished graduate school, I just got my MBA in Sustainable Business. And I'm in the process of looking for work.

Going to China: Being born in the United States, it was hard for me growing up, to figure out what was Chinese protocol. So much of it was unspoken. My parents couldn't walk in my shoes and I couldn't walk in their shoes. And that's the truth. Not for a long time. So going to China was to help me walk in their shoes.

I had lived in Taiwan for a year after my college days and I enjoyed the experience. I thought someday I'd like to go back to the real China, which is mainland China. I had this dream to go to Beijing to study Mandarin. So in 1999, I took my son, who was 16 at the time, and we spent three years there. I wasn't coming back to the States until I had crossed some bridges or come to some understanding about myself.

I got a second mortgage on my house. When I got there, I taught English for nine months. Then one of my friends said, Maybe you should check with the U.S. Embassy to see if they have any jobs for local hire. I knew when I read the job description that it was exactly what I wanted to do. I was working at the U.S. Embassy in public affairs as the voluntary speaker program manager which meant I recruited and designed programs to do outreach explaining American society to Chinese institutions and universities. I have to say I absolutely loved that job because it's exactly how I think of myself—as a bridge builder. Always between two cultures, two points, A and B. And the bridge is the person or the conduit that help creates understanding.

Living in China: Chinese Americans don't look like Chinese people that are there. There's something in my opinion about being Chinese American—we look a little too dairy. Whereas generally speaking Chinese people tend to look thinner and they don't

Candace Chin with parents Ark Chin and Winifred Chin

have that sort of healthy glow or body fat that Americans seem to have. People knew that I wasn't from China; they would always ask me where I was from. They thought I was from Korea, maybe even Japan. I don't think there was any particular sort of prejudice of overseas Chinese.

I found it really interesting because I lived in Chinese housing, among regular Chinese people. I didn't live in the foreign housing which is where I should have been living. I just felt that for me to learn Chinese, in some ways I had to fade into the background as much as I could—to not really stand out. There's kind of this sensibility being an American and being born in the United States; there's just an aura and a way of being as an American. It's about being fast, really kind of out there, quick at getting things; whereas in China the pace is kind of different. How I like to think of it is, in the United States I feel we have personal space that's maybe eighteen to twenty-four inches out. When you start to move into a person's personal space you begin to feel it. You can sense whether they want to talk to you or not. In China you can get up next to someone on the bus and you can actually touch them. So you can physically be there and you might think that we're friendly but you have no idea what they're thinking, not for a long time. Their personal space is actually inside. So I think that they've gotten used to having an internal personal space that they might let you in to if they wanted to.

Their ability to persevere through a lot of different situations— whereas in America we just wouldn't put up with it—made me think they know how to endure. I used to think it was passivity and I used to think, Well, they don't have feelings. Now I think it's because people have to hide their real feelings and they have to endure beyond whatever the situation is and just keep going. So I found myself thinking that's actually a good quality. A sort of American way of thinking and Chinese way of being and living in China—just kind of let me sit there and keep watching it over and over. People's ability to endure. You go to the train station especially before a holiday or Chinese New Year and you try to get a ticket— Oh my God. There are no lines, you just all push as hard as you can, and push to the front and get a ticket. It doesn't matter that it's not civil. In the United States if someone tries to cut in line everyone gives them a glare and they back off and move away. But in China there are billions of people and they can't take care of it. So if you can't get your ticket then no one's going to get it for you.

Being a Woman in Her Fifties in China: I think if I hadn't had the job at the U.S. Embassy, as a woman there wouldn't be much regard for me. It is still a sexist society. Now that we have a market economy, women who are young and attractive certainly have the possibility of getting men older or younger with money. If you're in your fifties, and a Chinese woman or Chinese American woman your chance of finding someone your age is probably pretty minimal because the Chinese mentality is if there's a man available in his forties or fifties there's something wrong if he's not married. It could be also the demographics. As a Chinese woman in my fifties I don't think people cared one way or another. But the fact that I worked at the U.S. Embassy gave me a little weight. As for older women, I don't think there are any advantages being in China. As for disadvantages—well, it depends on who you compare yourself to. If it's compared to a white American or Caucasian male that's a disadvantage. If it's to Chinese men I'm not quite sure.

I came back to the United States with a different mindset.

I was able to speak Chinese better, I had a stronger understanding of Chinese culture which helped me to understand my parents better, and thirdly I was able to kind of create that kind of network that I needed to get whatever I needed done. I wanted to come back to the United States, join the foreign service and return to work in China.

Hapa with Strong Chinese Roots

Susha Pratt

Susha Pratt, in her twenties, is Candace Chin's daughter and Ark Chin's grand-daughter. She gives her perspectives on growing up as a hapa with strong Chinese roots.

I was born in Seattle to my mom, Candace Chin, and dad, Tom Pratt. He was in Vietnam and was dispatched in Fort Lewis, Washington, and then met my mom. We moved to the Olympic Peninsula of Washington and I was five or six when they got divorced. So I grew up in Sequim, Washington. It was a fairly conservative, white rural town. But every other weekend I would come to Seattle and see my mom and half of every summer I would live with her. So, I got the best of both worlds growing up in a more rural place then coming every weekend to Seattle and seeing my mom and Chinese family.

I see myself as a third-generation Chinese. I see myself in the context of my mother and the way that she has sometimes struggled with being the first born in the United States and the cultural differences between her parents who are from China. She was the oldest and kind of the most rebellious. She was always kind of doing things that they didn't approve of so I think that was a real clash for them. I've heard stories of that and see that in the way they interact. I see the way that I was raised as being the second generation born in the United States, and the way they treat me is with much less strictness—they don't tell me who I can date or what I have to do at school. They're pretty much just supportive and loving. But I have seen that struggle in my mom's life and I can feel it to some extent.

You can feel pain through the generations to some extent. I feel very lucky to be raised in the situation I was raised in. And it hasn't been until very very recently that I felt really good about it. I've talked with Grandmother about her childhood growing up. Her mother was very protective, very incredibly protective of her. She came here and was the same with her children. And I can feel it lessening a little but I like to be connected to that and know where my roots come from. I've heard a lot of stories from my grandfather and grandmother and their childhoods and then from my mother's childhood.

I think of my grandfather's story—of coming to the United States with zero dollars and working in a restaurant as a bus boy and working his way up—pulling himself up by the boot straps and really becoming successful in American terms. He was an engineer and went to the University of Washington and did very well. That kind of industrious Chinese-ness brought him to where he is and he's comfortable; he's retired and he's set up and he has a wonderful family that loves him. He has a wife that loves him. I see them as very happy in their old age and it's really great to see. I mean we went to see the village that he grew up in and it was very rural; rice fields and farming. Just worlds away from where he's at now. I think he's very happy about that but also still very connected to his roots and where he grew up in China.

I speak a little Chinese. I definitely have a very good comprehension level just having heard it when I was growing up in the Chinese family. And I studied it for a year and a half at Lewis and Clark. My major was environmental studies. Just kind of a general look at environmental issues. I was more humanities-based and I also had a focus in gender studies or women's studies.

Now I live in Portland and I'm an Americorp volunteer. I get a stipend every month to work at a nonprofit bike shop. I'm the recycling coordinator, I recycle bicycles. I really love it. It's such an amazing experience to be involved with that I wouldn't have otherwise been able to do. So I feel fortunate.

I have two older sisters and a little brother, there's four of us. We're very tight. We have a very strong relationship. I look forward to spending time with them not just as my sister but as my friend also. So it's been really important.

Hapa: I feel proud to tell people I'm half Chinese. But in some ways I think of myself as hapa. It's a Hawaiian term that means basically "a mix." Specifically Asian/White mix. I grew up in a very white community so I take my hapa identity as a little bit separate from both of those, as my own. I really identify with my siblings and the way that we're in these two worlds.

For me being hapa is really unique because I am half Chinese and a lot of people actually think I'm white. I pass or whatever. But I feel very strongly about my Chinese roots. When I'm with my Chinese family eating Chinese food and hearing Chinese language the values that come with my Chinese side are very important to me. My favorite seasonings are always soy sauce and sesame oil. When I eat it I feel a part of my mom or my Chinese-ness.

On the Chinese side I would say the values are about family: the importance of gathering together, showing your support and love for family. We get together every Christmas and Thanksgiving and we have a family reunion which is pretty unique and awesome. Our grandmother and grandfather organize that—basically it's for all of us to come. I think that's something that's really important to them. Another value is being successful—being good at school, getting an education, getting a good job and just being able to support yourself financially.

I think of the white world as the mainstream, the norms of what it is to be white in this country. And I feel like I am quite a bit a part of that. Quite a few of my friends are white, Caucasian, yet I feel a difference within myself, a different plane of cultural understanding.

On the Chinese side I sometimes feel I've been not quite Chinese enough. I look different than my cousins and I understand it. That if you look different from someone then you are different. When we came together at family reunions we were all the same, we were all cousins. My cousin Yvonne is the same age as me. We have a lot in common, we're tight but we look different. So sometimes I feel I have a sense of not being 100 percent Chinese. Past issues come up and I see myself not feeling as Chinese as my cousins, but at the same time I'm starting to realize more that this is just who you are, and you are who you are. You can't try to be more Chinese or more white. They'll get over it and I'll get over it. I'm just a person.

But I think it's been lately in my life that I've been trying to take that position of not being fully Chinese, not really being fully white and really honoring it and trying to make it my own. My own position, my own hapa-ness, and who I am—almost my own culture.

I know there are other hapas out there that probably feel the same way and have maybe come to this sense of feeling good about it. But it was hard growing up in Sequim. I think I got racist jokes about my grandfather which I remember made me really angry. I guess for the most part in Sequim I passed as white because I look more like my dad.

Dating: I actually find myself very attracted to other hapa people, other half Asian people. I remember one time I was dancing in the club and I saw this very attractive guy. I went up to him and my pick-up line was, Are you half Asian? He said, Yeah, I am. I was like, I knew it. He said, What do you think my nationality is? And I was like, Chinese, Japanese, and I think I went through all of them. It ended up that he was half Filipino and I didn't get that one. I said, You're stumping me. So that was a funny thing and I found that I just am attracted to people who are mixed, not only half Asian, but half something. Half African American, half Venezuelan.

I find them attractive just physically, their skin color. And maybe just because they have a similar life experience as I do. I can see it being a struggle in life to be in between two worlds and I like to see how people deal with it. I have a friend who is half Chinese and he does not identify in any way to his Chinese roots. I think he doesn't even think, Oh yeah, I'm half Chinese. Just the community and culture he grew up in; he disassociated from his Asian roots.

When I'm looking to date someone I don't necessarily say it's a requirement. I just find myself naturally leaning towards people of mixed race and also of course the personality is really important. How I gel with them.

I think of myself as American and half Chinese. I just don't know if the title Asian American applies to me. I've never really thought of that. When I am abroad I often say I'm half Chinese, half American and I always include that in my identity but I don't say I'm Asian American. When I'm doing the census form I think about the boxes to check. I put Asian/Pacific Islander and often white.

Identity and Crossroads: I feel pretty content in that I've grown a lot in my racial identity and also my sexual identity, knowing who I am. Just becoming more confident in myself and recognizing that I can really honor my Chinese side. I think I used to maybe be scared of my grandma and grandpa, that I wasn't doing things quite right. I wasn't fully Chinese, I didn't date a Chinese boy, feeling a little bit like they wouldn't like me unless I did those things. Then I realized if I just love myself or I'm confident in myself they're going to love me if I'm happy. They're gonna be happy for me. I recently turned twenty-five so I feel like it's been awhile, twenty-five years of my life, to really get to know myself and feel like I can be confident in where I'm at.

I think it was easy for me to grow up in Sequim and not really have to confront my Chinese side. But it felt like a disconnect because I lived in a white community and there was nothing that reflected how it was a positive thing to be Chinese. But then I'd

Susha Pratt and Candace Chin

come every other weekend to my Chinese roots and be with my family and it was like I just left that behind.

I spent most of my time in Sequim where all my friends were. But I think moving away from Sequim made me realize that my real life is both.

On my dad's side, my aunt is a retired computer science professor and she has this knack for traveling. She was sailing around the world and my siblings and I went along. We were in the Mediterranean and we crossed from Spain to Brazil. We crossed the Atlantic. We stopped in the Canaries and in Senegal.

It was interesting to see the reaction from my Chinese side of the family, saying, Come on, Susha you need to get a job, what are you doing? I love them but I wanted to do this thing that seemed like such an opportunity—just going sailing on this boat. I don't have any kids or things to be tied to. I'm not so strapped so that I'm fortunate enough to go. To hear, Why can't you just get a job—I think of that as the Chinese side.

I see my cousin and she has a good job and is getting paid quite a bit. In my life when I was raised on my dad's side it was ok not to make all the money in the world as long as you're living happily and not taking too much from other people. So I grew up with the idea that you can live simply without making a lot of money and doing the things you love. But on the Chinese side it seemed like it wasn't the responsible thing to do. So that was a struggle, telling my relatives.

Overall, though, having the Chinese side, I would definitely say it gives me a plus; it's an invaluable part of my life that has just enriched it.

Notes

Answering the Call

1. *Korematsu v. United States*, 323 U.S. 214 (1944). Korematsu's conviction for evading internment was overturned in 1984. The federal district court ruling granted the writ because in Korematsu's original case, the government had knowingly submitted false information to the Supreme Court that impacted the Court's decision. Asian American Bar Association, http://www.aaba-bay.com/aaba/showpage.asp?code=korematsucase (accessed July 23, 2007). *Basic Readings in U.S. Democracy*, http://usinfo.state.gov/usa/infousa/facts/democrac/65.htm (accessed July 23, 2007).

2. Washington State had a 5 percent Asian population when Locke ran for governor. PBS, "Searching for Asian America," http://www.pbs.org/searching/gov_main.html (accessed July 23, 2007).

3. From 2000 census: 428,659 APAs call Washington State home. *The New Face of Asian Pacific America: Numbers, Diversity and Change in the 21st Century* (San Francisco: *AsianWeek*, 2003), p. 8.

4. "South Asia" is a flexible term that refers to the geographic area that extends from Sri Lanka and the Indian subcontinent north to the borders of Burma, China, Afghanistan, and Iran. It commonly includes

the countries of Bangladesh, Bhutan, India, Nepal, Pakistan, and Sri Lanka. The term "South Asian American" is not widely used by individuals of South Asian origin. More frequently it is used by community activists to forge solidarity. *The New Face of Asian Pacific America: Numbers, Diversity and Change in the 21st Century* (San Francisco: AsianWeek, 2003), p. 106.

5. The Immigration Marriage Fraud Amendments of 1986 amend the Immigration and Nationality Act to establish a two-year conditional permanent resident status for alien spouses. This was done to curb the influx of immigrants through sham marriages. The noncitizen spouse is issued a two-year conditional permanent residency status. At the end of the required two-year period, the conditions are removed after the couple files a joint petition and attends an interview with immigration officials. Library of Congress, http://thomas.loc. gov/cgi-bin/bdquery/z?d099:HR03737:@@@L&summ2=m& (accessed July 23, 2007).

Growing Up

1. When Laos fell to the Pathet Lao in 1975, Americans evacuated Hmong military leaders and their families from Laos to Thailand. At the end of 1975, the U.S. Immigration and Naturalization Service began to process Hmong refugees for resettlement in the United States, largely with support and placement by church groups. For data on population trends, see Hmong National Development Inc. and Hmong Cultural Resource Center, "Hmong 2000 Census Publication: Data and Analysis," http://hmongstudies.com/2000HmongCensus Publication.pdf (accessed July 23, 2007).

2. According to the 2000 census, there are 13,614 Asian Americans in the greater Des Moines area, comprising 3.5 percent of the area's population. Statewide, about 43,000 Asian Americans make up about 1.5 percent of the total population. Iowa Asian Alliance, http://www.iowaasianalliance.com/news_view.php?id=27 (accessed July 23, 2007).

3. Top Hmong metropolitan areas, according to the 2000 census, are
   1. Minneapolis–St. Paul, MN–Wisconsin—40,707
   2. Fresno, CA—22,456
   3. Sacramento–Yolo, CA—16,621
   Hmong Cultural Center, http://www.hmongcenter.org/top50metarby
   .html (accessed July 23, 2007). Total Hmong population in United
   States: 186,310, http://hmongstudies.com/2000HmongCensus
   Publication.pdf (accessed July 23, 2007).

4. On February 9, 2001, the USS *Greeneville*, a United States Navy submarine, struck a Japanese fishing vessel, the *Ehime Maru*, off the
   coast of Hawaii. The vessel sank and nine crew members onboard
   died, including four high school students. The *Ehime Maru* was a
   high school training ship for the Ehime Prefecture in Japan. American
   Society of International Law, http://www.asil.org/insights/insigh64.htm
   (accessed July 23, 2007).

5. The 442nd Regimental Combat Team in World War II was comprised
   of Americans of Japanese descent. In 1943 nearly 10,000 Hawaiian
   Nisei (second-generation Japanese Americans) volunteered, and over
   2,600 were accepted. The National Japanese American Memorial
   Foundation, http://www.njamf.com/hero.htm (accessed July 23, 2007).

6. After the bombing of Pearl Harbor, the government—unsure of the
   loyalty of Japanese Americans—considered them 4C (Enemy Alien),
   ineligible for the draft. In Hawaii, the 100th Infantry Battalion was
   formed by Japanese Americans into a special unit and was sent to the
   mainland for training. Approximately 33,000 Nisei served in World
   War II; close to 800 made the ultimate sacrifice. The National Japanese American Memorial Foundation, http://www.njamf.com/hero.htm
   (accessed July 23, 2007).

Views from Within

1. New York's Chinese American population is the second largest in the
   country. California has the largest concentration. Chinese Americans
   rank as the largest APA group, with 2.88 million nationwide. *The New*

Face of Asian Pacific America: Numbers, Diversity and Change in the 21st Century (San Francisco: *AsianWeek*, 2003), p. 40.

2. Japanese Americans, including those partially identified as Japanese, numbered 1,148,932 in the 2000 census. *The New Face of Asian Pacific America: Numbers, Diversity and Change in the 21st Century* (San Francisco: *AsianWeek*, 2003), p. 77.

3. In 1988 Congress passed the "Amerasian Homecoming Act" (PL 100-200). This law allows Vietnamese Amerasians and certain family members to be admitted to the United States as immigrants. The law took effect on March 21, 1988, and stipulated that Amerasians born in Vietnam between January 1, 1962, and January 1, 1976, would have until March 21, 1990, to apply for immigrant visas. The bill also provided refugee benefits for Amerasians and their families who were admitted as immigrants. University of California, Digital Library, Calisphere, http://content.cdlib.org/xtf/view?docId=hb9b69p28b&doc.view =frames&chunk.id=ch02&toc.depth=1&toc.id=&brand=calisphere (accessed July 23, 2007).

4. Through the 1980 Orderly Departure Act, the Vietnamese government allowed 20,000 family members of those already in the United States to leave for America. University of California, Santa Cruz, Southeast Asian American Communities, http://history.ucsc.edu/history80j/4-12outline.htm (accessed July 23, 2007).

5. The 2000 census recorded 1,230,000 Korean Americans. They rank as the fourth-largest group among APAs. California has the largest group of Korean Americans, 375,571. *The New Face of Asian Pacific America: Numbers, Diversity and Change in the 21st Century* (San Francisco: *AsianWeek*, 2003), p. 60.

After September 11

1. In the first two months after September 11, the Chinese American Restaurant Association reported a 40 percent drop in business among its members. Over 60 percent of its members experienced downturns of 30 to 70 percent after 9/11. *Chinatown after September 11, an Eco-*

nomic Impact Study (New York: Asian American Federation of New York, April 2002), p. 21.

2. In the three months after September 11, 7,685 people, or 23 percent of the worker population in Chinatown, were laid off. Total wage losses were estimated at $114 million. *Chinatown after September 11, an Economic Impact Study* (New York: Asian American Federation of New York, April 2002), p. 3.

3. Special Registration Program: This program requires registration with immigration authorities by nonimmigrant men (that is, those who are in the United States on temporary visas), who are aged sixteen and older and come from any one of twenty-five countries. The designated countries are predominantly Arab and Muslim, as well as states where Al Qaeda is thought to be particularly active. Special Registration is part of the National Security Entry-Exit Registration System (NSEERS). It was implemented September 11, 2002, at U.S. Ports of entry. In November 2002, the domestic call-in plan began. This was replaced by a new entry-exit system for foreigners entering the United States called the U.S. Visitor and Immigration Status Indication Technology System (USVISIT) in 2003. U.S. Immigration and Customs Enforcement, http://www.ice.gov/pi/news/factsheets/nseers FS120103.htm (accessed July 23, 2007).

Passages

1. The proposed Federal Marriage Amendment to the Constitution would define marriage as a union of one man and one woman. H.J. Res. 56, 108th Congress, first session. The Senate failed to pass the amendment, voted on June 7, 2006. Library of Congress, http:// thomas.loc.gov/cgi-bin/query/z?c108:H.J.RES.56.IH (accessed July 23, 2007).

2. *Goodridge et al. v. Department of Public Health*, SJC-08860, Massachussetts Court System, http://www.mass.gov/courts/courtsandjudges/ courts/supremejudicialcourt/goodridge.html (accessed July 23, 2007).

Index

Note: APAs refers to Asian Pacific Americans

education, 3, 26, 27, 42, 180–81,
193–194; Asian American studies
programs, 52–53; boarding schools,
116, 117, 137; gender and, 172–73;
learning English, 26, 37, 39, 41, 43,
64, 112, 193, 203, 229–30, 240;
racism in primary schools and
universities, 17–18, 28–29, 54,
126, 139; university, 27–29, 32–34,
54, 67, 92, 117, 120, 125–26, 137,
138–39, 143, 144, 149, 154, 168,
212, 250, 251, 254, 259; valuing
of, 18, 54, 67, 68, 121, 122, 129,
138–39, 143, 168, 180, 189,
260
English, speaking, see language skills
entertainment industry, 165; writing
about the, 153–56
Equality Maryland, 213
ethnic diversity, 14, 58, 112, 117;
in Hawaii, 133–34
Exclusion Acts, 163

Families With Pride, 213
family associations, 89–92
Federal Emergency Management Agency
(FEMA), 197
Filipino American Association, 128
Filipino Americans: cultural values of,
129; stories of, 128–32, 149–52
film industry, 114
films: Asian, 4; Bollywood, stories of
lesbians from, 223; Japanese culture
portrayed in, 164; stereotypes of
Asians in, 126, 145, 148
financial success, 12, 41, 260;
expectations of, 143–44
food stamps, 65
Fortune Cookies (girl singing group), 6,
107–10
Fresno, California, 114, 167–68, 175
friendships, 124–25, 126, 128, 138, 146,
230, 240–41, 260

gays, 2, 212–27; health insurance
benefits, 216, 217–18; immigration
problems, 218–20; legal rights of,

215–17; same-sex marriages, 4,
212–24
"Girl in Love," 110
grandparents raising preschool children,
3, 40
green cards, 85, 86, 115, 219

hapas (Asian/White mix), 260–64
Harlan, Kentucky, 115–17
Harvard University, 67, 143
hate crimes, 13, 57
Hawaiians, stories of, 101–6, 133–36
health insurance, domestic partners and,
216, 217–18
Hispanic Americans, 11, 13, 56, 156, 163
Hmong Americans: clans, 174–75;
gender issues, 172–73; holidays and
gatherings, 173–74; language and
internal divisions, 171–72; marriage
and cultural beliefs, 168, 169, 170,
172, 173, 175–76; political activism
and, 171; public assistance and,
167–68; religion and, 176–77;
stories of, 111–14, 167–77;
weddings, 176
Hoffman, Mr. (English teacher), 107
Houghton, Kristen, 3, 234–35, 239–46
House of Chang, 193
housing, 46; racism and, 35
Houston, Texas, 178

identity: Asian heritage and, see Asian
heritage, personal identity and; of
gays, 220, 225–27
immigration, 2, 9, 29–30; arranged
marriages and, 37–39, 42–43, 44;
children's adjustment to, see
children, adjustment to life in the
U.S.; detainment for interrogation,
16, 17; domestic violence and,
84–86; Exclusion Acts, 163; first
family members bringing over
others, 16–17, 24, 31, 37, 40–41,
59; gays and problems with,
218–20; green cards, 85, 86, 115,
219; jobs of recent immigrants, 3, 5,
27, 44–46, 59, 112, 139; language

immigration (*cont.*)
skills, *see* language skills; post–9/11
restrictions, 1, 2; race and U.S.
immigration policy, 12, 13, 18, 163;
Saigon evacuation, 23–24, 180;
sponsors, 24, 30, 111, 112; stress
on the second generation, 143–44
Immigration and Naturalization Service,
U.S. (INS), 219
Immigration Marriage Fraud Act, 85
Internet: activism and, 4, 15; in China,
46; music industry and, 104–5;
virtual communities, 15
internment of Japanese Americans, 13,
51–53, 57, 73, 124, 135–36;
assimilation and, 163, 164;
congressional hearings on, 51;
family recollections of, 55;
Korematsu v. United States, 52–53;
possibility of repeating internment
of a minority group, 56–58, 136,
148, 164; preserving firsthand
stories of, 136; psychological effect
of, 163–64
"It Should Have Been Me," 110

Japanese American Citizens League, 51
Japanese Americans: internment of, *see*
internment of Japanese Americans;
racially mixed children, 203–11;
stories of, 11–15, 51–58, 93–106,
133–36, 163–66, 203–11
jobs, *see* occupations; workplace, race and
racism in the
Jung, Daniel, 119–27, 183–85
Jung, Laura, 2–3, 142–48, 183, 184

Kamaka family, ukuleles manufactured
by, 102
King County Council, Seattle, 74–75,
76–77
Korean Americans: church-centered lives,
116–18, 146–47; cultural values of,
142, 143; expectations of females,
145; male role and culture of,
122–24, 142; stories of, 115–27,
142–48, 153–56, 183–85, 225–46

Koreatown, Los Angeles County, 183–85
Korematsu v. United States, 52–53

language skills, 39, 79, 118, 179,
183–184; bilingual balloting,
160–61; English in school, Asian
language at home, 6, 46–47, 121;
helping parents with, 143; Hmong
dialects and internal divisions,
171–72; knowledge of Asian
language by acculturated APAs, 5,
26, 118, 129–30, 136, 142, 189–90,
203, 230, 242, 254, 255, 257, 259;
learning English, 26, 37, 39, 41, 43,
64, 112, 193, 203, 229–30, 240; as
occupational barrier, 37, 39–40, 47,
71; songwriting and, 96; teaching of
English in schools, 26, 64, 203
Laos, Hmongs of, *see* Hmong Americans,
stories of
Latino Americans, 11, 13, 56, 156, 163
Lau, Joanne, 107–10
Lau, Rose, 107–10
Lee, Albert, 2, 115–18; on being gay,
225–27; entertainment industry,
writing about, 153–56
Lee, Bruce, 75, 103
Lee, Corky, 157–62, 195–97;
photography of, 157, 161–62
Lee, Joann Faung Jean (author):
childhood of, 6; Fortune Cookies
and, 6, 107–10
Lee, Sue Jean, 107–10
Leung, Veronica, 191–94
Liang, Qing Shan, 3, 37–43
Liu, John, 160
Locke, Emily, 70
Locke, Gary, 4, 59–70, 79; background
of, 59–60; childhood of, 66–67; on
education, 67–68; on personal
identity, 63–64; politics and, 60–70;
on role models, 68–70
Locke, Mona, 70
Los Angeles, California, 119–27, 146,
163, 165
Ludwig, Jay and Joan, 229, 231, 232,
240, 241, 243–44, 246